Foreign Threat

by

Mitchell Goldstein

Mitchell Goldstein

Published by: Elevation Book Publishing
Atlanta, Georgia 30308
www.elevationbookpublishing.com

Contributors:
Author: Mitchell Brian Goldstein (1960 -)
Editor: Courtney Elizabeth Taylor (1984 -)
p.c.m
ISBN 978-1-943904-15-0 (pb)

BISAC DRA001000
BISAC FIC002000
BISAC FIC006000
BISAC FIC035000
BISAC FIC038000

Prologue

The phone rang. This call would change the course of history.

He answered, and an Afghanistan operator completed the connection. "I've been waiting for your call, but we have to make it brief. I'm concerned that—"

"Stop, my friend," said a calm voice with a Middle Eastern accent. "It's time to begin work. I think I have found the right doctor to do our little chore. Now we must wait for the right guinea pig. We need to move this along. It has taken entirely too much time."

Too much time? The American thought the entire process was moving too quickly. Their first meeting had been only six months ago. A great deal of planning still needed to be completed. So many questions with not enough answers. How in the world did this Afghan nut think this was the time for action?

The American pleaded, "I need more time. I have not yet made the contacts that we discussed. I can't move too quickly or I will stick out like a sore thumb."

"My friend, you do have time. We have only found the doctor, and now we must find a patient. This may take some time. But I must urge you to begin making your contacts. When our patient arrives, we must move swiftly."

The American again tried to make his point clear. "On the contrary, I think you already have moved too quickly. If this pace continues, there will likely be mistakes, and the mistakes will lead to bigger problems. Perhaps the entire operation will be discovered."

"Please, my friend, understand that my people don't make mistakes. There is no cause for alarm. My people have done this for years. They are what you call…professionals. They have been well trained. You, my friend, are new to this activity. I wish for you to be patient. Please make your contacts. I will speak to you soon."

A click sounded on the other end.

Be patient…make the contacts…no mistakes… This was not Iraq, Iran, or Afghanistan; this was the United States of America. Mistakes were made all the time, every day, by very careful, organized, and cautious people.

He grabbed his overcoat and hat and crossed his small apartment. He looked through the peephole into the hallway: nobody around. He slowly opened the door and then scurried to the back stairwell. He raced quietly down the stairs and out the side door leading to the busy street.

He raised the collar of the coat and joined the crowd on the sidewalk. Many people were walking to work, to lunch, to the stores, and he soon was lost in the crowd.

After a few blocks, he passed his car. The tires were still there, no scratches along the doors, and the dark blanket was still lying partially over the passenger seat. No obvious markings suggested that someone had tampered with the car.

He walked one more block, looked around for anyone suspicious, and started back toward his car.

Out of nowhere, he felt a tap on his left shoulder.

His heart rate raced, and adrenaline leaked into his blood stream. He gently slipped a hand toward his inside coat pocket. Just before he drew his weapon, he heard the small voice of an elderly woman.

"I'm sorry, young man, but you dropped your gloves on the street. They look very nice. I didn't think you would want to be without them."

He nearly collapsed with relief. "Thank you, ma'am."

The woman smiled and continued on her way.

He finally reached his car, constantly looking over his shoulder for someone threatening. He was trained to identify what didn't belong in the quickest of a glance.

He checked the car again, concerned that something had changed while the old woman was distracting him. Nothing was extruding from the end of the tailpipe. No wires showed along the lower edge of the bumper. The tires were fine.

Everything inside the car appeared to be equally intact. He placed the key in the ignition, closed his eyes, and slowly started the ignition. As the engine rolled over, he relaxed in his seat, shifted the car into drive, and drove away.

At the first red light, he pulled out a file that read, *University Hospital*. Inside was a list of doctors with a brief history about each person. He had read the files carefully again last night, and the number of potential candidates for the job was down to three. After this morning's phone call, he had just one day to select someone and make contact.

Plenty of hungry doctors were out there. He only needed one.

Chapter 1

It was the last question of the last exam of medical school, and Steve Carmichael was about to finish. *The most important indication for preoperative antibiotics in a patient suspected of having appendicitis is: A. To decrease the incidence of intraabdominal abscess formation; B. To help reduce postoperative pneumonia; C. To decrease the incidence of postoperative wound infections; D. To alleviate the need for postoperative antibiotics.* He had no difficulty with this last question. He was asked a similar question by his chief resident just last week. Preoperative antibiotics would help reduce the incidence of postoperative wound infections. He marked answer C, collected his belongings, and handed in his test to the proctor.

After taking three surgical rotations as a medical student, Steve had decided to pursue a career in general surgery. While in the operating room, he was amazed that the human body could be opened and taken apart – and still function a few hours later.

As he finished the last moments of medical school, however, his thoughts weren't on the miracle of medicine. Instead, he was focused on Joe's Place, a small bar on the edge of campus. This was the traditional meeting place after finals. Nothing fancy: just a few pool tables, a 1950s jukebox with more recent tunes, and lots of beer.

When Steve arrived, half of his classmates were already past the point of no return. Six people were dancing on tables. Several others were playing billiards, about to lose their vacation money. The rest were just plain drunk.

What a sight for any patient of these future healthcare providers.

The future was not a concern for these young med school grads, though. They had waited so long for this moment: to finish their final exam, to be done with the tormenting abuse from their residents, and to graduate from medical school. The end was in sight.

Steve sipped his beer and reflected on the path that had brought him to this point.

When he was young, he had often visited the practice that was run by his father and grandfather in northern Minnesota. They practiced at a time when doctors managed the whole patient, anything from delivering babies to removing gallbladders to treating asthma.

Steve recalled one episode with his father at the grocery store in their small town. An obese man had fallen to his knees and then onto the floor. The loud thump of this giant collapsing resonated in Steve's memory. His father ran over to the man and put a hand near his mouth to check for breathing. The man's skin turning purple confirmed that he was not breathing. Steve's father yelled for the cashier to call the ambulance.

In the minutes before the ambulance arrived, Steve's father saved the man's life. Because the man was a patient, the doctor knew his last cholesterol level, his blood pressure, and his battle with obesity. He knew about the diabetes, the gallbladder surgery, and the concern about a heart attack several months back.

The doctor knelt alongside the unfortunate man and carefully tilted his head upwards with one hand on his forehead and the other on his chin. The doctor proceeded to give the man mouth-to-mouth breathing.

Dr. Carmichael had paused to check the man's pulse and then placed his hands on the monstrous chest. Palm over palm, he started the chest compressions. He had asked Steve to continue the mouth-to-mouth breathing.

The boy froze in his spot. He was just ten years old. He knew how to ride his bike, he could fly a kite, and he handled fishing just fine, but mouth-to-mouth breathing? No one had ever addressed that topic.

But somebody needed to get oxygen into the man's lungs.

Steve tried to follow his father's instructions. He gagged at the idea of putting his lips on this man's mouth, but as he lowered his face, he realized that if he did not breathe for him now, the man would never have a chance to breathe again.

Young Steve leaned over the man, plastered his lips against his, and blew as hard as he could. He repeated the maneuvers, correcting his technique until he saw the man's chest rise. Dr. Carmichael continued to provide instructions as they alternated breathing and compressions. Steve realized that he and his father were working as a team to save this man's life, something the boy would never forget.

While Steve took breaks between breaths, he watched his father. He had never seen his dad work before. Sure, he went to the office to sit in the big desk chair and listen to the nurses say cute things about him, but never before had he been given the opportunity to watch Dr. Carmichael practice medicine. At that moment in the supermarket, he was proud of his father.

After what seemed to be hours, the ambulance arrived. The ambulance driver replaced Steve at the patient's mouth.

Steve watched and admired how quickly and efficiently his father and the ambulance crew took care of the patient on the floor. They quickly secured patches on his chest to monitor his heart. They transferred him to a gurney and wheeled him to the ambulance.

Dr. Carmichael took Steve by the hand and knelt down to his eye level. "I have never been so proud of you as I was just now. You are the best partner I could have ever asked for in this crisis. Now, go straight home and tell your mother what happened. I will call her after he stabilizes."

Steve knew then that he was going to be a doctor just like his father.

As Steve drank from his third beer, his friend Mary sat next to him. She threw her arm around him and offered her warmest congrats. They'd had lockers next to each other during their first two years. This may not have been a big deal in grade school, but in med school, it was important: you learned a lot about your neighbors. Not about their childhood or their last date, but what underwear they wore or if they wore any at all.

As far back as anatomy lab, everybody had to change into old clothes. Dissecting cadavers was messy business. Since there were no changing rooms, most people would undress right in the hallway. The few more discreet students would walk to the bathroom on the opposite side of the building, but by the end of the first month, nearly all students would strip right at their lockers.

That was how Steve and Mary had met.

She leaned over to his ear now and asked, "Are you wearing the boxers with hearts? You know they're my favorite."

They both laughed.

As Steve took another drink, he looked up at the T.V. A young female news anchor was educating the world on the latest headlines. "For further details regarding the U.S. embassy bombing in London, we'll go to Sam Forsyth. Sam, what is the damage there, and do you know of any casualties?"

The screen cut to a male reporter who was facing a spotlight with a darkened city behind him. "Well Jane, there is a lot of confusion at this point. What we do know is that, at 3:05 P.M. Eastern time, there was a loud explosion from the front entrance of the embassy. The explosion caused major structural damage. Three are feared dead, and thirty-six are wounded in this devastating tragedy. At this point, the most concerning issue for authorities is those three missing people. We just discovered from an undisclosed source that one of those individuals is Phil Wells, who is believed to be connected with the CIA. At this time, no journalist or civilians are allowed within a one-mile radius of the embassy for fear there may be additional bombs planted in the building. No group or individuals have claimed responsibility, but the speculation is…"

At 2:00 local time, Steve had just walked into the Clarence Simmons Hall for the last final exam of his medical school career. As he tried to come up with the correct answers for clinical problems, a U.S. embassy was being bombed. Lives had been shattered.

He could spend hours reflecting on this matter, but not tonight. This was his chance to celebrate. He grabbed Mary's hand and pulled her to the center of the room to dance.

The time passed too quickly. Before anyone realized it was late, the lights at Joe's were turning up, putting an end to the celebratory ambience. Like any other med school celebration, no one was ready to stop partying.

Don Smith offered to perpetuate the party by moving it to his house. "Well, it's the house that I rented. Well, it's not exactly a house, but more like a two-bedroom guest house that belongs to an elderly couple."

Steve knew that Don helped out with a few chores on this ten-acre estate, and for his help, he got room and board for a ridiculously low fee. Everyone in the class was envious. Fortunately, Don was a man of generosity and had offered his home for numerous parties in the past. The best thing about having parties at his house was not the ten acres of beautiful rolling hills or the secluded location of this dream house, but the fact that the backyard had a lake.

Everybody thanked Joe drunkenly. A bus had been arranged by Joe to take everyone home after the bar closed. Instead of touring the neighborhoods, the bus just had to make one stop.

As he rested his head on the back of the seat, Steve tried his best to keep his head from spinning. He listened to the all of the commotion around him. He knew most of these students relatively well, but there were a few with whom he had never studied or socialized.

Tonight, though, everybody was everybody's best friend. No competing for the best score on the physiology exam, no challenging who could offer the most information on medical rounds, no showing off for chief residents or staff doctors. They were all the best of buddies, celebrating the accomplishment of finishing a grueling four years of medical school together.

Deagan O'Brian sat next to him on the bus. Deagan looked at Steve, gave him a big hug, and collapsed on his shoulder.

Steve smirked and gently pushed his best friend against the window.

Deagan had also elected to enter the surgical career. Although they shared the same interest in surgery, Deagan had decided to go into the field from the moment he was born -- or at least early in life. Maybe it was all the knot tying as a Boy Scout or part time work as a carpenter, but whatever the reason, Deagan knew all along that he was going to be a surgeon.

He had decided to attend a plush training program. The program was somewhere in North Carolina. It only took two residents a year, then treated them like kings and queens. Every fourth night, the residents had call with teams to draw all the blood. They had technicians that would get EKGs at any time of the day or night, and they provided unlimited food, twenty-four hours a day. Whether it was post-call, pre-call, or no call, the resident always had access to gourmet food.

Steve's decision to enter the surgical field was not determined prior to medical school, and he had elected to stay at the university to complete his surgical training.

As it turned out, after the first week of his general surgery rotation, he wasn't impressed with the field. He witnessed fatigue, emotional abuse, intimidation, and general displeasure among the residents on his service.

Each surgical service or team was comprised of several people, beginning with one or two staff surgeons who almost never spent time with the team or their patients. Next in the hierarchy was a chief resident, someone in his or her final year of training for general surgery. Depending where one trained, this could happen anywhere between their fifth and eighth year of training. He or she could make your life miserable or wonderful during this unique experience. Then there would be one or two junior residents, people training in general surgery who had already completed four years of medical school and one year of surgical internship. The junior residents were a variable group of people. Some were nice, and some were jerks. The team would have one lonely intern, a poor soul fresh out of medical school, ambitious yet usually the scapegoat. It was much more appropriate to chew the intern out because the medical students were not expected to know all the information, and the junior residents had already been there. The team was rounded off with one or two medical students. Usually one was a third-year student on his or her first surgery rotation, the greenest of green, and the other student was a fourth-year taking extra surgical rotations to determine whether or not to pursue surgical training after all. Medical students were not abused on the surgical service, or at least not as badly as the residents were.

Although most students feared the surgical clerkship, Steve's third-year experience started out wonderfully. No abuse, no intimidating attitudes, no condescending remarks – for the first six hours or so. Then the chief resident had finished his surgery. He introduced himself as Jeff Levinsky but did not shake hands, did not smile, and did not seem to like Steve. He gave his staff a list of things to do and then disappeared. The residents took off to get their work done so they could get home before midnight.

The intern showed Steve where the blood-drawing cart was and instructed him to draw labs on fifteen patients. Steve had never drawn blood before, but he didn't have a chance to tell the intern. As a result, his first day on surgery was spent teaching himself how to draw blood.

In the second day on the service, things only got worse. During rounds, Dr. Levinsky inquired about a patient who had been admitted on their service during the night. She was a 32-year-old with right lower quadrant pain.

The chief resident turned to Steve and asked, "Stephen, what is your differential diagnosis?"

Steve was humiliated by some stranger calling him Stephen, but he responded, "The woman could have appendicitis."

"That's all?" screamed Dr. Levinsky.

Steve was still recovering from the Stephen thing when a new wave of redness and heat rushed through his body. Everybody, including the nurses, could hear the conservation, more commonly known as grilling.

"I thought you medical students would know a little more," Dr. Levinsky shouted. "Maybe you should spend a few hours in the library and determine other probable causes for this woman's problem."

Steve walked away from the team like a whimpering puppy with his tail between his legs. His wounds were deep, and the scars were sure not to heal anytime soon. He looked back as he walked away and saw the group smirking and laughing at him. He just hated this rotation and the people who went with it. He had spent the entire day in the library looking up information about right lower quadrant pain. He looked at surgical texts, medical texts, and anatomy books. He was so full of knowledge about the right lower quadrant by the end of his study that he could have given a lecture to fellow students. He was so pissed at his team that he was determined to show them when he met up with them during evening rounds.

Dr. Levinsky was still set to make his life miserable. "I thought I told you a few hours, not the entire day! Well, did you find out if you can save this woman, or do you need to refer her to a real doctor?"

Steve refused to let the intimidating remarks of Jeff, the shit head, bother him. "In a normally healthy female, this most likely is appendicitis. It could also be inflammation of the small bowel or infection of the small bowel called terminal ileitis or Crohns Disease. Then it could be Meckels diverticulitis or gastroenteritis. Since she is female, we have to worry about twisted ovaries or cysts on the ovaries. If she is sexually active, she may be pregnant and may have an ectopic pregnancy, which could lead to severe problems. Along the same line, endometriosis could be causing her this pain. Now, in a patient who may be infected with T.B. or H.I.V., there may be a host of other conditions that may account for her symptoms including-"

"Okay, enough!" shouted Dr. Levinsky.

The other residents stood with their mouths hanging open. The intern looked down in embarrassment, hoping the chief resident would ignore her instead of revealing her lack of such thorough knowledge on this topic.

Steve was relieved that the conversation ended there.

Dr. Levinsky found Steve again after rounds that evening. He put his arm around him and told him he was very impressed with the wealth of knowledge that he offered the team. He invited Steve to scrub on a bowel case the next morning.

Steve was happy as a clam. He spent that night reading at

home about the case for the next day.

His learning experience only continued to flourish on that rotation. The chief resident continued to challenge him throughout the clerkship, and he was forced to study a great deal of new material. He became increasingly interested in the field of surgery. By the end, there was no doubt: he would be a surgeon.

Deagan was just coming to as the bus pulled up to Don's house. Everyone ran into the house and grabbed a fresh beer. Some ran to the lake, took off their clothes, and jumped into the water. Deagan was among those who proudly whipped off their clothes.

Steve and Mary laughed at their classmates for being so drunk.

As the crowd got larger in the lake and smaller on land, however, Mary made a bold move. She grabbed Steve's hand and dragged him to the beach. Without flinching, she began taking off her clothes.

He guzzled his beer and took his clothes off as well. He ran into the cold water with a sense of apprehension.

As the moon shed light on the lake, Steve treaded water and watched the others for a while. Then he lay on his back to float. Staring at the moon, he acknowledged what had been his biggest accomplishment yet.

Chapter 2

The alarm clock wailed.

Jake Douglas tried to find it so he could slam it into the garbage. He kept his eyes closed and felt around his bedside table before realizing that no clock was in the vicinity. Instead, he felt a small, hard square.

"Damn it!" he yelled. He was still in the hospital, still on call, still answering stupid pages that his intern should have been taking. He felt like throwing the pager across the room, but he had tried that once before, and they still found him.

He tried to muster enough energy to open his eyes so he could see the page. The pager showed the numbers he had grown to despise over the last twenty-four hours – 323-2266…4:10 AM. "Shit, those fuck wads just called ten minutes ago," he grumbled.

As he dialed the number, he thought about the incompetent intern he had been assigned over the last two months. The guy was never around, difficult to keep track of, and never managed any of the patients. In other words, he was useless.

But this was Jake's last day as a resident. He could tolerate eight more hours of call.

Then he would start the final year in his surgical training program. He would finally be a chief resident.

A warm pleasant voice answered the phone, "Hello, Dr. Douglas. This is Sarley Anderson."

"What the hell do you want this time? You know there is an intern taking call tonight. You could bother *his* ass every ten minutes."

"I'm so sorry. I have one more question. That patient, status post a colon resection from a few days ago, is still having pain, and I wondered if you wanted to give any other pain medication."

"Shit, Sarley, you just asked that twenty minutes ago!"

"Well, actually, it was three hours ago, but you wrote for meds to be given every four hours and, well, it is only three hours and…"

Before she could finish her sentence, Jake barked, "Just give him the damn Demerol! And next time call Andrew Johnson. He is the intern on call tonight." He slammed the phone down.

At 5:30 A.M., the phone rang again.

"Now what?" Jake screamed.

"I'm so sorry, Dr. Douglas, but this is the operator, and you wanted to be called now. Is this the wrong time?"

Jake rolled his eyes. "That's fine. Thanks."

He dragged himself out of bed, brushed his teeth, and splashed water on his face and hair. This was the closest he could get to a shower post-call. He forgot his deodorant, but that wasn't his problem. The poor intern in the operating room would have to suffer with his smelly armpits. It would serve him right if that intern were the useless Andrew Johnson.

Jake rushed down to the cafeteria so he could grab a cup of coffee before six o'clock rounds. As he waited in line to pay for the drink, a smile formed on his face. He would scrub on this early morning case and try to get his floor work done by a reasonable time. Then he could get home and plan the next several months as chief resident.

"Hey, Jake. How you doing? Look like you may need more than that one cup of coffee," the intern said with a smirk.

"Fuck you, Johnson. Where the fuck were you all last night?" demanded Dr. Douglas.

"I had an unstable patient in the Intensive Care Unit, someone the other surgery service dumped on me last night. The guy was status post a triple A repair that would not stop bleeding. We were afraid that he was going into DIC," Andrew replied.

"Fuck you, Johnson."

Jake had a unique way of dealing with people. He treated them as if they were his worst enemy's pets. Not too many people really cared to be in the presence of Jake Douglas. New medical students who didn't know any better sometimes dared to hang out with Jake, trying to kiss up to him, but after two or three days, they usually couldn't take his abusive behavior anymore.

By the time Jake arrived in the ICU to start rounds, Andrew was already gossiping with the other staff.

"What are you all smiling about?" asked Jake as he walked up to the group.

Evidently, no one could muster up a fake answer.

"Fine. Andrew, you write the notes, and George, you write the orders."

This wasn't Jake's responsibility, but he was glad to step up. During the last two weeks, Chief Resident Tom Peters had been mentally moving on from residency and preparing for life as a staff surgeon, so he was regularly late for morning rounds.

Jake didn't mind. He liked to be in control of the team. Besides, in less than twenty-four hours, this would be his team to command.

The entire group followed him into the first room. "Good morning, Mrs. Hartman. How are you feeling this morning?"

After rounds, the team moved to the cafeteria for a quick bite to eat. Here they would delegate all the floor work and divide all the tasks amongst the team members.

Chief Resident Peters finally caught up with the team. He spoke with Jake, who filled in all the pertinent details of all the patients on their service. The briefing took five minutes.

Then Dr. Peters shook Jake's hand and left.

Jake returned his attention to the rest of the team. "Tom probably won't be here the rest of the day. George, you organize the management of the patients. Make sure you check the cultures on Mr. Killman, and get the CT scan on room 204. Don't forget to get Mrs. Hartman extubated and transferred out of the ICU. Andrew, you lazy sack of shit, you get to hold retractors for the next six hours." Jake left for the operating room.

The day went by quickly. The staff was content to let Jake do most of the work, and the operations went well. At 4:00, the team met at X-Ray to go over any important films and discuss the patients. This was supposed to be a learning time for the medical students, but as usual, Jake elected not to provide them with any surgical pearls. Jake knew that most students complained to the staff surgeons about his lack of teaching, but no action was ever taken. The resulting perception was that all the staff surgeons were just as much assholes as Jake, except worse.

After X-ray rounds, the team rushed up to the ICU to begin evening rounds. These were always briefer than the morning rounds. As they left the last patient's room, they all paused just outside the room. Jake went over all the remaining tasks for the evening with the team. Chores, blood draws, and lab research were delegated again just like in the morning. When all the assignments were divvied, Jake turned around and started for the elevators.

John Knudson, the most naïve medical student God could ever create, yelled down the hall, "Dr. Douglas, thanks for a great rotation! It's the last day of the rotation."

Everyone stopped in their tracks. Even Jake was stunned. What was this guy doing? Thanking the biggest jerk ever for being the most complete asshole one could ever imagine? Everyone else on the team could not wait for this moment to come. They were all excited to be off the service of Dr. Douglas, and this stupid idiot wanted to give him a big hug and kiss goodbye.

Jake shook his head from side to side in disbelief and continued his path into the elevator.

Jake spent the ride home thinking about the coming year. It was what cach surgical resident eagerly anticipated: the chief resident year. This was the year that the resident would do most of the surgery, spend as little time as possible with patients themselves, and have full control of their surgical service – or at least most of the control. The staff surgeons that were assigned to each service would ultimately be responsible for the patients. This was somewhat of an irony since the staff rarely had any contact with the patients. They might meet them once just before surgery so the patient could put a face to the name on the bill that would arrive in two or three weeks, but otherwise, the staff usually kept their distance.

Driving down the interstate with the window open to stay awake, Jake planned out the next day. The new surgery interns would have orientation in the morning in order to fill out their W-2 forms and learn the boring details of being a surgery resident. Jake would have to make rounds with the two new junior residents assigned to his team, Sally Jenson and Tom Formin.

Sally was a fourth year resident and was good at her job. Jake had worked with her in the past, and she did everything with great confidence. Most of the staff liked her, which made her a great spokeswoman for his service so that he would not have to deal with those egotistical assholes more than necessary.

Tom Formin was a little greener. He had just finished his internship year and had been known to falter under the stress of surgical residency. He would show up to work, but that was about it. No one felt comfortable having him responsible for the patients on the floor recovering from surgery. He would routinely get labs mixed up, forget to order important studies on patients, and take forever to get the work done. He even had to have help getting the history and physicals done when there was too much going on. Still, Jake felt that a little Dr. Douglas guidance would help Tom shape up.

Jake was not sure which medical students he had been assigned, but he couldn't care less. He was so removed from the med students that he didn't know if any particular one was better than the others. As long as they didn't mind getting up early, going home late, tolerating any dull or obscure assignment he gave, and basically disregarding life outside of surgery for the next two months, Jake didn't care anything about the students. It was well known that, while on the surgery clerkship, they would eat, sleep, and shit surgery.

Jake turned off the interstate and pulled into the grocery store near his apartment. He picked up the bare essentials, strode to the checkout line, and asked the clerk to charge the total to his account.

As she recognized him, she said, "One moment please, Dr. Douglas." She went to the office to get the manager.

"Well, hello, Dr. Douglas," said a stern voice.

Jake turned to the manager of the store. They had met several times over the last four months. "Hello, Joel."

"Your account still is not paid, Dr. Douglas. You have told me many times over the last four months that the check is coming. We have yet to receive this payment."

"I get paid this Thursday, and I will make this wonderful

grocery store my first stop. I appreciate the fact that you and your staff have been so patient, and-"

"Cut the BS, young man. If you don't pay the bill by the end of the week, I will turn your account over to a collection agency," Joel promised.

Jake signed for his purchase and left without another word.

What is one more collection agency? He had promised himself not to go to that market ever again after Joel had given him a hard time six weeks ago. The post-call exhaustion must have caused him to have a minor brain infarct, and he forgot to go to the market on the other side of the interstate. Next time he wouldn't forget. He'd have to write a reminder to himself and leave it on the steering wheel.

Jake turned the knob to his apartment. As he opened the door, he could already smell the stench. He switched on the lights and saw the mess he had left behind two days ago. Clothes, clean and dirty, laying over chairs and the sofa. Old pots and pans still on the stove.

He thought for a moment. He didn't recall what meal he had cooked prior to this last call shift. In fact, he remembered eating a frozen pizza. The pizza box that lay on the kitchen table with three uneaten pieces was confirmation. That would also account for the smell in the apartment, or at least part of it.

He walked over to the refrigerator, closed his eyes for a second, and opened the door. Three beers and an apple. What a pitiful way to celebrate the beginning of his chief year. At least he had a few beers. He opened the first can, stared at the pile of dishes in the sink, and turned toward the sofa. He shoved all the clothes over to one side, sat down, and looked at the picture on top of the television.

It was a photograph of four people at a water park. Jake stood with the beautiful young woman who had been his wife until eight months ago. Between them was a little girl with long brown hair and a golden tan and a little boy who very much resembled his father.

Jake remembered the picture, the day, the park, and the family vividly. It was one of only a few vacations that his young family could afford. They went to a water park in Wisconsin for just a few days, but the children had a lifetime of entertainment. Soon after that trip, though, he and Claire began to struggle with many issues. They had married when they both were seniors in college. They quickly had Brittany, and Claire decided to stay at home with the baby. They used school loans for living expenses until they were dried up, and credit cards became the next best solution. Soon they were in major debt, and he had not yet finished medical school. By the time Jake started his surgical training, he owed the credit card companies more than $50,000. This put quite a strain on the family, not to mention their relationship. As Jake continued with residency, his long hours, sleepless nights, continued debt, and lack of time spent with his family, the stress on his marriage became just too much. Consequently, Claire decided she could not take it anymore and had asked for a divorce earlier in the year. She won custody of the children, and he got visitation rights one weekend a month as long as he was a resident. Hopefully that would change after he got a real job as a general surgeon.

While Jake finished his last beer, he continued planning the year. He still had to juggle his finances so he could cover child support and alimony and attempt to pay off some debt. It was a depressing situation but one to which he had grown accustomed. He tried to create a financial plan as he was slowly getting drunk. It did not prove to be a good time to figure this out.

He changed gears and started to go over the list of members

of his surgical team who would be his slaves for the next two months. He would find out which unfortunate medical student was assigned to his service in the morning. He already knew that he was fortunate to get Sally Jenson. He could tolerate Tom Formin, someone who would require a little polishing but should do fine. His intern was Steve Carmichael. He remembered a presentation that Steve did for Grand Rounds. It was actually quite good, but that didn't matter. The transition from a medical student to intern is tremendous. One moment, you could be the most energetic student who looked up all the obscure topics and did all the scut work without a flaw. Then you're finishing medical school, and you're the doctor. The doctor is supposed to have all the answers to all the problems, but the lack of sleep combined with the long hours of being degraded and slammed from all the staff could make the best medical student appear just shy of inadequate as an intern.

While he thoughtfully analyzed his team, Jake fell into a restless sleep. Today had been the last day of pure hell, and tomorrow would be the first day of his chief residency. The advantages it promised would include power, respect, and more operating time.

Chapter 3

As Jake made his way to the Surgical Intensive Care Unit, Tom and Sally were finishing pre-rounds. By the time the chief resident was ready to make rounds, all the little problems of the night were identified and resolved. It was important for the residents to know everything about the patients before the chief. This way they would look as efficient as possible, and the more organized the service, the more surgery they would get to do.

When Jake walked through the electric doors to the Intensive Care Unit, Tom and Sally gathered several pieces of paper with patient data and hurried to the first bed. "Good morning, Jake," they greeted.

"Yeah right," replied Jake. "Let's get on with it. Hey, where the hell is the intern?"

"Steve has orientation with all the interns for the first part of the day." Sally didn't wait for Jake to start in on her before going over the patients. "This is Mr. Gordon who found himself in an awkward position last night as he sold his crack. It appears the buyer felt he got screwed on the price and wanted it all for the preferred rate. So he decided to blow a few holes into Mr. Gordon's chest and abdomen to remind him the next time he is in the area that all the buyers with guns get the preferred rate."

"That is really too bad, but why the hell is he on my service?" demanded Jake.

"Well, as far as I know, the operating surgeon has full responsibility for managing their patients. And since I spent eight hours operating on this lowlife, I expect you to spend the next several weeks taking good care of him. And if he dies, Jake, my boy, you'll be back to a junior resident faster than you can say *oh, shit*," spoke Dr. Rosberg.

"Sorry, Dr. Rosberg, I had no idea you operated on him!

And-"

"Save it, Jake. Just don't let him die. I missed my daughter's birthday party for this shithead. If he dies, it really would make it that much more painful." With that, Dr. Rosberg walked out of the ICU with a smile from ear to ear as he chuckled about Jake stuffing his oversized foot into his mouth.

"Why didn't you shitheads tell me he was behind me?" snapped Jake.

"It was too late. You already had your whole leg in your mouth before we could hint anything to you," said Tom.

What a great way to start the chief year, thought Jake. Making a complete idiot of yourself to your staff before the year gets started. It's one thing to jerk around your residents, but to jerk around your staff is not good etiquette. "Well what did they do to this guy last night?" he asked.

"They did a thoracotomy on the left side and wedged out the part of his lung that had a bullet hole through it," Sally narrated. "Then they opened his belly and repaired several holes in his small bowel. He also had his left colon penetrated with a large amount of stool in the belly, so they left a colostomy for the time being."

Jake thought that was quite a bit for not getting the preferred rate, but Sally was not done.

"They also repaired his Vena Cava for a through and through injury just above the renals. And finally the best for last, they packed his liver for several penetrating injuries to the right lobe."

"No wonder Dr. Rosberg made such a big deal about this case! It's miraculous the guy is alive this morning," said Jake.

Tom gave a brief update, recent vital signs, urine output, lab values and medications. They spoke a little more about the case while Sally finished the daily note and wrote several orders. Then they moved to the next patient.

Foreign Threat

Rounds in the Intensive Care Unit always took a long time because the patients were so sick and complicated. Fortunately, Jake only had three people in the unit this morning. The two others he knew from last rotation. One was an eighty-three-year-old man who had come in with bowel obstruction the previous week. He had undergone surgery to find an obstructing colon cancer. Surgery went well, but because the man had surgery emergently, his heart was not evaluated fully prior to surgery. Consequently, he suffered a heart attack one day after the operation. Nevertheless, the man was doing well but needed close follow up for the next several days.

The other patient on Jake's service in the unit was a young woman in her early thirties with severe pancreatitis. Jake had operated on her twice in the last week. She was better this morning.

Sally began giving a brief update, "Mrs. Johnson had a fever last night up to 101.8 degrees Fahrenheit and was given some Tylenol, and then-"

"Was any physician contacted? Was there a fever work up conducted? How about a chest X-ray?" yelled Jake.

"Actually, we just found out about it this morning. We were also confused why a doctor didn't get called either."

Jake knew Sally was covering her tail, and besides, he didn't mean to scream at her the first day. There would be plenty of time for that later. He looked around and yelled for the charge nurse.

Agusta Simpson was a pleasant nurse who had worked in the ICU for the last million years. She was a rather overweight woman who walked from side to side. She knew the ICU like the back of her hand. Whether the patient was an elderly person having a myocardial infarction, a gangbanger with multiple gunshot wounds, or a young child involved in a motor vehicle accident, Agusta was the most skillful in managing patients.

When she found out that Jake Douglas was tracking her down, she produced a small evil smile. “Oh, the time has finally come: we must put up with Dr. Douglas’s attitude for the next year. We will have to set that boy straight from the get-go; otherwise, this will be a very long and difficult twelve months,” promised Agusta. She strode out of the charge room to see what the commotion was all about. “Good morning, Dr. Douglas. What’s all the fuss about?”

“Well, for starters,” yelled Jake, “no doctor was notified about Mrs. Johnson’s fever last night. If someone had been contacted, we could have started a fever workup with blood cultures, a CBC, a urine analysis, and probably a chest X-ray, not to mention we could have taken out the central line that is in place. And-”

Agusta quickly and sternly stopped the doctor from exploding right in front of Mrs. Johnson. She raised her hand as to quiet the very dramatic Jake Douglas and walked out of the room. She turned around and motioned for him to follow.

Jake shamefully followed her commands.

Once out of earshot from the patient’s room, Agusta started in on him. “Well, it seems we have a problem your first morning as the big chief Jake. I’m sure this won’t be the last display of fondness expressed toward the hardworking and devoted nursing staff. But I promise you that neither I nor the other charge nurses will tolerate your abusive behavior.”

“Yeah, but the problem here is-”

“Shut up, Jake,” demanded Agusta. “The problem is you. Now to explain the situation from last night, well, that is actually quite simple. The nurse’s aide got that temp on Mrs. Johnson and told me immediately. I realized the patient was under several blankets and the room temp was turned up to eighty degrees. Apparently Mrs. Johnson likes her room warm. I rechecked her temperature fifteen minutes later, and it was back down to 98.8 degrees."

Jake looked down at his shoes for a second and then started to walk backward as to leave the area.

"Not so fast, young man," said Agusta. "In the future, I would like to know how you want the nursing staff to deal with this problem. That way we can attempt to please the majesty as best we can."

"I like that attitude." Jake smiled. "Why don't you have your nurses call me anytime they get an abnormal temp or lab value? In fact, why don't you just have them call me anytime they feel uncomfortable with a particular situation?"

Agusta crossed her hands around her stocky body and rolled back and forth on the balls of her feet. She smiled. Then she clarified Jake's statement. "You mean you would want the nurses to contact you with any situation they feel uncomfortable with at any time. Is that right Dr. Douglas?"

"That's perfect," replied Jake.

"Then you want the nurses to contact you as they did the night before last? Is that perfect Dr. Douglas?" As Jake struggled for a rebuttal, Augusta smiled, turned around, and proudly walked back to her office.

Tom and Sally tried their best to hold back their laughter as the team walked out of the ICU. Just as the automatic doors were swinging open, two very nervous medical students entered. They asked frantically where Dr. Douglas's team was as they gazed around the unit looking for a group of people that resembled a surgical team.

Sally grabbed one by the arm and whispered, "Are you Mike and Roger?"

The boy with a rather large earring in his left ear answered yes.

"Boy, are you two in trouble, not to mention you picked the wrong day to be late. Dr. Douglas has already had a difficult morning. Just do as he says and apologize profusely that you guys were late. And stress to him you will never ever be late again on this rotation." Sally put her long, thin arms around each boy and added, "Good luck!"

Sally walked quickly to catch up with Jake as he dashed to the general care floor where the rest of the surgical patients were located. "JAKE!" she shouted as she raced up to him. "The medical students are here. It appears they went to the wrong ICU and started rounds with the medical ICU service instead of starting with us. Is that right, guys?" she asked with a wink to Mike.

Jake was still so pissed with Agusta that he didn't notice the nonverbal communication.

"Ahh, yes. We are so sorry, Dr. Douglas. It was really stupid. It won't ever happen again, Dr. Douglas. Not while we are on your service, sir."

Sally thought, *What a sweet kiss ass. He will make an excellent surgeon some day.*

Jake looked at them both like he was going to explode. "Which one of you is the fourth year?" he demanded.

"Well, actually, sir," Mike stuttered, "we both are third year students. They must have made a mistake, but if you like, I can run up to the office to see if one of us can be exchanged for a fourth year student."

"That's fine," mumbled Jake. "Just hang out with Dr. Jenson. She will show you both what your duties are on this service. She also will fill you in on all the little secrets that you need to know to survive this rotation, just like the ones she gave you a few minutes ago." Jake smiled cleverly and continued his trek to the second floor nurses station. The entire crew followed close behind.

The rounds on the general care floor went quickly and without too many problems. Jake and the rest of his service hurried to the cafeteria to get a bite of breakfast before surgery. They all sat down at the same table. It was uncomfortably quiet for the first few minutes, but then Tom began to make small talk.

Soon after the ice was broken, Jake gave orders for the day.

"Tom, why don't you scrub with me today, and Sally you take the medical students this morning? Show them all they need to know about taking care of the patients and looking up their labs. And Sally, don't forget to schedule that ICU patient for the OR today so we can take out his liver packs." With that, Jake and Tom went to the operating room.

Sally and the students stayed at the cafeteria for a few more minutes. After Jake left, there was a feeling of relief. Sally told the students about the events of the morning and gave them more hints on how to survive the rotation with Doctor Jake Douglas.

Chapter 4

Steve looked around and saw a few familiar faces, but he didn't recognize the majority of people. There were two guys from his medical school class that he knew were going into Urology, and there was one girl going into Ortho, but other than that, he didn't see anyone else he knew. Sitting back, he wondered how Deagan was getting along. Deagan started his internship two days earlier. Steve would have to e-mail him later.

The room became quiet, and a large figure in a white coat walked to the front of the room. As he faced the crowd, Steve recognized him as Dr. Musso, the chairman of the Surgery Department.

"Good morning, people," he announced. "I would like to welcome all of you to our surgery training program here at the University Hospital. I assure you that you will discover the challenges of internship during the next twelve months. But I also know that everyone sitting in this room will deal with these difficult issues with great maturity. I know this because I selected each and every one of you to be a part of this training program. I wish you all the best. Dr. Goldman is the Residency Coordinator. He will fill you in on several other issues to be discussed today. If you have any questions about the year, your schedule, or problems that arise during the coming months, please feel free to contact him. Good luck!"

Steve leaned over to the guy next to him and said, "Short but sweet, huh?"

"Yeah, no lie. Not like I was expecting a big hug or anything, but a few words of wisdom or encouragement would have been nice. Hey, my name is Dennis Burrows. What's yours?"

"Hi, Dennis. I'm Steve Carmichael. I'm one of the surgery interns tracking for general surgery. How about you?"

"That's great! I'm going in general surgery too. Maybe we will have a few rotations together."

A calm and quiet voice began speaking in front. Dr. Goldman had arrived and started to inform the group of the expectations of the year and of other pertinent information that the interns needed to know.

Dr. Goldman spoke for about two hours. All his words seemed important, but it was difficult to stay awake for the entire time. At the end of the presentation, Steve and Dennis went to lunch at a small bar and café a few blocks from the hospital. As they sat down, Steve glanced at the T.V. up on the wall.

A CNN reporter informed, "There is no new information regarding the whereabouts of Phil Wells. There is great speculation that he was injured during the latest attack this week. The importance of this remains unclear, and the authorities are still not giving out too much information. Reporting live for CNN news, I'm Alan Paridy."

A new voice said, "Thank you, Alan. Today the world trade market continues…"

"Isn't it weird that those attacks are getting closer to us?" questioned Dennis.

"Yeah, but that would never happen," Steve replied. "The security at all of those government buildings is so strict that the president probably has a difficult time getting into the White House."

They both laughed.

A few other familiar faces from orientation came into the bar, and Steve motioned them to sit with him and Dennis. The group of people introduced themselves and then took turns criticizing the orientation thus far. It continued throughout lunch and on the way back to the orientation room.

Upon returning to the lecture hall, Dr. Goldman distributed W-2 forms for the interns to fill out, the first item in a ton of documents to be completed. After the paperwork was finished, Dr. Goldman took center stage again. "Well, that is about it. If any of you have any questions that your chief can't help you out with or you are having some other problems, please feel free to contact me. You can get a hold of me either by paging me or making an appointment through my office. When we are done here, please report to your service. Good luck, people."

With those delightful words of bullshit, Dr. Goldman was gone. Steve and Dennis remained in their seats and looked over one another's schedule.

"Quite frankly, I'm not in a hurry to do scut work for Jake Douglas. I think I'll just stay here for another two to three hours. Do you think anyone will notice?" Steve asked jokingly.

"I heard Dr. Douglas is a complete dick," replied Dennis. "I'm glad *I* don't have him this year."

Eventually they both felt it was time to start their internship. They exchanged phone numbers and went their own way.

Steve stopped at the elevator and looked out the large glass windows. Dressed in his finest suit and a perfectly ironed white lab coat, it would appear to any patient walking by that he was an exceptional young doctor, one who could help a child overcome appendicitis or relieve a man with terrible diverticulitis through a colon resection or find a safe way for an elderly diabetic to revascularize a leg that had been in pain for more than six months.

The truth of the matter was that Steve really didn't feel comfortable with any of those scenarios. It was true that he completed four years of medical school, not to mention two of those years spent on clinical rotations, but during those rotations, he was never totally responsible for the patients. He was involved with their care and management, but he didn't have to take all the phone calls about their problems after hours. He sat by the residents as they answered their pages and heard them order certain medications. He had stood in the corner once while an older man had a cardiac arrest; the residents did CPR and revived him, but Steve had never had to take on that responsibility.

In fact, during one code when a young kid was shot in a drive by shooting, Steve requested to do the CPR. Because the kid was in extremis and about to die, the residents pushed him away and told him to stand back. He wondered then how was he supposed to handle the situation if it happened to him while he was a resident. That scenario would certainly occur during the course of a surgical residency. How was the brand new doctor to assume full responsibility for a sick patient without having managed those patients in the past?

As Steve continued to stare out the window, he began to feel faint. His skin color turned pale.

One nurse walking by asked if he was all right. "Dr. Carmichael, are you OK? Do you want to sit down?"

Steve forced himself to the present. "No, uhh, how did you know my name?"

"The nametag was a big clue," answered the nurse with a small smile.

Steve looked down at his nametag. Sure enough, below his picture was printed "Dr. S. Carmichael." The second line read, "Surgery Department." The nurse was right. What a smart nurse. "Uhh, no, I'll be fine. Thanks anyway," said Steve. As he moved toward the elevator, he saw that a few other people must have been concerned. A group of nurses, probably on their way to the cafeteria for their break, was staring at Steve. So were several visitors.

"Maybe he has the flu," said one lady.

Her husband added, "Those doctors shouldn't work when they're sick. They'll just get the rest of us sick. You think they would know that."

This older couple continued to comment back and forth to each other as they walked down the corridor.

Steve stared at the crowd blankly and turned toward the elevator. He pushed the up arrow and crossed his arms over his chest as he waited for the elevator.

He thought about the orientation process. It seemed that there should have been more practical information provided to the interns. After all, this was only the first day of internship. They were still just medical students, or close enough that it sure didn't feel any different. He certainly didn't feel that he possessed all the knowledge that he needed to be considered a doctor.

Maybe it wasn't the orientation process. Maybe the medical schools should have encouraged more practical experience on the clinical rotations instead of so much basic science instruction the first two years.

Maybe the problem was Steve himself. *Should I have spent more time in the hospital, hanging out with the residents? I should have never gone on my vacation. My time would have been better spent learning how to manage post-operative patients!*

When the elevator doors opened, Steve subconsciously walked in, paying no attention to the others entering. As he reached out his hand to push the second floor button, a quick hand raced in front of him and pushed it for him.

"Hi, my name is Erica, Erica Miller. How about you? Does the ozone man have a name?"

"Yeah, uh, yeah. My name is Steve Carmichael. I'm one of the new surgery interns. Sorry, I was just thinking about something."

"I figured as much. It looked as if you were freaking out about the beginning of your internship. Either that or your chief just grilled your ass. Either way, you just look like you were doing some major freaking."

Major freaking, that was an understatement. Steve was in total shock about the next several days. "Well, you're correct on one account: I am a little concerned about the transition from medical school to being an intern. I mean, the next time I'm on call and there's a code, I'll have to run it myself. I'm not sure I'm ready for that! You know-" Steve cut himself short when he heard Erica laughing. "What's so funny?"

"I'm sure you're really good and all, but I can assure you that the chief on call won't let the intern run a code. At least not the first night on call. Maybe by the second call night…naw. I'm just joking! That's why you take call with a junior and chief resident. They won't expect you to handle those situations by yourself for a while."

"Hey, thanks," said Steve, much relieved. "That makes me feel better. I really was starting to freak there a little bit."

After a short pause, Erica added, "Of course that may be different for surgery interns. They do have such a more vigorous internship. I'm sure the demand of a surgery intern is much greater than any other intern. I would really hate to be in your shoes!"

Steve looked down and had that queasy feeling all over again. "I liked what you said in the beginning of this conversation better."

Erica asked, "Hey, when is your first call night anyway? I'll need some time to warn all of my friends to get off the streets, refrain from shooting and stabbing each other and if they must do all of that, well, at least request to go to the county hospital that night."

Steve slowly looked up and saw Erica smiling. He bowed his head again and shook it from side to side as he started laughing.

The elevator door opened on the second floor, and Steve walked out. Erica stayed inside. "Hey, aren't you coming?" asked Steve.

"Nope, this isn't my floor. I'm not one of those strong, invincible surgery interns. I'm just a little lowlife second year medical resident. I transferred from Chicago this year to finish my residency."

"Oh, that's cool."

"Yeah. My dog ran away. The strangest thing happened, though: someone found him up in Minneapolis. I figured, well, if he wants to come up here so badly that he ran away, maybe I should follow. I guess he had enough of the gangs, violence, and drugs that were down in Chicago."

Steve looked at her, confused.

"Hey, lighten up, man. It was a dumb joke. It was really my cat that ran away."

Steve laughed. He then placed his foot in front of the elevator door to stop it from shutting. He was grateful that the elderly woman in the elevator just smiled at the two of them. It didn't appear she was in much of a hurry but was amused at how the two were flirting.

Erica continued, "Actually, my two kids wanted to come up to Minneapolis. Since their father found a job up in Minneapolis, well, they thought they should move too."

Both Steve and the elderly lady in the elevator looked disappointed. "Well, it was nice to meet you. And thanks for the words of encouragement. Actually, that was more than the orientation program had to offer today. I guess I'll see you around."

Erica picked up on the disappointment from both Steve and the lady. "It's OK, we've been divorced for about three years. I just thought the kids should be by their Dad. How about lunch some time?"

Steve perked up at the idea. "That sounds great."

As the elevator door closed, Erica shouted out, "Hey, I'll look for ya at the next code!"

Steve turned around and walked toward the nurse's station. He had a grin on his face that could have been seen for miles. Although a very handsome man, he had never really spent much time seriously dating women. There were always other important things to do. For example, the last four years of medical school had been his first priority. There were a few women who attempted to establish a relationship, but school, studying, and surgery always interfered. It wasn't as if Steve didn't want to have a relationship, but with everything going on, arguments soon focused on time spent with his girlfriends versus time that should be spent on school or other activities. Steve was the type who didn't like to argue and face any confrontation. Consequently, it was much easier not to date.

But there was something different about Erica. He sure hadn't known her for very long, but something made her stand out from other girls he had dated.

As he strolled to meet his residents at the nurse's station, he continued to think about this new woman. She had a very warm sense of humor. It was like she had this compassionate side to her, but before anything would get too serious, she would calm everything with a joke. That was refreshing. Everyone he had dated before was always too serious about life. They were worried about this and that, anxious how other people felt about them, and mostly upset that Steve wasn't spending enough time with them. Erica, on the other hand, appeared to be more calm and relaxed in just one wonderful encounter. She could lighten the most serious conversation with a joke. She recognized Steve's anxiety about his first day and took a moment to calm his fear as no one else could. Besides her sense of humor, she was beautiful.

Steve entered the nurses' station, wondering how someone so beautiful, smart, and funny could be divorced. How could some idiot let that perfect person go?

"Dr. Carmichael, we have been waiting for you. Where the hell have you been? Orientation finished twenty minutes ago!" yelled Sally.

"Uh, hi, yeah. I, uh, I just met a friend in the elevator, and, uh, we got to talking and one thing lead to another and-"

"Shut up, Carmichael! I've been taking care of all the patients and floor work, and you've been socializing. There seems to be something wrong with this picture. Let me assure you that while you're on this surgery service, I will not do your scut work for you. And furthermore-"

Before Sally could finish chewing Steve out for being late, a firm but calm voice interrupted her over the loud speaker. "Code Blue, Room 204. Dr. Jenson stat to room 204. Code Blue, Room 204. Dr. Jenson stat to room 204."

"Shit!" screamed Sally. "That's Mr. Springer. Come on, Carmichael, help me run this code!"

Steve froze. He could not move. The adrenaline pushed his heart rate to speeds he had never experienced before. His face, hands, and back became sweaty and warm. He felt as if the room was spinning around him. There was this rush of nausea that crept within his stomach. He felt like he was going to faint.

Just then, he heard an incredible scream that got his attention. It was Sally. “Carmichael! Snap out of it, I need your help!”

Steve looked at Sally for a few seconds as she ran down the hall. He had no choice but to follow. By the time he arrived at Room 204, a number of people were already there. Steve was grateful that he wasn’t the only person present, but when Sally yelled for Steve to do chest compressions, the nausea and dizziness came back in a flash.

Chapter 5

It was almost 9:00 P.M., and he had just finished reviewing the final applicants for the job. None of the people really applied for this position, but he took the liberty of analyzing their lives, including foolish economic mistakes. He found the three who needed money more than anything. However, he also had to find someone who would be willing not to ask too many questions. Of the three who were broke, one stood far above the others for this job: Dr. Jake Douglas.

Dr. Douglas was the perfect screw up who needed money so badly that he would probably not ask many questions. If he did, he was the type not to care about the social and professional immoralities that were associated with this job. Unfortunately, as with any half-wit with a conscience, if he discovered the truth and implications of this project, he would not only turn down the offer but would most likely reveal the entire project to the appropriate authorities. In fact, most of the applicants would do the same.

As he gathered all the information on Jake, he looked at his watch again. He needed to make contact tonight or else they would call him again at his home. The more they called at home, the more likely he would be exposed.

He put on his overcoat and grabbed a manila folder. He walked out of his apartment and to the elevator. As he approached the elevator, he saw two men come down the opposite hall. They both wore dark suits that he knew too well. He quickly turned around and headed toward the door for the stairs. He took one more glance before the door closed. They were nodding to each other. One walked down the hall, and the other headed toward the stairwell.

He couldn't wait any longer. He spun on one foot and raced down the stairs, jumping three to four steps at a time. While going down the four flights of stairs, he considered why these men in dark suits were already following him. He didn't think any mistakes had been made. There were no reasons for them to be suspicious yet…or were there? Maybe he wasn't being cautious enough, or maybe he hadn't realized that he was leaving behind a trail of clues.

At the ground level, he reached for the door to the street as he had done so many times before. This time the door was locked. He was left with no time to understand the change and no other choice but to walk through the lobby. He peeked around the lobby door and didn't see anything out of the ordinary. Two parking attendants loitered at the bell stand. One he recognized, and the other one he could not make out fully but looked like the new guy they had hired three weeks ago.

He suddenly realized that the new hire might have been a way for them to follow him more closely.

Since there were no other people in the lobby, he dared to walk through. He heard footsteps coming down the stairwell. This made him move quicker, but he didn't want to attract attention to himself. Raising his left hand to the men at the bell stand, he made a gesture to say hello and act composed. "How are you gentlemen doing tonight? Looks as if it will be a good night for dinner at Pasal's. See you when I get back."

Pasal's was a small Mexican restaurant that had outdoor seating. It had a nice ambiance with good food, good margaritas, and a nice atmosphere. Tonight it would serve as a testing ground to see if any unusual people showed up. For the most part, the clientele were all regulars around the neighborhood. If unusual diners showed up, they would stand out like a sore thumb. If by chance some people were there asking about him, well, two parking attendants were the only people who knew he was going to be there.

"Do you need your car tonight?" asked one of the attendants.

"No, I think I'll walk on such a beautiful night." He didn't need to stick around and wait for the guy coming down the stairs anyway. He continued to walk toward the doors. He had never appreciated the mirrors alongside the double arched doors, but now was a perfect time to make use of them. As he pushed one of the doors open, he glanced at the mirror. Sure enough, the new attendant was picking up the phone. A phone call to his girlfriend, a phone call to order pizza or a phone call for back up at Pasal's?

When the door was fully open, the mirror was not visible. He didn't want to stop his stride to continue to look at the mirror, but he wanted to notice anything else he could without making it too obvious. He glanced at the glass door and saw a reflection of the entire lobby. He saw the stair door opened, and out came a tall man in a dark suit. The man on the phone made eye contact with the tall man coming through the stair door, and he pointed a finger toward the double arched doors as he placed the phone back on the receiver. That was certainly not enough time to talk to a girlfriend or order a pizza.

Without any further hesitation, the man with the overcoat continued through the door and ran to the corner. He ran halfway down the block, and turned up an alley that led to a neighboring street. He quickly glanced over his shoulder but did not see a soul. No men in dark suits, no vendors, no street cleaners, no one. He continued up the alley to the next street into a busy area of town. A taxi was parked just in front of the alley. He opened the back door and jumped in.

"Hey, mister, the light's not on! Can't a guy take a break?" the driver complained.

The man in the overcoat pulled out a hundred dollar bill and shoved it through the partition between the back and front seats.

The driver saw it and his eyes opened widely. “I guess I can take that break later. Where to?”

“Let’s start by going to Sixth and DuPont.”

The driver looked confused. “That’s way on the other side of town! It will take at least-”

“Shut up and start driving. I’ll double the rate if you get me there in twenty minutes. I’m late for a meeting.”

As the taxi took off from the corner, he looked back. Still no one. *Great,* he thought. *Now we’ll see who shows up at Pasal’s for dinner.*

The ride was not the most luxurious as the taxi bounced him around the back like a sack of potatoes. Someday soon, very soon he would be able to ride in a beautiful car with a chauffeur driving him to his golf games. Until then, he was stuck in the back of this dirty, smelly taxi.

When he was not being bounced so badly, he took out a manila folder and began organizing some papers. One sheet had all sorts of fun-filled facts about Jake Douglas, things that Jake probably would not even remember, horrendous facts that he would have struggled to forget. But the man with the overcoat sitting in the back of this taxi had a large smile as he reread some of the information contained in the files. He especially was amused by the amount of financial debt Jake had accrued in his short, screwed up life. The man was over four hundred thousand dollars in debt in addition to alimony and childcare. The taxi passenger couldn’t help laughing as he read this number over and over again. There was no way Dr. Douglas would turn down his offer.

If Jake *did* turn down the offer, the man in the overcoat would have to resort to plan B. It was simple: expose Dr. Douglas and make public his attempt to sell hospital narcotics to lowlifes for enough money to cover his childcare payments.

If that weren't enough to sway him, then his patients and his future employer would hear about his drinking problem. Most damning was the time he operated while drunk on a five-year-old girl for presumed appendicitis. She never had appendicitis, but she did have an outrageous scar on her lower abdomen to remind her of that unnecessary surgery.

The taxi driver looked confused as he turned on to DuPont Street. There were hardly any occupied buildings. The streetlights were few, providing an eerie aura.

The man in the overcoat sensed the driver's uneasy feeling about the area. "Relax," he said from the back seat. "This area has always given me the creeps as well. Don't worry; I'm not planning to sacrifice you for this wonderful palace on wheels. I just need to take care of some business, and then we can head back to town. Now, if you would kindly stop the car right here, I'll be back before you can say oh shit."

The man got of the taxi in the middle of the street. No one was there. Nothing seemed alive in this part of town.

The driver called after him, "Hey, how about you call another taxi when you're done with this meeting? I'm sure they can get you a driver in just a few minutes. And if not, just give me a call and I-"

The man in the overcoat leaned into the taxi through the passenger seat window. "How about if you stay and give me a ride to dinner at Pasal's when I'm finished with this meeting? I'll make this worth your while." With that, the man in the overcoat opened his left hand, holding another hundred-dollar bill.

The driver quickly reached for the money, but the fist closed before he could grab the bill. The driver looked up at the man in the window.

The man just smiled and took two steps back from the car. "I'll see you in a few minutes." He walked down to the corner and turned right down the next street.

As the man with the overcoat reached the payphone, he cautiously turned around to make sure no one was nearby. This phone was a good spot to call because it always seemed to be deserted, especially at night. The only people out were usually gang-bangers. He wondered if the taxicab driver would actually stay around. There had only been a few drivers who had stayed for the entire phone conversation in the past. Usually he returned to discover that the driver got scared away by kids looking for trouble.

He pulled back his overcoat to retrieve the phone number and then reached for the phone. It was coated with some slimy, sticky scum that was left by a piece of candy. He wiped it off with a Kleenex before dialing.

It was difficult at times to get through, but tonight there were no delays. The operator came on the line with a strong Middle Eastern accent and verified the number. After a short pause, the man heard the familiar voice.

"Hello, my friend. I've been waiting so patiently for your phone call. We have located a doctor here that I think will be able to do the job. How about you? We need a doctor from your end to complete the mission."

The man with the overcoat responded, "I have also narrowed down my applicants to just one. I think he will work out great, but I need to meet with him. I need to discuss the details and go over the initial plan with him. But I'm sure he will accept our offer, and according to his files, he really could use the money."

"You know if the money is the issue, my people can make sure he never has a chance to make it to the bank."

The man in the overcoat cautioned, "I don't think it would be a good idea to make this a bigger deal than needs to be."

As they talked, the man glanced down at the phone timer.

Fifteen seconds left. He had to end the conversation quickly, just as he had so many others before. “I need to go, but I will talk to you in a few days. I plan to meet with him tomorrow.”

“Very well, my friend. We shall talk soon.”

There was a click on the end of the line. The man was relieved and surprised that they’d had another four seconds left. This had to be one of the first times in a long while that he hadn’t needed to hang up on his contact midsentence. He hung up the phone and started to turn around when he felt a light tap on his shoulder. His heart rate shot up, and he quickly reached for his gun before slowly turning around.

Standing in front of him was a young punk. “Hey mister, got any spare change in that pocket of yours?”

“Sorry I used it on the phone.” He headed back toward the taxi. At the corner, he saw a few gangbangers giving the driver a rough time. He was amazed that the driver stayed, noting that the guy really must be hard up for money. “Hey, this one is taken, so get lost,” he told the group of kids.

“Well, maybe we’re not ready for you boys to leave quite yet,” announced one of the kids in the crowd.

“Sorry, but I am ready to leave.” The man in the overcoat pulled out his gun and shoved it between the kid’s eyes. He cocked the trigger with his index finger and asked, “Do you have any problems with that?”

With fear in his eyes, the kid stared down the barrel. He quietly shook his head from side to side.

The man proceeded to get into the taxi. “Let’s get back to Pasal’s.”

“Two hundred, fifty-three times,” said the driver in a very disgusted tone of voice.

“What are you so upset about? I just saved your little ass from those hoodlums.”

Again, the driver repeated, "Two hundred, fifty-three times. You assured me that you would be back before I could say 'oh shit.' I said it two hundred, fifty-three shit-ass times!"

"Oh so sorry about that. Here is a hundred dollars for your trouble and another hundred dollars if you can lose those gangbangers."

The driver quickly glanced up at his mirror, and sure enough, there were two cars behind him. He made a sharp turn down Sixth Street, another turn down an alley, and then behind a warehouse. As the taxi came out from behind the warehouse, it nearly collided with a gold Cadillac. The rear windows were down, and a gun of some sort was brought into view. The driver of the taxi didn't waste any time before making a quick left followed by another right. The Cadillac was still right on their tail as both cars approached a railroad crossing with the wooden gate down. The whistle of an oncoming train sounded. Both the taxi driver and the man with the overcoat looked to the left to see a train only a short thirty yards away going at least forty miles per hour.

The passenger in the back yelled, "Don't even think about it!"

There was a moment of deceleration as his foot came off the gas pedal, but the taxi driver felt that there was no other choice to escape the Cadillac. He slammed his foot on the gas pedal, and the instant acceleration slammed both men against their seats. As the taxi broke through the first wooden gate, they both looked to their left to see a huge white light speeding toward them. They both let out a terrified scream. The sound of the train whistle roared past them as they broke through the second gate. They heard the sound of the train wheels going over the train tracks behind them. They glanced back to look at the train and see the Cadillac on the other side. Without hesitation, the taxi driver sped away toward the highway ramp.

After about five minutes of silence, the man in the overcoat yelled, "I told you not to do it. I specifically said not to think about it! What the hell were you thinking?"

"You saved my little ass, and the least I could do was save your *dumb* ass in return," replied the driver. "Do you still want to go to Pasal's?"

"Yes," replied the man in the back seat.

They did not talk again until they neared the restaurant.

Just as he suspected, several unmarked cars were in the neighborhood of Pasal's. The stakeout started two blocks away from the restaurant.

"Do you want to be dropped off at the front door?" asked the driver.

"No, just drive slowly by the front door and then continue on."

The driver was confused and looked up at the mirror to stare at the man in the back.

The man in the overcoat didn't care. His hunch was right: they were on to him. At this particular moment, he couldn't figure how they discovered him. He covered his tracks very well, but somehow they found out. As the taxi slowly drove down the block of Pasal's entrance, he saw several agents in street clothes. He recognized three of them. Unmarked cars, undercover agents, they were definitely on to him. From now on, he would have to be more discreet.

"You know, I have kind of lost my appetite. Why don't you take me to the Whitefish apartment complex downtown?"

As they drove, the man looked through Jake's file again.

Chapter 6

The room was still. What seemed like a brief period of time with everyone who was involved in a code on Mr. Springer was actually two hours spent trying to save Mr. Springer. From the time Dr. Jenson called the code and declared him dead, the room was silent. It was always difficult to bounce back from a failed code.

The crowd that had gathered in the room a short two hours ago now moved as if in slow motion. The nurses from the Emergency Room began to pick up some of the debris left in the middle of the bed. The nursing supervisor, who had been present to help coordinate the nursing staff, began to go over the flow sheets with the nurse who had recorded all of the activity over the last few hours. The respiratory therapist began to disconnect the ventilator.

Then there was Dr. Jenson. Sally walked over to a chair in the corner of the room, sat down, and held her head as she rested her elbows on her knees. She stared out the window as if she were somehow removed from the cleanup activity going on.

Steve, although still numb from the experience, felt sad for Sally. He walked over to her and knelt next to the chair. "I'm so sorry, Dr. Jenson. You really did a great job running the code, and I'm sure the family would appreciate how much you did in here today."

"Yeah, well that's nice and all, but he still came in for an elective procedure and died shortly afterwards. And he still has a family." She looked at Steve and added, "You just don't see the whole picture here." She proceeded to explain her extensive experience with Mr. Springer.

Mr. Springer was a very pleasant man who looked to be in

his thirties but was actually fifty-two years old. He had been blessed with a youthful appearance that so many people admire. His charm was pleasant as well. When he first saw Dr. Jenson walk into the office at his first appointment, he made a small joke to break the ice between the new patient and doctor. It had something to do with a small child and a clown, but Sally couldn't remember the details.

Mr. Springer and his wife sat across from Sally and told her about the troubles that had been bothering him over the last several months. Sally recalled his history of severe constipation for many years, and the use of laxatives and stool softeners in order to have bowel movements. The Springers had discussed the problem without hesitation, as if they felt this unusual comfort with Sally. Upon further questioning, Sally learned he had developed severe left sided pain after eating popcorn. Every time he and his wife went to a movie and stuffed themselves with the goodies at the concession stand, he would get this severe pain on the left side. The pain seemed to move to the lower area of the left side. Mr. Springer said that he would occasionally get fevers and nausea after the movies. Sally remembered his story so well because it was so typical for diverticular disease.

Diverticula, small herniations of the colonic wall, can form small out pouchings from the colon and can cause a host of problems, including infection and bleeding. Sally told the couple about a man who had elected to let his infection go on without any treatment but developed an abscess along the diverticula, which eventually ruptured. The man almost died and required a few extra operations to resolve the problem. Of course Mr. Springer was concerned, so Sally placed him on some antibiotics and ordered some tests, including a colonoscopy. After just the first visit, the patient, his wife, and the doctor felt at ease with each other, and the Springers asked Sally if she would do the procedure. Sally smiled and, without hesitation, gladly accepted the opportunity to evaluate Mr. Springer's colon. She turned to his wife and suggested a two-for-one bonus deal, but his wife just laughed and shook her head no.

The colonoscopy was not scheduled for a few weeks, but when it was done, many diverticula were discovered. A CT scan did not reveal any abscess formation but did show areas of acute and chronic inflammation. Sally and Mr. Springer discussed a diet plan that included no nuts, no foods with seeds, and definitely no popcorn. The plan worked for a while, but then Mr. Springer grew frustrated with the new diet and began cheating every so often. This every-so-often was when he would get the recurrent pain in his left side. Eventually, he and Dr. Jenson agreed to remove the portion of colon with the diverticula present.

Since the surgery was not emergent, Sally stressed the importance of abiding by the diet plan for diverticular disease, and she scheduled the surgery electively with Dr. Jake Douglas. The couple was confused by the switch in doctors. Sally tried to describe how the system worked. She explained that the chief resident got to scrub on all the bigger cases as he had more experience. The Springers would have none of that and requested that Dr. Jenson be their surgeon. Sally discussed the scenario with Jake. He didn't seem to have a problem with it, so Sally called scheduling to tell them she would be the operating surgeon. There was a moment of silence on the other end of the phone. Then the scheduler congratulated her on a job well done. She told Sally she never recalled when a junior resident was able to be the surgeon on such a big case.

During the next several days, Sally met the entire Springer

family as they came in for pre-operative testing and workup. They were a wonderful family, two teenage boys and a ten-year-old daughter. They all seemed to be a close family, but there was a special bond between Mr. Springer and his daughter. Sally empathized with the little girl as she recalled her relationship with her father. "My father is the best father ever," his daughter said during one visit. Sure enough, there was something very special between Mr. Springer and his baby.

The morning of the operation, Sally went over the plan for surgery with the Springers. They discussed what she was going to do, the small chance for a temporary colostomy, and the risks of surgery. She hated this part because, no matter how you brought it up, people focused the most on the risks and possible complications of surgery. Nevertheless, they got through the discussion without too much trouble. The Springers had all the confidence in the world of Dr. Jenson, so they had no doubt that surgery would go just fine.

In fact, surgery went better than fine. It was perfect. Sally was able to resect the affected colon without a problem and was able to connect it together without the need for a colostomy.

The first several days passed without a problem. Mr. Springer was out of bed the first day and walking the hallways by the second. The nursing staff was impressed with his sense of urgency to get better and out of the hospital. He pushed himself so hard the first few days that on the third day, his incision was tender, so he just lay in bed. Sally thought that resting would be sensible after he worked himself so hard the first couple of days.

But the next day, postoperative day number four, Mr. Springer woke up feeling unwell. He was not able to describe the discomfort to his nurse that morning. He said he felt a little nauseous, a little short of breath; his legs felt a little tired, and overall he just didn't feel well. When Sally saw him that morning, she agreed that he didn't look like the upbeat Mr. Springer she knew. Everyone including Sally felt that it was merely a result of his hard work on postoperative days number one and two.

Sally didn't think twice when she saw him on morning rounds because the fourth day after colon surgery tended to be a difficult hurdle to get past. Unfortunately, Jake never rounded on Mr. Springer. His reasoning was that since Sally declared herself the primary surgeon, she should then manage the patient after surgery. He thought it would be a good learning situation for her, and if she had any problems, she would ask.

She had no questions until she heard the overhead page to Mr. Springer's room. She wondered desperately why he would code. Could it be a heart attack, could it be a pulmonary embolus, could it be late postoperative hemorrhage, could it be, could it be, could it be? The fact was that it could have been any number of things, and without an autopsy, no one would ever know.

At this moment, Sally could not even think about asking the family for an autopsy. She could not even imagine the difficult conversation that lay ahead when she had to tell the family what happened. His wife and children had left around lunchtime to complete some errands. They left unexpectedly because he was doing well. Sally was in the room when they all were saying goodbye. No one could sense this was their last farewell to their father and husband.

Dr. Jenson slowly turned to Steve and said, "So now you know the whole picture. Once you know these patients, it's not just a code. It's a heart-splitting challenge to save someone who you grew to care for as a person, not just an operative case." She put her head back into her delicate hands and began to sob.

Steve didn't know what to do. He looked up to see if one of the nurses would be able to console Dr. Jenson, but no other warm human being was even paying attention to the two of them. He slowly raised his arm to put around her slumped shoulders but suddenly stopped. *Wait,* he told himself, *Just a few hours ago this bitch was reaming you over the coals. And now she wants some sympathy? Well, screw it.*

But Sally didn't want sympathy; she needed it. Steve, a sincere person, perceived her pain and slowly put his hand around her shoulders. He leaned over and said in a very gentle way, "I'm so sorry, Dr. Jenson. I didn't realize the attachment you had with Mr. Springer."

Sally responded, "I can tell you just started your surgery residency." She sniffled. "You're still nice and compassionate."

They both giggled.

Steve was thinking as he consoled Sally. She was right. He just saw this code as an adrenaline stimulating experience. He hadn't given a moment's thought to the fact that the patients were real people involved with families, friends, husbands, wives, and children. He was so scared about his own risks that he didn't realize the true implications of a code.

Steve attempted to recount the ordeal from his point of view.

When he had dashed into Mr. Springer's room behind Dr. Jenson, he saw several nurses doing this and that. He saw a respiratory therapist trying to bag the patient. The ambu bag was filling with secretions rapidly, and the RT yelled at Sally that she could no longer bag him anymore. This just added to the mayhem. Sally scrambled to the head of the bed and asked for an endotracheal tube. "Give me a size 8 ET tube and a laryngoscope, now!" she screamed. It must have been a difficult intubation because Sally kept on yelling for suction. "Why don't you people ever have the fuckin' suction ready in these codes? Damn it, where's the fuckin' suction? I needed it yesterday!"

Once Mr. Springer was intubated, Sally took the stethoscope and listened to both sides of his chest. "All right," she said. "Let's get him hooked up to the ventilator." She stepped back to the foot of the bed and anxiously folded both her arms around her chest. She looked up at the monitor to follow the rhythm. It looked as if he was in Vfib. Even Steve could see that. "Ok, Carmichael, start compressions."

"Me? Me, Dr. Jenson?"

"Are you Carmichael?"

"Uh… yeah, but I …"

"Shut up, Steve, and start doing chest compressions! You'll never learn anything standing twenty fuckin' feet from the patient."

Steve realized she was right. He had barely made it in the door of the overcrowded room but reasoned that he could learn more by standing in the doorway. The fact was that he was scared shitless.

"Carmichael, or whoever you are, you're right. You are absolutely correct. This man does not need compressions.

What does he need, Carmichael?"

Steve stood over the bed in a full panic sweat. He could feel his pulse racing and was sure everybody in the room could hear his heartbeat.

"Carmichael!" screamed Sally. "Don't freak on me, boy! I can only handle one code at a time. What does this man need? Now!"

Steve looked at the monitor and then at the vital signs. He took the back of his left hand and wiped the sweat off his forehead. As he did this, he discovered more moisture than he had anticipated. One of the nurses handed him a towel. "I think we should shock him," whispered the petrified intern.

"What, Steve? What did you say? Speak up. This guy is dying, and his hearing is a little shitty. He won't care if you speak up a bit."

Steve was upset with the way Sally was treating him, but she was probably right. He was pussyfooting his way through his first code. Speaking of which- where was Erica? She had promised to be at his first code.

"We need to shock the shit out of him!" yelled Steve.

"Let's try to leave the shit in him. The nurses would really appreciate that. Come on, Carmichael, let's do it."

Steve looked over his shoulder, saw the paddles, and reached for them. He placed them on the patient's chest. In the correct position, one paddle was in front and the other along the patient's left side. His hands were shaking as the paddles rested on Mr. Springer's chest. He screamed at the nurse standing near the defribulator, "Charge at 300!"

A soft voice responded, "Charged."

Steve leaned into the table, ready to charge.

"Stop!" yelled Sally. "Didn't you forget something? You are about to make a few enemies."

"Oh, yeah – clear!"

With that, all the people at the bedside moved back a step so they wouldn't feel the electrical surge delivered through the paddles to the patient's body. Steve pushed the small red buttons on the paddles, and Mr. Springer's body jolted off the bed a few inches in a spasmodic manner.

Steve glanced at the monitor and smiled. Everyone in the room cheered as the patient showed a normal sinus rhythm. The sweat was dripping from Steve's face, but that didn't matter, he had just saved Mr. Springer.

Dr. Jenson felt much better, too. She thought that was all Mr. Springer needed.

About twenty seconds later, one of the nurses shouted that his pressure was back down. The only IV he had was a small one, so Sally asked for a central line kit. She pushed her way to the front of the bed and evaluated the vein situation on the patient. Both of his arms had already been bruised from multiple IVs during the past week. Sally pulled the hospital gown off his broad shoulders and looked at his clavicles.

While Dr. Jenson was assessing his subclavian vein situation, another nurse shouted, “Vfib, he’s back in Vfib!”

Dr. Jenson looked at the monitor, and sure enough, he was back in that rhythm that would not allow the heart to adequately pump blood through the body. She checked his blood pressure: 55/20. “Shit! Start the compressions again, and Carmichael, get ready to shock him!” She was no longer in the teaching mood. There was definitely something failing Mr. Springer, and she could not determine the cause. “Someone call Dr. Douglas, NOW! And get a drip of Dopamine started at five mics.” Dr. Jenson, in the midst of a panic attack, began to place a central line.

Steve thought, *Dr. Douglas?* She must be totally freaked.

For Dr. Jenson to call in the reinforcements meant she was in dire need of assistance. Steve knew for a surgical resident to call for help was a sure sign of a major problem. Surgeons never felt like they needed any help, and the residents were proud of the fact that they took care of most of their problems by themselves.

But this was not a typical problem. The patient was trying to die.

Dr. Jenson grabbed a bottle of Betadine and splashed a bunch on the left clavicle. Then she slammed a drape over the area and inserted a long needle into the skin toward the clavicle.

The patient didn't move. His pressure was only in the fifties.

"Someone get lab up here and draw a CBC, chemistries, and a blood gas. Then get X-ray up for a portable chest. Come on, Carmichael; shock the shit out of him! Someone give one amp of epi and then another amp of sodium bicarb. Now!" Dr. Jenson was beginning to unravel, and the others in the room noticed.

The charge nurse leaned over to another nurse and whispered, "Find out who the attending is, and get his butt down here now!" The nurse scrambled toward the door and ran to the nurses' station.

Steve shocked Mr. Springer repeatedly, but he didn't respond. Dr. Jenson finally secured the central line, despite being interrupted several times for the shocks that Steve delivered.

Dr. Rosberg burst into the room. "What the hell is going on in here? Jenson! Why didn't you call me when this happened? Shit, it looks worse than a fuckin' MASH unit. Did anyone get a blood gas?"

Dr. Jenson, as upset as she was, filled Dr. Rosberg in on the details as best as she could remember. Steve could sense both a feeling of remorse and relief that Dr. Jenson expressed while talking to Dr. Rosberg.

After almost two hours of coding Mr. Springer, Dr. Rosberg checked the patient's pupils. He turned from the bed and walked past Dr. Jenson. "Next time you decide to kill one of my patients, inform me first." He walked solemnly out of the room.

Dr. Jenson was even more determined to save Mr. Springer, but after several more minutes, she too checked Mr. Springer's pupils. Fixed and dilated. Over the last few hours, there had not been enough blood pumped to his brain. Not enough oxygen had been delivered to his brain cells.

Dr. Jenson turned and quietly glanced at the clock. “Shit,” she whispered. “Time of death is 4:32 PM.” She took Mr. Springer’s hand and said, “Sorry.” She roamed the room quietly for a few minutes and then sat down to put her head in her hands.

As Steve sat with Sally, he thought about his perception of the code and death of Mr. Springer. What the code meant to Steve versus Sally was clearly different.

Steve sat with Dr. Jenson for five minutes before she said, “Alright, Carmichael, now you’ve seen surgery at its worst. There are a few other patients on the floor that need scut work done. Why don’t you find Tom? He will orient you to our patients and what needs to be done. I guess you won’t have to worry about writing a progress note on Mr. Springer.”

Steve stood up, patted Sally on the back, and repeated his condolences.

Later while walking down the hallway with Dr. Formin, Steve saw Jake and Sally talking. She was crying again, and he was comforting her with a hug. Steve never thought surgery residents needed hugs, but then he never saw a resident so upset before, nor had he ever witnessed a patient dying right before his eyes. Steve was impressed that both residents were able to express their feelings so openly, but he knew that they were surgeons and that it would be short lived. By tomorrow, both Jake and Sally would be just as demanding, just as egotistical, and just as condescending as they had been before.

Chapter 7

It was pitch dark out as Steve drove home. It was not the beginning of a beautiful sunset or a romantic twilight. It was just late at night. He, of course, had been forewarned about the long hours spent training to be a surgeon, but he thought it would somehow be different for him. When he left for orientation this morning, it had been dark as well. This would be something to which he could adjust, but the real problem would be the lack of sleep that accompanied such long hours of training. He'd had his chance to select a different specialty, but surgery was what appealed to him the most. So for the next several years, at least until he became a chief resident, residents above him would dictate his life; his days would be painfully long.

As he turned up the driveway and shut off the engine, Steve had to admit it was a wonderful night. No clouds in the sky and all the stars one could ever imagine. The temperature was still warm, and he heard some neighborhood dogs barking to each other. He was happy that he decided to rent a duplex in a family neighborhood. He had felt it was time to move away from college apartments. While in both college and medical school, he lived where all the action was, but now he needed a place to hang out quietly after long call nights. He needed a place to be able to study without a loud party blasting his eardrums until the wee hours. He needed a place to call home and not share it with three other guys who had girls gallivanting around the place, left dirty clothes on the stairs, or ignored three-day-old pizza laying on the kitchen table.

The duplex he had found was in a very quiet area and near most of the hospitals that he would have to work, specifically the University Hospital. The family below him was very pleasant and kept to themselves. They had two small children, both boys, and one golden retriever. Steve thought the father worked nights and the mother stayed home, but he was not sure. They owned the complex, and Steve could tell they were good managers as everything appeared clean and well kept. Whenever he had a problem, the husband would be up the next day to fix it. In fact, when he first moved in, the stairs up to his front door squeaked. The next day, they were fixed.

Tonight the stairs were quiet as ever. He looked through the front door window and noticed everything was pretty much how he had left it that morning. He bought an automatic light switch so when he came home on nights like this he would not have to walk in to a dark house. He put his key into the lock and was glad that the owners installed a new deadbolt since the previous occupants had run off with one of the second set of keys to the old lock. The landlord tried to assure Steve that they were fine people and would never bother him, but Steve felt more secure knowing that he held the only keys to his home.

As he swung the door open, he heard this clatter coming from the living room. He stopped in the doorway and stood still. Sudden the scurry of feet hitting the hardwood floor sounded. One second later, a big yellow lab raced around the corner and almost flattened Steve. “Down boy, down boy! That’s a good dog. How was your day, Pudge?” Steve called his dog Pudge because the dog never stopped eating. From the very beginning as a pup, Pudge always chowed on anything and everything. He had earned the name Pudge.

It was nice to have Pudge greet Steve after his first day of residency, especially since there was no one else to do the chore. After letting the dog out, Steve opened the fridge and pulled out yesterday’s meatloaf and warmed it in the microwave. Steve was not a gourmet chef, but he knew how to cook the basics. In college, he always did the majority of the cooking. It never bothered him. In fact, he rather enjoyed it.

While the meatloaf was warming, Steve sat at the dinner table and began making a list of the things he needed to get accomplished that night. He always made lists to help him stay organized. Tonight the list was short, but his late start time was a problem. He had to go over the orientation material, make a list of the patients on the surgery service and read about their problems, read at least ten pages of his surgery text, and then talk to his best friend. He had never actually met this lady before in person, but he knew her well from chatting on the internet.

She entered his life about three months before med school ended, about the same time he found out where he was going to complete his surgery residency. It was strange at first, talking to a stranger, but they were like best friends after just a few encounters. Steve was usually very cautious, so when she first entered his cyber world, he was reluctant to converse with her. However, she coaxed him into chatting with her, and eventually they developed a private chatroom so no one would snoop on their conversations. This made Steve feel more comfortable with the conversation, but then he went through a phase where he thought she might actually be a he. He stopped talking with her for about a month after that. She never sent a picture of herself but assured Steve that she was, in reality, a woman. She referred to herself as Sweetpea. Tonight, though, Sweetpea might have to take second fiddle to all the things Steve needed to get through before morning. They had talked almost every day since he had gotten over the gender doubts, only missing a day talking to each other for really special occasions. But Steve had to get through his orientation material and learn about his patients. He had also promised himself that he would read a little every day from his surgery text so that he could learn as much as possible before his surgery inservice exam, a yearly test surgery residents had to take.

After letting Pudge back in, he made a pot of coffee and took his meatloaf to the living room. His TV was up on a meticulously organized entertainment center. On one shelf, he had a few art sculptures, and on another, he had several hard cover books that were neatly sitting upright against each other.

Steve sat down with his plate of food and turned on the TV to listen to the news. He took a drink of coffee and began to go through his packets of material from orientation.

After twenty minutes going through boring orientation materials, Steve had enough. He made a file with a manila folder and titled it "Surgical Orientation." He carried the heavy folder into his second bedroom, which was converted into a small office. A two-level file cabinet stood next to his large oak desk. He sat down and found a place for the orientation file in the file cabinet.

A framed picture of his family sat on the file cabinet. Steve gazed fondly at his father, mother, and two sisters posing in front of a fountain at a family wedding. It had been too long since he had spoken to any of them. He made a mental note to call his mother in a day or two.

On his desk were neatly organized papers describing his medical school graduation and information on his medical boards. To the right on his desk laid a beautiful laptop computer. It was a gift from his parents for graduating from medical school. His desk, like the rest of his office and living quarters, was quite organized.

It was not as though Dr. Carmichael was some obsessed neat freak, but he was brought up in an organized home, and the pattern stuck. When he first left his parent's home, he couldn't wait to get to a place where he didn't have to make his bed every day, but as soon as he moved into the college dormitories, he found himself making his bed every morning out of habit. It was one of several habits he had planned to break once on his own, but they were so engrained in his everyday life that they could not be broken.

After filing his orientation material, Steve turned around to a matching bookshelf and pulled out a surgery text. He grabbed several index cards and wrote the names of a patient on each card. He put down their primary diagnoses, their medications, allergies, their past medical history including operations, and any relevant social or family history. Steve reviewed all of the different problems the patients had. Those he didn't recognize, he looked up in his text. He continued until his eyelids were heavy and about to close. Finally, he gathered the cards together neatly and placed a clip on them.

The time was 11:25 PM. He still wanted to chat with his friend online, so he organized everything for the morning, got ready for bed, and turned on his computer.

Steve and Sweetpea met in a private chatroom. They tried to connect together around eight every night, but Steve had warned her that he was about to begin a new job that would have some terrible hours. She asked him what was so demanding that they would not be able to talk to each other every day. Steve was reluctant to tell her about being a doctor and a surgeon, but just before school ended, he told her that he was a med student about to graduate. She took it much differently than Steve imagined. She was just every bit as excited as Steve was. He figured that was probably why they were such goods friends. They talked a lot about medicine and Steve's career in surgery. He confessed right before his internship was about to start that he had fearful thoughts on the surgery training experience. Sweetpea talked him through it and made him feel like he could accomplish anything.

As much as they talked about Steve and his plans, he still didn't know exactly what she did. He asked several times, but she always evaded the question and managed to get them on to a different topic, yapping about the Bahamas or skiing in Colorado. Nonetheless, Steve wanted to fill her in on the details of his first day, so he signed online and went to their chatroom.

She was waiting for him. "Hi, Steve. You must be really tired. I mean, it is almost midnight. Don't those residents you work with have any heart? You're just an intern in his first week."

Steve replied, "You would think they would give us a little break, but there is so much to learn about how to take care of patients. The more senior residents feel that the sooner they teach us how to handle all the everyday pidly stuff, the sooner they can do other things like enjoy surgery and not have to worry about taking care of the patient because that's the job of the intern. In other words, the better the intern is, the more surgery the senior residents can do."

"Well still," typed Sweetpea. "They should cut you guys a little slack the first couple of weeks."

Steve didn't want to explain the surgery hierarchy tonight.

There were too many other things on his mind. "Yeah, you're right."

He rambled about his day, including the boring start with orientation and then about his surgery service. He didn't bother her with the details of meeting Erica. Tonight probably was not a good time to discuss other women, whether they were online or not.

Steve saved the most exciting for last. "And just as I was getting off the elevator and arriving on the surgery floor, there was a code called in our hospital wing. Unfortunately, it was a patient from our service. We coded him a long time but were unsuccessful. I had to do CPR and shock him. My poor resident felt really bad as she did all his surgery and postoperative care…" He paused for a moment again and thought how sick it was that what was a terrible event for a family was his most exciting part of the day. "I know it is kind of sick to think that my most exciting experience of the day had to be somebody else's misfortune. But I was able to participate in the thing that made me the most anxious about starting my internship: a code." He stopped typing and waited for a response.

After a short while came a response. "It must have been difficult for you and your resident to attempt to save the life of another person. I'm sure you will lay awake tonight in bed and sort out your emotions. You will probably replay the code minute by minute and realize the excitement of the entire event. And after you have gone through the code and all its details, you will encounter two issues. One, in order to learn to be an excellent doctor you will have to take care of and manage many patients. Some will not do well and continue to be very sick, and some will do fine, but you will definitely learn medicine from both groups of patients. Second, you will learn from very unpleasant situations. Like tonight, you learned to be involved with a code, and you found out that when put in a certain stressful position you can still function and provide excellent medical care…at least to your ability. You learned this tonight at the expense of a patient's life. But the experience will hopefully provide you with some new knowledge so that the next time you're in a code situation you will have gained new insight so that the outcome will be different. Most importantly while you're lying in bed tonight thinking about that gentleman's family, don't get too sad because it sounds as if you and your resident did everything you guys could do. Just the fact that you were thinking about the unfortunate fate of the patient while you were learning shows me that you have great sensitivity…which I already knew. Don't lose that… that sincere sensitivity and wealth of medical knowledge will make you an all-around excellent physician. I need to go, Steve. It's late and I need to work tomorrow too. I'm glad you had an exciting day and learned a lot. When you're seeing your patients tomorrow, don't forget about the person inside. See ya, Sweetpea."

Wow, thought Steve. That was exactly why he loved talking to her. She always knew the right things to say to make him feel better. "Thanks for your warm thoughts," he typed. "You always know what to say. Talk to you tomorrow, Steve." He signed off thinking about all the comments Sweetpea had made.

After letting the dog out, he got ready for bed. As he lay in bed for a while, he did think about the day's events and everything that happened. Then he thought how lucky he was to have a friend like Sweetpea.

Chapter 8

The music from the radio seemed to be at concert decibels. At 4:30 in the morning in the middle of a good dream, it was bound to catch anyone's attention. Steve rolled over, saw the time, and thought for a moment there was some mistake, like maybe he was supposed to get up at eight to round at nine or ten in the morning.

But there was no mistake. His plan was to preround on all of the patients on Dr. Douglas's service. If he had a chance to see all the patients before they started their formal rounds, then he would know about any problems that had occurred during the night. The more he knew for rounds, the better the chance he would get to operate.

Steve had been awake several times during his short night. He had too much nervous energy and lay in bed at times thinking about the day before and the day ahead. He thought about Sweetpea and Erica. He thought about Dennis Burrows, the new friend he had made in orientation, and wondered if he had just as much anxiety as Steve. He thought about Sally and Tom and wondered what time they got up to round. He thought about the medical students, Mike and Roger, and remembered how it felt to be at the bottom of the hierarchy. He thought… and thought… and thought… and only slept occasionally between his moments of insomnia.

He lifted his lean body from the mattress, but just as he was about to stand, he slumped back down into the nice warm, cozy blankets. *Just a few more minutes,* he thought to himself. Then he could rush his shower and still make it on time. But as his eyelids began to gently fall closed, he jumped out of bed. He definitely did not want to be late, at least not the first week.

There were stories about residents who were fired for being late continuously, but it only took one morning to start a bad habit.

He took a quick shower and made a light breakfast. He let Pudge out, made his bed, and tidied the house. It was pitch dark outside as he locked his apartment and made his way to his car. As he reached for the door handle, he heard a familiar, distressed noise. "Oh shit, Pudge!" Steve ran back up the stairs into his house and let the barking dog inside. "Sorry, pal." He only paused a moment to pet Pudge before leaving for the hospital.

The hallways of the hospital at 5:30 in the morning felt lonely. Few other people were walking around. The nurses on the night shift were finishing patient baths or charting their notes for the shift. A single resident must have been on call; he walked down the corridor with a large cup of coffee in his hand. Other than that, no other residents were visible.

Steve started in the ICU, visiting Mr. Gordon first. His head was buried in the flow sheet when he heard a voice over his left shoulder.

"Hey, top of the morning to you."

Steve swung around to find Dennis standing behind him. "What are you doing here so early?" he asked.

Dennis shrugged. "I thought I would follow your footsteps as a good surgery intern and pre-round on all of our patients on the surgery service."

"Hey, that's what I'm doing, but it looks like I'll only get through the ICU patients," said Steve. "So how was your first day? Did you get some assholes for residents?"

"I actually think I have a great team. My chief, Linda Kaplan, seems really cool. She didn't yell at all yesterday and was even nice to the students and let them leave early. Maybe it was just show for the first day, but that's ok. I'll take whatever

I can."

"Yeah, you're pretty lucky. I remember her from last year. One of my friends had her as a senior resident. She was very cool last year too. I think she is a civil person in general. I wonder what she is doing in surgery!"

They both laughed.

Steve and Dennis lost track of time as they compared their first day on the job. Just as Steve mentioned the code, a voice boomed from behind him.

"Come on, Carmichael, we don't have time to wait for you while you get a date for Saturday!" Tom Formin yelled across the ICU. If there was any doubt, it was gone: Tom was a dick like the rest of them.

Steve turned and looked at Dennis, "I guess my residents have a civil nature about themselves as well. I'll see you later, Dennis."

"Hang in there. I'll talk to you later."

"Alright, Carmichael, you write the notes while one of the students does the exam," said Tom. "Let's get started. I don't know where Sally or Jake are, but if we don't move along, we'll never finish before the operating room starts." Tom looked over the flow sheet and noticed that Mr. Gordon had a slight temperature last night. "Shit, Mr. Gordon spiked a temp last night."

"Yeah, but it was only a low-grade temp, and his white count was still normal at 9900," responded Steve.

Tom looked in amazement at Steve. "So you were doing more than getting a date for Saturday. Good job, Carmichael! That should land you in the OR today. At least hat would be *my* decision, but we both know that I'm not the commander in chief of this service."

While they were laughing, Sally approached from behind.

Somewhat short of breath, she pleaded her case. “Sorry I was late. First my alarm clock didn’t go off and then I couldn’t find my notes for the Morbidity and Mortality conference so I can discuss Mr. Springer and then…”

“It’s okay, Sally,” said Tom. “It’s just us. Remember that we’re on your side. The enemy has not arrived yet. Actually, Jake is late, too.”

“Yeah, and when he does get here, he better have a good excuse why his ass was so late,” said Steve in a stern voice.

Tom, Sally, and the students looked at Steve, shocked by his comment.

He added with a straight face, “What? Jake should have to answer to somebody. We do. And from now on, Jake Douglas will have to answer to *me* when his sorry ass is late!” Steve could no longer keep his composure and began laughing, the rest of the team added to the laughter.

After a few seconds of fun, Sally broke in and said, “Jake is not late, at least not late for making it to the hospital. He is outside the ICU talking to some lawyer. So how is Mr. Gordon doing this morning?”

Tom explained that he and Steve had noticed low-grade temps from during the night, plus the normal WBC.

Sally walked over to the patient and drew out her stethoscope while she listened to their report. She examined the patient herself while Tom spoke. He stopped when Dr. Jenson listened to Mr. Gordon’s lungs, heart, and abdomen.

When she was done, she turned around and asked who had examined the patient.

Mike, looking as if he had done something wrong, answered, “I did.”

“What did you find? Any abnormalities or was everything the way you would want for your mother?” Sally smiled.

"Actually, I thought his lungs were clear and his heart was sinus. I didn't appreciate any murmur."

"Would you expect to hear a heart murmur in a post trauma patient if they didn't come in with a murmur?"

Mike was beginning to feel warm, "Uhh, I don't think so."

Sally continued teaching rounds. "Are you sure? Are you absolutely sure? This is your mother we're talking about now. Why don't you listen again just to make yourself absolutely certain?"

Mike grabbed his stethoscope and placed it on Mr. Gordon's chest. The ventilator continued to make his chest move twelve times a minute, but in between the movements, Mike listened carefully. The distraction of the vent made it difficult to hear clearly, but he was certain there were no murmurs. He moved back from the bed shaking his head as he removed the stethoscope from his ears. "No, definitely not. No murmurs."

"How about his lungs? Any findings on his lung exam?" continued Sally.

"No, I think the exam was just as I stated at first."

"Well, that is a very confident statement, especially for a third year medical student."

Mike looked down at his feet as if he had just been scolded.

"As a matter of fact, I agree," stated Sally.

Mike looked up and produced a slight smile of relief.

"Now, Dr. Carmichael, in the face of a life threatening trauma, do you think Mr. Gordon had a thorough exam when he came in to the trauma room? I mean, most likely this guy was about dead when he arrived, and tubes, IVs, catheters, and fingers were already going into his body. Most likely, a medical student at best put a stethoscope to this guy's body. Do you think the exam would have been accurate?"

"No, but if there *was* a murmur, I think it probably would have been noticed."

"Really? You think above all that commotion and noise someone with the best set of ears could hear a murmur? Carmichael, grab your scope and listen to my chest. Now! We don't have all day."

Steve timidly walked toward Dr. Jenson and hesitantly pulled out his stethoscope. He wondered at first if she was joking, but Sally did not even hint a smile. He placed the scope over her heart and began to listen. Sally grabbed the scope off her chest. With his ears ringing from the amplified crash on his stethoscope Steve took off the scope.

"Do you always do your heart exam through someone's clothes? That is a sure way to miss a finding." Sally unbuttoned the top three buttons of her blouse.

Steve, now totally embarrassed, had to put his stethoscope on the upper part of her bare breast. He could feel his skin warm up quickly, but he listened carefully. After what seemed to be an eternity, he removed his scope.

"Well what did you hear?" asked Sally impatiently.

"I heard a normal sinus rhythm with a normal S1 and S2 and no murmurs."

"You sure? Absolutely sure just as if your mother's care depended on it?"

"Yes. I didn't hear any murmurs."

"Well, how about that, Mr. Know-it-all. During a trauma code you missed a grade1 murmur from a mitral valve prolapse!" As Sally buttoned her blouse she asked, "So how does that affect your assessment of Mr. Gordon this morning, Steve?"

Steve was not sure where to go with the question and he stared at her with a blank look on his face.

Sally helped out. "Let's say this guy is indeed the druggie that he was made out to be. Then he probably uses too, right?" Sally waited for a response after her large hint.

"There is a small chance that he might have a vegetation on one of his heart valves."

"A small chance? I'm not sure that it is necessarily a small l or a large chance, but doing IV drugs certainly increase the chance that vegetation could develop on a heart valve and cause a bacteremia. That would certainly cause a low grade temp."

Continuing the role of chief resident, Sally turned her attention to Dr. Formin. "So Tom, since you were the highest in ranking here this morning, what did you attribute this low grade temp to?"

Tom searched for the right answer. "Well, as you mentioned, he could have bacterial endocarditis-"

"Very original Tom, but your astute medical student tells you that there is no heart murmur, and I agree."

Mike let out another proud smile, also revealing gratitude that the grilling was not directed at him any longer.

Tom continued. "Since he is only a day out of surgery, he might have developed some atelectasis in his lungs. That small amount of lung collapse could certainly cause his low grade temp."

"Very good." said Sally, "Keep going."

"Uhh, he could have, uhh…"

"Dr. Formin, before you get into another 'uhh' fit, review the exam that you recorded in his progress note."

Tom reviewed the note that Steve had written but could not find any culprits that would cause the temp. Finally, Tom looked up, shook his head, and said, "I just can't find another reason for his temp."

"That's it? You just stop there and accept the fact that he

has a low grade temp that could develop into a major septic episode?"

Tom stared at Sally.

Glancing at her watch, Sally realized the time was getting short and she had to wrap up teaching rounds. "Tom, what did the wound look like?"

"I'm not sure."

"Why is the wound important, Dr. Carmichael? Does it make a difference the first few days out of surgery?"

Steve had assumed that his grilling was done, but now he realized that he had a few more years to suffer the unusual teaching method. "It is my understanding that it usually takes up to a week to develop a wound infection, but there are a few organisms that may cause a wound to get infected the first couple of days after surgery."

"Very good, and what would those bugs be?" demanded Sally.

"I think Clostridium and Streptococcus could cause an early wound infection."

"Good. So should we look at the wound today, guys?"

Steve walked over to the bedside, put a pair of gloves on his hands, and removed the dressing. The wound looked fine, without any redness or warmth over it.

"Ok," said Sally. "The wound looks good. We need to wrap this up. Mike or Roger, could you two think of any reason why Mr. Gordon has a temp?"

The two students looked at each other and shook their heads no.

Sally turned toward Steve again.

"It's probably too early for a urinary tract infection, but that could be a possibility," he said.

"Doubtful," replied Sally. She finally looked at Tom, but he didn't have the answer. "What is he scheduled for today?"

Suddenly Tom and Steve knew where Sally was headed with her questioning.

"The packs could be a source for the temp," Steve blurted out.

Sally nodded dramatically. "You've had a foreign material stuck in this guy's belly for 24 hours, not to mention his trauma and hypotension. What more do you want? We need to get the packing out today. His WBC is okay, but what about his diff? Is his differential abnormal? Are there any bands?"

Steve looked at his notes and then at the lab sheet, "No, that was all fine."

"Good. He will probably do fine. Let's make sure he is typed and crossed before he goes to the OR. Steve, please order that. All right, that's enough teaching for this morning. We need to fly to get through the rest of these patients."

The team looked over the two other patients. The elderly man was doing well. Dr. Jenson thought he could be transferred out of the ICU, but to be safe she would run it by Dr. Douglas. Mrs. Johnson also was doing well, but Sally wanted to keep her in one more night. They finished with the notes and headed out of the ICU toward the surgical floor.

The team bolted through the doors of the ICU. Sure enough, Jake was down the hall talking to a guy. The team continued walking the opposite direction toward the surgical floor.

Steve began to follow the pack but then stopped in his tracks. The team started to leave without him, so Tom asked Steve if he was okay. "I'm fine. I'll catch up with you all in a few seconds. I forgot my notes in Mr. Gordon's room." Steve paused until the team was out of sight and then backtracked to near the ICU doors. From afar, he studied the man who was talking with Jake.

A lawyer didn't seem to be the correct profession for this guy. Steve felt like they were both aliens in the hallway of a major hospital. Something didn't fit. The guy just didn't have that attorney look. He had the overcoat, something not seen much inside a hospital unless of course an attorney was present. But the man was too stocky, too unprofessional, too…too much like a detective, thought Steve. Maybe he was a private detective doing some work for Jake. Maybe Jake's ex left the country, and this man was helping locate his family. The guy certainly did look like a detective, but whatever they were talking about was no business of Steve's.

The two men began shaking hands. A bright sparkle from the man's ring caught Steve's eye. Jake turned toward the ICU, and Steve quickly jumped back. He ran into the ICU to grab his notes and then chased after the rest of the team.

Chapter 9

Sally kept her pace at top speed while doing rounds, and Dr. Douglas never caught up. He wanted to see all the patients himself. By the time he was done visiting with one patient, Dr. Jenson and the team were on to the next patient. None of the other members of the surgery team minded since Sally was a little more pleasant to be around. The bonus of teaching the residents and students also made rounds more tolerable.

Jake finally caught up with them as the team sat down for a bite to eat before the OR started. "Thanks for taking care of rounds," acknowledged Jake.

Sally just nodded her head.

"It looks as if the only case today is removing the packs from Mr. Gordon. That shouldn't take too long. Tom, how would you like to help out with that?"

"I would love to, but Jake, Carmichael came in early to pre-round on all of the patients," Tom confessed. "If it is OK with you, I think he earned the OR today."

"Just because he did his job you think he should get rewarded? All right, that's fine with me. Steve, I'll see you in the OR at 7:30 sharp. Don't be late! I'm sure Dr. Rosberg will be there, and you will want to show him that you are an excellent and punctual intern." Jake smiled to himself and walked off.

Steve was not sure whether to thank Tom or flip him the bird, but going to the operating room was always better than doing the scut work on the surgery floor. Steve put half of his bagel in his mouth at one time and began to stand up.

"Where are you off to, Carmichael?" asked Sally. "We haven't gone through the patients."

"Yeah, I know, but if it's okay, I would like a few extra minutes to review Mr. Gordon's injuries and read about anything I don't understand, if that's okay with you Dr. Jenson."

"Fine, you little brownnoser."

Everyone laughed, including Sally, but she remembered all too well the first few years when she would do the exact same thing. If she didn't know something, she would thoroughly research it so she wouldn't look like a fool in front of the attendings when they asked her questions.

Steve looked at the clock in the cafeteria while walking out. It was 7:15. He had ten minutes to go to the ICU to look through Mr. Gordon's chart and still make it down to the OR by 7:25 to change into scrubs. Steve ran up the stairs to get to the ICU and walked through the doors to find that Mr. Gordon was gone. Steve looked around in disbelief.

"Can I help you?" asked Agusta Simpson.

"Yeah. Where the hell is Mr. Gordon?"

"They already took him down to the OR."

"Shit!" exclaimed Steve. "Is his chart still up here?"

"Sorry, they took that down with him."

Steve looked at the clock. 7:20. He turned around and ran down to the OR. He quickly changed into his scrubs and hurried to the pre-operative area. He looked around to locate Mr. Gordon. *It shouldn't be tough with the guy on a ventilator,* thought Steve. But as he looked over the pre-operative area, there was no sign of a vent or Mr. Gordon. Steve heard a soft voice from behind the nurses' desk.

"Can I help you find someone?"

"Mr. Gordon. Do you know if he came down already?"

"Yes, they did, but he was on a ventilator. They take those patients directly to the room. He is in…" The nurse studied her sheet of paper in front of her. "Um…it looks like operating room four."

"Thanks." Steve quickly headed to OR 4. As he left the pre-op area, he glanced at the clock again. 7:24.

Steve put on a facemask and hat and walked into the room. He looked up and nearly fainted. In the corner was not only Jake Douglas, but also Dr. Rosberg. Dr. Rosberg was flipping through the pages of the chart.

Great! thought Steve dryly. *Now what, just grab the chart from Dr. Rosberg and say excuse me, but I need to look through that thing too?* No, that didn't sound right.

"Good morning, Dr. Carmichael," greeted the senior doctor. "Welcome aboard. I heard you earned the right to scrub in the OR today. That a boy! I know you'll do as good of a job as a resident as you did while you were a medical student."

Steve was not certain what else to say, but before he could think about it, words came out of his mouth. "Thank you, sir. I'm looking forward to the challenge."

Dr. Rosberg got up and put the chart down. "Jake, don't get started until I get back. I need to talk to scheduling for a minute, and then I'll be ready to go."

While anesthesia put Mr. Gordon to sleep, Steve finally had a chance to glance through the chart. Just as he was in the middle of a paragraph, Jake tapped him on the shoulder.

"Come on, let's go and scrub."

Steve hesitantly put the chart down and followed Jake to the sink. While washing, Jake apologized for the boring case. "This is all I got for you today, but I'm sure there will be other more exciting cases soon. All we have to do is remove the packs and irrigate. It shouldn't take too long."

A scrub nurse poked her head through the door, "Come on, guys, we're ready."

Steve followed Jake into the room. After the patient was draped, Jake asked for the scissors.

"Don't you want to wait for Dr. Rosberg?" inquired Steve.

"Nah, we're just wasting OR time waiting here. This should be simple. Just remove the liver packs, and irrigate."

"Yeah, I know, but Rosberg stated specifically to wait for him," pleaded Steve.

Jake looked up at Steve and stared at him. "If you don't think you can handle a little blood, doctor, then you better leave!"

Jake grabbed the scissors and cut the suture holding the patient's skin together, exposing the whole belly. "All we've got to do is remove a few packs, irrigate, and get out." Jake poured saline over the packs to make them easier to remove. Slowly and very carefully, he pulled the first pack out. "See? Not a problem. I wonder how many packs they left in this guy."

Steve looked up at Jake and could not believe his ears. "Didn't you read his operative note from the trauma?" he asked.

"Nah, I didn't have time. Rosberg had the chart, then it was time to scrub in, and here we are. We just have a few more packs left."

Steve was shocked. Here was a chief resident who spent years of training before entering the private sector, and only a year away, he didn't find the time to review old op notes. *Shit,* thought Steve. *I'm just an intern just a few days, and I know better than that!* "Six," he answered.

"What? What do you mean six?" asked Jake.

"Six. There were six packs placed at his surgery."

"Oh, that's good to know," said Jake. He continued to work.

Steve shook his head in disbelief but made certain not to make it too noticeable.

Jake poured more saline in the abdomen to loosen the packs.

Next, three packs were removed fairly quickly. Not a problem. But then Jake stopped and studied the situation. Two more packs were left, but they appeared to be deep and behind the liver. Jake took a deep breath and began to pull the next pack. A little red fluid was building up next to the liver, but that could be saline mixed with old blood.

The OR was incredibly quiet as the fifth pack came out.

"See? Not a problem. You just have to take your time and be patient. This way, when Rosberg comes back all the dirty work will be done, and all he'll need to do is put on gloves and gown, peek in, and say okay. Then he can turn around, leave the OR, and bill the big bucks." Jake laughed to himself as he looked at the last pack.

Steve was not as content. He didn't have much time to look over the chart, but what he did read through was concerning. The trauma team had encountered a difficult time to stop the bleeding from what they thought might be hepatic veins behind the liver. These were incredibly difficult to reach unless you were doing a liver transplant. But that was not the plan today.

As Jake began to pull the last pack from behind the liver, Steve took a small step back and squinted, as if waiting for a disaster to occur. At last he couldn't take it any longer, "Uh, Jake, don't you think we should wait for Dr. Rosberg for this last one? I mean you did most of the work, but he could be here for this last pack. That way he wouldn't feel guilty about charging the patient, and-"

"Rosberg feel guilty? This is an attending we're talking about. There are no guilt feelings in their conscious. And besides, he…OH SHIT!" screamed Jake. "GET ME SUCTION! SUCK, SUCK!"

Steve couldn't believe his eyes. He had never seen the abdomen fill with that much blood so quickly.

"PACKS! Get me packs now, damn it! Shit, where is all that blood coming from?" Jake's voice was filled with panic.

Steve tried to help. "The op note said that there was a lot of bleeding from the hepatic veins, and that is when they-"

"Hepatic veins? They never told me about fuckin' hepatic veins! Shit, we'll never get to those." Jake quickly started to freak out and lose it.

"WHAT THE HELL IS GOING ON HERE?" shouted Rosberg as he burst into the OR. "Douglas, what the hell are you doing? Do you not understand the English language? What did you not understand about DON'T GET STARTED UNTIL I GET BACK?! Is there any blood available? Send for it, NOW, DAMN IT!! Get me a gown! Jake, you stupid shit, pack that belly, NOW!" Dr. Rosberg quickly gowned up.

The rest of the room was silent as could be.

Then anesthesia yelled, "We've got a drop in blood pressure. We need some time to catch up. Let's get two bags of LR while we're waiting for the blood. How come the blood is not in the room? How long before the blood is available?"

Great, thought Steve. Not only did he earn this bullshit operating room experience, but also he was going to witness several grown adults freaking out.

"Carmichael, move down!" Dr. Rosberg shouted as he stepped toward the table.

Steve thought for a second that he could earn major brownie points by telling Rosberg about the op note, number of packs, and the source of bleeding, but then he would have to answer to Jake for the next several months. Steve still had to respect the hierarchy of authority.

"Jake, how come you have an intern scrubbed on this trauma case?" Dr. Rosberg demanded.

"Well, he earned the privilege to be in the OR and-"

"That's exactly right, you moron. It is a privilege to be here in the OR. I'm not sure YOU have earned that privilege!"

Dr. Rosberg packed the wound with about ten packs and put pressure on them as they lay over the liver. He turned toward the head of the bed and asked, "How are you guys up there? Are we caught up yet?"

"We need the blood up here before the packs come out, and let's get some fresh frozen up before we let the dike out," replied Dr. Lee, head of anesthesia.

"Fine. Someone call Dr. Jenson and get her butt down here, NOW! Steve, it's nothing personally, but I'll need some experience for the remainder of the case. Don't you worry, young man. The next appendectomy I have, you will be the first person I call. Besides, you learned just about everything you could learn from this case, especially not to be a stupid asshole while in surgery. Speaking of appys, I think the intern lecture today is on appendectomies. Why don't you listen carefully today so the next appy that comes in can be yours?"

Steve felt awkward with the situation but took his cue. "Thank you, sir. I guess I'll see you later. Good luck." He had a feeling of relief as he exited the OR.

He couldn't believe how careless Jake was with patients.

No wonder Sally thought the guy Jake was speaking with this morning was a lawyer. Jake seemed to find himself in these situations a lot, per the last poll from junior and senior residents. From their analysis, Dr. Douglas not only needed a lawyer but a small firm to take care of his legal matters. He had the divorce, his kids, his stupid ass mistakes in the OR, and his financial difficulties, to name a few.

Steve was thinking about Jake when he almost bumped into Sally.

"What the hell happened?" she demanded. "It was supposed

to be a simple procedure, remove a few packs, irrigate and get out. How the hell did you guys get into so much trouble so quickly?"

Oh no, not her too. "Just remove the packs and irrigate" seems to be the resident thing to do, thought Steve. "Jake removed the final pack, and the hepatic veins showed themselves."

"Great!" said Sally, rolling her eyes. "Now the floor work will be delayed by an hour."

"An hour!" laughed Steve. "If you guys are out in one hour, I'll do your scut work for a week."

"Scut work? That's your job anyway. How about you wash my car for a month if we're done in less than an hour?" dealt Sally.

"Fine, that sounds like a good…" Before he went on, he had to rethink what he was betting on and the possibilities. "In less than an hour is a deal, except the man needs to come out of surgery alive and stay alive for at least a month."

Sally considered the bet as she continued toward OR four. She shook her head violently from side to side. "No, absolutely not. There is not a bookie in town who would take that risk."

They both giggled. Steve departed the operating room as Sally continued in.

The lecture series was put on by attendings and their chief residents once a week. The lectures were usually presented by chiefs, but Jake had other plans today. When Steve got to the lecture hall, only a few interns and students were there. He looked for Dennis but couldn't find him, Mike, or Roger. Steve picked a seat in an empty row.

Finally, a familiar face joined him. "Hey, great OR experience so far this morning," Dennis said. "The whole hospital already knows about it. I think they e-mailed most of the personnel just to forewarn the good human beings, as well as the assholes, to stay away from Jake the flake."

"You could say that I now know what to do when your attending says wait for him," said Steve. He and Dennis compared notes on their mornings before the lecture began. As they were talking, Dr. Jones approached the podium.

Dr. Jones was known as the chief resident who was the epitome of a surgeon jerk. He made Jake Douglas look like an angel. "Good morning, lowlifes. It has come to my attention that some of you green interns went to either very prissy med schools or just skipped out on all the essentials to making a good surgery intern. But for you wimps who didn't put IVs in while you were students, you need to face this horrible event so that you won't bother me anymore with the bullshit phone call that you can't get an IV."

Dennis leaned over to Steve to whisper, "I heard the intern on last night couldn't put an IV in for the life of her. Jones got so pissed he made her go home."

"What? No way."

"Yeah way. She has to make the call up later. But he got so pissed he told his team that he was going to bore us with the art of placing IVs instead of teaching us the art of performing appendectomies."

"Just my luck," said Steve. "Today Dr. Rosberg felt bad for kicking me out of the OR, so he said the next appy that comes in I'll be able to do."

"That's great! Maybe you'll be the first intern to do an appy this year."

"That *is* great, except I was planning to learn how to take out an appendix today in the lecture. I guess I'll have to show up to these lectures for the next few weeks, at least until they discuss the appendectomy."

Dr. Jones explained the art of putting in IVs, the pearls or tricks to make certain they were placed correcting in the first attempt, and the complications of IVs. After going over everything in painful detail, Dr. Jones made the participants practice on each other. Steve and Dennis got IVs into each other very quickly and were instructed to leave after passing the practical exam.

The exam was controversial, at least in Steve's mind, but it was very simple: place an IV in Dr. Jones. The controversy existed because there were a few residents who would rather fail on purpose in order to make a mistake or two on Dr. Jones, just to cause him pain. Since Steve and Dennis did such an outstanding job on each other, Dr. Jones elected to dismiss them without placing an IV into his thin vessels.

Steve walked out grinning with Dennis. "Hey, hope to see you at the next appy lecture."

They laughed and departed in opposite directions.

Chapter 10

The Whitefish apartment complex was definitely not paradise, but it was a place to call home until one could *afford* paradise. The front held a large white-lighted sign. If it weren't missing half the lights, it probably would have been a halfway decent sign. The peeling paint from the sides of the building gave it a certain raunchy look. Passersby stared at it as they walked past, but they were not admiring it. It often helped them realize that they weren't so bad off after all.

The man in the overcoat had selected an apartment with a fantastic view. It enabled him to look out the window and see the three feeder streets that connected into the street outside his apartment building. It allowed easy visualization of the entrance to the front lobby. There were no back exits; he had checked before signing the lease.

His apartment was on the top floor of a four-story building, providing a clear view of the surrounding neighborhood. His place was the only apartment in the complex to have easy access to the roof directly from his bedroom. He had already organized an escape plan to the roof where he had stored a long ladder so he could cross between buildings. He had obtained the key to open the rooftop door to the next building.

The rundown apartment had an unexpectedly terrific security system. The man could watch anyone come through the front lobby doors as well as look at the underground parking and outside parking ramps. This was all he really needed to monitor his building. There were no security guards or doormen like at his last residence, eliminating the chance of enemies entering the workforce at the Whitefish. Certainly if any new people started to work at the Whitefish, they would stick out like a sore thumb. The man would be able to recognize it and move on.

The place didn't have much furniture, but then he didn't really need a lot. There was a bed, a couch, and some other miscellaneous items. He had not bothered to purchase a television yet, but he had arranged to rent one for several days until he took time to buy one. This way he could watch the news and see how far the mission had progressed.

Tonight, though, would not be good for T.V. shopping. He had to make another phone call abroad. He thought about his last phone call, which had gone well. Actually, the phone call itself went well, but afterwards the gangbangers made everything a little tough. He was glad he would not need to make many more phone calls. The plan was almost all set up, and the contacts were being made.

He thought for a moment about how nice it would be if the mission were already completed. He would be able to retire in some beautiful paradise and not worry about a thing. He would be able to sit on a beach, sipping margaritas with a straw hat and some funny sunglasses. Gorgeous women would bring him drinks and kiss up to him.

He woke himself up from this daydream. Time to figure out how to reach his phone on Sixth Street. It was definitely too far to walk, but he didn't want to take a chance with the bus in case he needed to flee quickly. If he took his own car, the kids surely would destroy it. The taxi the last few times worked out well, but the most recent experience had been a close call. Unfortunately, it was the best option to have a getaway plan, so he called for a taxi.

As he waited for the ride, he checked all the cameras for suspicious characters lurking around. He sat in a recliner chair and used the remote to view the channels with the different camera angles. The basement parking lot had a few places someone could get in and hide. The lobby and outdoor parking lot were straightforward with few places to hide. The lobby had a large floor plant but not big enough to hide a person.

He saw the taxi pull up on the lobby camera. As always, he locked his room with both the dead bolt and the door handle lock. The elevators in this building made him a little nervous, so whenever possible, he took the stairs. It was much easier going down the stairs than climbing up.

The lobby was deserted, and nobody was behind the front desk. There were two chairs in clear view of the camera. They were also empty. He pushed the lobby doors open and walked to the taxi. From the doors, he glanced to see the driver's face and stopped for a brief second thinking the driver was the same man from his last phone call. But when he got in the car, he decided it was definitely not him. In fact, the ID pictured in the back was that of a Margaret Sinville. Nothing to worry about.

After he shut the door, the driver released the brake and started on her way, "Where to, mister?"

"Sixth and DuPont," replied the man.

"You gotta be kiddin', man. That is like the worst part of town. Of course, you're not leaving paradise here, are ya?"

The man knew she was referring to the apartment building where he was staying. He sat back and smiled. He wanted to tell her to treat a future millionaire with a little more respect, but he bit his lip and made no reply. He just leaned back into his seat and watched the buildings go by.

This whole project made him a little uneasy, but it made him feel powerful, too. The plans could not advance without his help. There were a lot of people depending on his resources. If he wanted to, he could demand more money, demand more time, demand more people power, demand this and that. But the fact of the matter was that if held up the plans, the entire project could be delayed indefinitely. That would mean that he would have to work a real job longer and be out of millions of dollars. So the show must go on.

As the taxi turned down DuPont, he got that queasy feeling he always did in this area. It truly was the slimiest part of town, but for his phone calls, it offered the most private moments. No one in their right mind would come out to this place and stake him out.

The driver also felt the uneasy vibe of the place. As she spoke, her voice had less confidence than when she first had the man enter her taxi. "Uh …uh, so where would you like to be dropped off in this pretty part of town? Will you be staying for a bite to eat after your movie?"

The man smiled, "That's funny, but if you would be so kind, I would like to go over to the next corner. I should only be a few minutes, and if you wouldn't mind waiting, I'd-"

Before he could finish, the tough little taxi driver saw the writing on the wall. "No fuckin' way am I hanging out here while you get yourself laid!" she shouted.

"First of all, I am not getting laid, and second, I will make it worth your while." He leaned over the seat and dropped a hundred dollar bill on to her crossword puzzle from the newspaper.

She looked down at the money and then grabbed it.

She slowed the car down in order to inspect the bill. She held it up into the light and glanced at both the front and back of the green paper. Without any further hesitation, she smiled and said, "Thanks, but no thanks." She threw the bill back at the occupant in the back seat.

He was astonished. This had never happened before. The drivers always took the money. There were never any questions or hesitation. They just took the money and waited. The last visit was nearly a disaster, but even that still turned out ok.

This would cost him more, but it was certainly better than hanging out on Sixth and DuPont waiting for another cab in the middle of the night. "Fine! You win. I'll give you two hundred bucks to stick around."

"No fuckin' way," she said.

The man started to get worried and hyperventilate. "OK, what do you want?" he shouted from the back seat.

"I want to let you out and get the hell out of here. Here is Sixth and DuPont, sir. That will be $37.50."

Not only had this never been an issue before, but also the man was unusually uncomfortable with the fact that he may not have a ride home and would be stuck out there with the gangbangers. He certainly would not stand a chance out on the street for more than an hour.

The driver knew this. She had heard from a few fellow drivers about an incident a few days ago with a driver and a client being chased by some gangbangers. "I'll tell you what, mister. The way I see it is you had to come down to beautiful Sixth and DuPont to make a very important phone call that you could not make at your wonderful apartment. There probably are not any phones there, but whatever. So now you're stuck down here, and you need me to stick around while you make this all-important phone call. In fact, you are probably so scared that I might leave that you would pay a lot of money for me to stick around and put myself at risk for serious injury or harm."

He could see where this was going. "So how much do you want?"

"Well, taking account the fact that the risk of personal injury or death is high, I think five hundred would be acceptable."

"Five hundred dollars? No fucking way, absolutely not,

forget it."

"Here you are, sir, Sixth and DuPont. Have a great day!"

"FUCK YOU!" He counted five hundred dollar bills and slapped them into her hand.

She smiled back at him.

"If you decide to split while I'm on the phone I'll look you up Ms…" He turned sideways to see her name again. "Ms. Margaret Sinville. I'll look you up and make your life miserable."

The taxi driver stared at him through her rear view mirror and smiled. "Do you have any other threats? Because if you do, I just want to remind you that if I did leave your sorry ass here on Sixth and DuPont, you most likely would never get a chance to make my life any more miserable than it already is! Any other warm fuzzies before you get out of the car, darlin'?"

The man opened the car door slowly and looked at her and then all up and down the street. She was smiling, and for good reason. She had him where she could manipulate the situation to her pleasure, and he knew it. He just never before had a driver that would take advantage of the situation. This was definitely getting to be an expensive phone call.

He stepped from the car and cautiously walked over to the phone. He picked up the receiver and began to insert the money that he had already counted. It was the exact amount to keep the line open for 45 seconds. The man glanced at the driver and saw her shit-ass grin. It pissed him off even more. He listened for the international operator. He asked for Afghanistan and then dialed an international number. All the while, he was looking up and down the street watching, not for troubled youth, but for any suspicious characters lurking behind cars or garbage cans and staking him out.

Finally, a familiar voice came on the phone. "Well, my

friend, I think we are ready here. We have all the essential ingredients to make this work. We need to know the name of a fine young American doctor for my friend in case he gets sick."

"I think before we get to this point, I need to make absolutely sure this doctor will take on new patients," said the man.

"Listen, my friend…"

As the foreign voice continued to ramble on, the man looked down at his stopwatch to check the time remaining. As he did, he noticed the mouthpiece to the phone was slightly loose. He started to tighten it thinking that one of the kids in the neighborhood was playing with it.

Then, as he was screwing the mouthpiece, he was hit with a sinking feeling. He quickly glanced up to the street. Again, he looked up and down the road, but there was nothing suspicious. He stared at the mouthpiece as the voice on the other end babbled. He quickly unscrewed that part of the phone, examined it, and nearly collapsed. He could feel his heart pounding. He was sure that the driver of the taxi could probably hear his heart racing. He looked around again as he felt himself beginning to panic. He started to hyperventilate again.

He interrupted the voice on the other end of the line.

"Listen, I have to go. I- I have an emergency. I mean, I- I have a situation here that I need to correct before I give you any names of doctors here that your friend can see. I will call you when the time is right!"

The man in the phone booth pulled the receiver down while holding the phone in his hand. He laid his head on the side of the booth with his heart racing. He was beginning to get a nasty headache. Then there was this rush of nausea and light-headedness. He felt faint and started to sweat. The street began moving in all different directions.

The man looked again at the phone and the mouthpiece. Without any further hesitation, he opened the door to the booth and threw up until dry heaves were audible from the taxi in the street. Finally, the man took the micro bug off the mouthpiece and threw it on to the pavement. He slammed his heel on it and heard the crisp sound of the mechanical device break into tiny pieces.

He nonchalantly wiped the phone off with a cloth and hurried back to the taxi. "Take me back to the Whitefish Apartments." The man was pale as a ghost.

"Are you okay, mister? Do you need to see a doctor first?"

"No!" screamed the man. "Just get me back home, and I'll feel better, thanks." As the taxi sped along DuPont, the man searched for a stakeout vehicle. He looked up at windows in deserted buildings. He looked down the cross streets. He looked and looked but could not find a soul.

But that didn't matter. He knew they were on to him.

Chapter 11

The alarm clock went off again. Much too early, but that was part of the deal for surgical training. Steve had only been a resident for a short week, but the long days were already taking their toll on him. He could tell he was becoming impatient with people and situations. Just last night at the grocery store, he scolded a checkout clerk to hurry up with his checkout because he was in a hurry to get home so he could get some sleep. It was little incidents like these that were beginning to mold his personality into that of a general surgeon. As much as he tried not to become a typical egotistical doctor, the trap was set, and he was about to fall right into it.

His apartment, which was usually tidy and well organized, was now looking more like a tornado flew by. Although it had been only a few short days since he started his residency, he found less and less time to take care of everyday tasks. His laundry was beginning to pile up next to the hamper. The dishes were stacked in the kitchen sink. In the bathroom, he had a brand new roll of toilet paper on the counter top because the roll in the dispenser had been empty for three days now. There was just no way of denying it: his precious time was a thing of the past. When he did have a moment or two to himself at home, he felt obligated to read from his surgery text. In fact, it had been almost three whole days since he corresponded with Sweetpea.

When he got up out of bed, he kicked some clothes lying on the floor across the room in order to make room for a path to the bathroom. After his shower, he went to get dressed. As he reached for the usual tie and shirt, he remembered this was the day. This was going to be the very first day. He broke out in a cold sweat. This was the day he had been frightened of since his last two weeks of medical school. Today was going to be the very first call day. He had heard horror stories about interns' first night on call.

The surgery interns' last year filled his head with so many fears. Fears like managing a fresh postoperative patient by himself. If anything were to go wrong, it was always the interns' fault. Life was no longer like a medical student, where the blame was always directed to a person of higher authority. As an intern, you were the responsible physician giving orders and taking responsibility for your decisions.

As he thought about this, he became more and more anxious. He tried to focus instead on breakfast. As a med student, he would take time to eat a fortifying breakfast, but the last few days, he had filled the coffee mug to the rim with caffeine and grab a bagel as he was leaving the house. He was out of bagels today, so he found a few slices of bread and dashed out of the house.

He locked his apartment door and headed down the stairs. However, there was this noise coming from his apartment, and it was getting louder. "Oh, shit," he said to himself. "Pudge!" Steve ran back up the stairs and fumbled with the keys as he tried to open the door. He dashed in and found Pudge whimpering. He had totally forgotten about the dog. While he let Pudge run around outside, Steve loaded a bowl with a generous supply of dog food for the day.

He had previously given a copy of his call schedule to his landlords so they would be able to let Pudge out during the times he wouldn't be around. He thought about calling them to remind them that he would not be home later tonight, but it was much too early. Anyone in their right mind would be sleeping at five in the morning.

Pudge started to whimper outside the door, so Steve let the dog in and showed him his food. Then Steve turned around for his second attempt to depart, leaving the animal devouring his meal.

It was pitch dark out. The sun was nowhere to be found, and the moon was on its way to another part of the sky.

Steve had trouble finding the keyhole on his car door in the darkness. As he struggled with the key, he thought he heard some noises in the bushes near the house. He stood up straight, eyes wide open. His heart began to race. He strained his eyes in the dark to see if there was anyone around. He could not find a soul, and there were no more sounds, so he continued to work the key into the door. Once opened, he grabbed the coffee and bread and hopped into the car.

Traffic was always light on the interstate at this time of day. That was probably the only good thing about leaving so early every morning. The music was playing on the radio, but Steve was not listening. He started to plan his day and imagined what it would be like being on call. He was role-playing all sorts of scenarios in his head. What if he got to the hospital and there was a major trauma before the chiefs arrived? Since this was his call day, would he have to place the IVs or the foley? Would he have to make the decision to crack a chest in the emergency room? How would he explain the situation to the little girl's parents that she had major intra-abdominal injuries and would need emergency surgery?

The DJ on the radio yelled "Gooooood morning" in a voice loud enough to jolt Steve back to reality. Steve realized that there would also be a junior or senior resident with him on call, so all those difficult decisions would be made by a more experienced doctor. A more realistic thought was what to do if the nurses called about patients on the floor. He started to think what questions he might be asked while on call. "Good morning, Dr. Carmichael. I have Mr. So-and-so, and I just noticed him throwing up gross amounts of blood, and his urine output has dropped significantly. Also, during the last hour or so, he developed a maculopapular rash over his torso and became diaphoretic. Oh, and by the way, his pressure dropped to the sixties, but now it's back up to the low one hundreds." Steve thought and thought about this hypothetical patient situation he had created and tried to come up with a diagnosis and treatment plan. As he pulled into the parking lot, he realized he couldn't come up with a good diagnosis, but he then started to master a treatment plan to deal with the problem at hand.

First, the blood pressure would need to be corrected with fluids. He would give the patient a bolus of IV fluid, probably Lactated Ringers, probably 500 milliliters. No, maybe that would be too much, maybe only 250. Whatever the amount, it would probably help his urine output as well. Steve thought about the rash as he slammed his car door shut. What could be causing the rash?

He was pondering this thought when an arm reached around his shoulders, "Good morning, Steve."

"SHIT!" he screamed.

"Sorry, I didn't mean to scare the shit out of you," said a friendly voice. Dennis Burrows felt bad that he had scared his friend but still managed to get a few chuckles from the moment.

"Very funny," said Steve. "Next time why don't you bring the defibrillator with you so that when I have a coronary, you can just shock me out of Vfib right then and there!"

"I'm so sorry, but I didn't think you would get so spooked. Next time I'll just wave hello from across the parking lot."

Steve nodded but continued, "I can't help it. Today is my first call day, so I am a bit on edge."

Dennis knew exactly what Steve was talking about. "Oh, it's your turn tonight. My first call was two days ago, and it actually wasn't too bad. I got a bunch of calls from post ops and then one ER consult."

"Wow, that was really sweet! You lucked out. We'll just

have to wait and see how tonight goes."

"Alright, I hope your call day goes smooth. Maybe I'll see you later. Good luck!"

"Thanks, I'll need it. See ya later," replied Steve.

The two of them entered the hospital together, but once inside, they quickly went different directions. Steve wanted to make sure that he was able to pre-round on all of the post-op surgical patients. He ran up the stairs to the locker room and dropped his stuff off. Sincc hc was on call, he thought it would be a good idea to just change into scrubs now rather than wait until some drunk in the ER lost his stomach on him.

After changing, he dashed to the ICU so he could go over the sickest patients on the service. As he was going over the vital signs of the last patient, Jake and Sally walked into the ICU. Steve saw the two of them together and for a split second, he thought they were becoming a hot item. This type of thing happened all the time in the hospital and especially during residency. He had even heard of a staff surgeon having an affair with one of the younger female residents while his wife was being treated for breast cancer. Certainly long hours in the hospital and time spent away from loved ones could lead to encounters such as this, but that relationship never sat well with him. Not that any encounter outside of the marriage was appropriate, but to cheat on your wife while she was being treated for cancer was pathetic.

The fact that Jake and Sally walked in together probably meant nothing, but Steve was grossed out by the thought that any woman could stand to be with Jake Douglas if she didn't have to be. The more Steve thought about it, he figured they probably happened to ride the elevator together.

"Good morning, Carmichael. So this is the big day, huh? I just hope you don't bug me all night with sorry ass little things that should be taken care of by the intern," squawked Jake.

"I won't bug you if you let me do an appendectomy," joked Steve.

"What is it with all you interns? You come out of medical school expecting to do appys your first day out. Well, I'll tell you when I was an intern, we had to show our dedication to the chief before we ever saw the inside of an operating room let alone performed any surgery. And Carmichael, this is only your first day on call! Let's see how you do first before we have you cutting up people," said Jake.

Steve thought to himself, *Dedication? Doesn't working alongside Jake Douglas show dedication?!*

The ICU rounds went as usual: short and sweet. Jake never wasted any time with nonsense. He would get the vitals and talk to the patient. Dr. Douglas would quickly complete the pertinent physical exam, review the labs, and make a management plan for the day. There were only three ICU surgical patients for Dr. Douglas's service today, so the rounds in the unit went exceptionally quick. Steve made sure that he paid special attention to everything that morning since all the phone calls would be directed to him throughout the day. For that matter, it would last all night. The floor rounds went just as quick, and Steve made mental notes on each patient so that when he got phone calls about the patients, he would be able to respond with some recollection of their status.

The day in the OR was scheduled to be very busy for Dr. Douglas and his team. Consequently, when the team finished with rounds, they ran off to the operating rooms and left Steve with the patients. All of the patients. Steve counted the list of names. Eighteen patients! That would be no big deal if there was another body to help manage them, but everyone else had gone to the OR, even the medical students.

Steve found his way to the cafeteria to grab a cup of coffee and collect his thoughts. He wanted to organize his morning in order to get all the scut work done. As he sat down with his coffee, he heard a friendly voice.

"Well, good morning, stranger."

Steve looked over to the next table and saw Erica having breakfast by herself. "Hey, how ya doing? I've been meaning to talk to you this week, but the time…well, the time just slipped away from me."

Erica laughed, "Yeah, that's what they all say. At least you surgeons do. They never have any time to themselves once they start their careers. But that's ok, you just miss out on life. But hey, there is life after death, so when you do unexpectedly pass up on this life, you can enjoy that life, unless of course you provide surgical services for the dead too."

Steve looked at her in a confused sort of way, and they both laughed.

"So what do you have there?" asked Erica.

"Oh, this is my patient list with all the things I need to get done today before Dr. Douglas gets out of the OR. I just have eighteen patients with four discharges to complete, three NGs to take out, two chest tubes to remove, two IVs to place, and a bunch of labs to review. Then I need to-"

Before Steve could continue, they heard an all too familiar sound, the sound that most medical students love and most residents grow to despise. That sound would only be that of a pleasant little box clipped to the waistband on your pants or scrubs. That magnificent music could only be that of a pager.

Steve jumped straight up into the air as his beeper went off for the first time. "Shit!" he screamed.

Erica just giggled.

"I guess I wasn't ready for the first page of the day." Steve nervously hurried over to the phone as if he were keeping whoever paged him waiting too long. There were four phones in the cafeteria so that residents and doctors could get their pages while eating. After all, why should one enjoy a meal when they could be paged constantly?

Erica watched the very innocent and green intern answer the page. He tried to write some info down on a piece of paper with the phone balanced between his shoulder and right ear. He looked very serious as he listened to the call. Erica tried not to laugh when he came back to his table.

"Well, let's add two admissions and a consult to that list of chores to do for the day," Steve griped.

"Don't complain, Dr. Carmichael," said Erica. "If you stay busy like this, think of how fast your call day will go. You'll never be bored, and you'll probably learn a lot, which is really why you and I are both here anyway."

"Yeah, you're probably right," acknowledged Steve. "But it would be nice to sit down and have a cup of coffee before all the shit hits the fan."

"Shit hits the fan?" exclaimed Erica. "If you think one page equals shit hitting the fan, you better hang on tight for a long and bumpy ride!" She rolled her eyes. "Or you could change to Internal Medicine where we start each and every day with a cup of coffee."

Steve smiled back at Erica. As he got up, his pager went off again. "Shit!" He looked at the pager but didn't recognize the number. "2004?"

"Ah, you might want to get that one right away. That's the ICU," Erica calmly suggested.

Steve rushed to one of the phones with a frightened look on his face. As he quickly dialed the number, Erica walked by and grabbed him. She gently but firmly shook his arm and said, "Chill out, Carmichael, if you freak out like this all day long, you will be on anti-acid medication by the end of the night. If they really wanted you, I mean *really* wanted you for a serious problem, they would have overhead paged you. So just relax.

They probably need TPN orders or something like that."

Steve nodded his head as he put the receiver to his ear. "Hello, this is Dr. Carmichael. Were you looking for me?"

Erica stared at Steve and silently lipped, "Hello?" She just shook her head and said, "Let's meet for dinner down here tonight."

Steve again nodded yes and then listened to the voice on the other end. "Hi, Dr. Carmichael. This is Nina Rogers, and I am the nurse taking care of Bed 4. Could we please have a TPN order?" Steve looked at Erica as she walked out of the cafeteria. He smiled.

The morning was going well for Steve. He calculated TPN orders on all of his patients in the ICU and then made sure they were all taken care of before he moved out to the floor. There he had to take care of the admissions as well as the discharges. It seemed for every person he sent home, there was another one being admitted. Looking up lab information was also important because if someone had low potassium or an elevated bilirubin and he didn't discover it, then it would be his fault whatever happened to the patient as a consequence of the abnormal lab value.

Just about lunchtime, he seemed to be nearly caught up when he got two new calls for IVs. He didn't plan on lunch anyway. He got all the items he needed for placing an IV, including a hep lock, lidocaine, a tourniquet, and of course the IV. He would always bring different size IVs in case he couldn't get a larger size in.

He could not help himself thinking of the lecture when they all learned about IVs and then placed them into each other. Steve was still upset about that, not that they had to practice on each other, but that it was supposed to be the lecture about appendectomies. All of the interns routinely looked forward to that lecture because they all want to do appendectomies. Steve was no exception. An appendectomy was almost always the first operation interns were allowed to perform. The appendectomy lecture would be the first step to get there.

After the IVs were successfully placed into the appropriate patients, Steve was about to sit down for a caffeine break when he heard his name overhead. "Dr. Carmichael, stat to the ICU! Dr. Carmichael, stat to the ICU!" Steve instantly felt his heart rate accelerate, adrenaline release throughout his body, and nausea hit his stomach. Before he had a chance to throw up in the cafeteria, he took off for the ICU. He arrived in time to see a large commotion in Mr. Gordon's room.

"What is going on?" demanded Steve.

One of the nurses started to explain, "Gordon's blood pressure began to drop, and his fever is now 103.2 degrees. His pulse is in the 130s, and his last blood pressure was only 74 over 46."

"What was his last hemoglobin?" asked Steve.

"13.2, after the blood he received yesterday."

The young doctor felt frantic. "Did anyone get a hold of Jake yet?"

"Not yet," replied one of the nurses. "We haven't had time."

"Shit, shit," muttered Steve.

"Dr. Carmichael, what do you want hanging? Any meds you want pushed? Do you need anesthesia? What do you want to do about his blood pressure? What do you want to do about his temp?" The nurses' stream of questions was endless.

Steve was in a daze. He felt as if he was in a make-believe story. He didn't want this to be true. As a medical student, he had witnessed such scenarios with other residents but hadn't thought it would happen to him so soon in his residency. Steve walked in small circles looking at the monitors, hoping everything would suddenly get better. Maybe if he ignored the situation and all the nurses, this disastrous situation would just disappear. It would become another daydream: you think about the worst-case scenarios and what you would do. When you came up to something that was uncomfortable or hard to handle, then you could jolt your thoughts to something else like what you were going to do Saturday night.

But this was no dream. Mr. Gordon was crashing.

"Dr. Carmichael! Dr. Carmichael, what the hell do you want to do? Is there anybody else around? Where is Sally or Tom?" asked Agusta, the veteran ICU nurse.

"Uh, they are still in the OR." Steve took a big deep breath in and started belting out orders. "Let's make sure we have two large bore IVs in and get a central line kit ready for me to put in! Next, give 500 of LR. Just push it in, and if that doesn't bump his blood pressure, then repeat that bolus. After a liter of LR but still no improvement in his blood pressure, let's start Dopamine at 5 mics!" He continued dishing out the orders. "Since his temp is sky high, let's give 1000 of Tylenol. And while we're on that topic, what antibiotics is he on?" One of the nurses showed him the med list. Steve read the list and then re-read it two more times. "What antibiotics is this guy on?" Steve shouted in a panicked voice.

The nurse who handed him the meds list looked over the list just as Steve did and then quickly replied, "None! Douglas discontinued them yesterday."

"What?!" questioned Steve. He had grown to not really respect the patient management plans devised by Jake, but now he had to deal with consequences for the chief's poor medical decisions.

"Dr. Carmichael, his pressure is down to the 60s, and hat bolus of LR is in!" a frantic nurse exclaimed.

Steve thought for a second. He remembered from a Morbidity/Mortality conference one resident whispering to another as a third resident was getting chewed alive by the staff for a bad choice he had made. The guy had whispered, "If you're going down, drag as many people with you as you can." The other resident leaned over and whispered in reply, "Never go swimming in shark infested water alone." They both had laughed as the conference continued.

Steve did not want to face the M/M conference by himself to explain why a fresh one-week-old intern was taking care of a complicated surgical patient that was crashing, and crashing bad, without the help of any senior residents. He shouted, "Let's go ahead and start that Dopamine at 5 mics, and Agusta, call the OR and let me talk to Jake, now!" The ICU was in a blur of constant motion. The nurses were great, trained to go autopilot when situations like these developed. In fact, Steve was sure these ICU nurses could handle this crash better than most interns. It didn't take much time to realize that they had much more experience than most interns just coming out of med school. Steve might be able to recite the biochemical Cori cycle and those nurses probably didn't even have a clue as to what the hell it was, but the Cori cycle was not going to save the patient's life at this particular moment.

As Agusta walked over with the phone, a nurse reported that the blood pressure was back up to 104 over 65. "Here is the king prick for you," said Agusta, handing the phone to Steve.

"Jake? Yeah, hi, this Steve, and we have a small problem over here with Mr. Gordon." Steve was very careful to select his words to not incriminate Jake. He continued, "Uh, it seems that his blood pressure dropped with a sharp elevation in his temp. It looks as though he may be crashing from septic shock."

"Oh, great!" exclaimed Jake. "Just give him a lot of fluids, and I'll be there in about fifteen minutes." With that, the other end hung up.

Fifteen minutes? thought Steve. That was a great deal of time where a lot could go wrong, and Steve didn't trust Jake's decision thought process anyway. As he scratched his head and thought what would be politically correct, a nurse came running and screamed his BP was back down to 72 over 48 and his pulse was 135. "Shit, alright, let's get ready for a swan ganz catheter, and Agusta, call Dr. Rosberg and tell him that we are crashing and Jake is busy in the OR. Hey, you!" Steve called out to anyone who would listen, but specifically to a nurse near the bedside. "Let's hang a liter of Hespan and push it in!"

Agusta had been around the ICU scene for a long time, and she had seen her share of green interns. Through what she was able to observe thus far, however, she was quite impressed with young Dr. Carmichael. She knew he was placed in a horrible situation, made worse by having to work with Jake Douglas. She would have no hesitation relaying that to Dr. Rosberg.

As Steve was scrubbing the right clavicular area, he could hear the conversation between Agusta and Rosberg. "He is doing the best under the circumstances. It seems that Douglas stood him up and left him in this mess by himself. I think Mr. Gordon needs a little help from senior staff…all right…uh-huh…ok…great. That sounds just perfect. We'll see you soon."

Agusta placed the phone down and said to Steve, "He will be down in just a second. Just hang on tight!"

Steve smiled to himself, but not for long as he continued to try to save Mr. Gordon. Steve took a large needle and inserted it into the skin just under the right clavicle. The needle was long and connected to a syringe. All of a sudden, he noticed the syringe fill with blood. He thought to himself, "Great, that was easy!" But as he continued to look at the syringe, he realized that the syringe was filling too quickly with pretty red blood. He figured that he was in an artery instead of a vein, but just in case, he disconnected the syringe from the needle itself to see if there was any bleeding. Sure enough, he saw an episodic arterial pumping of blood and quickly removed the needle from the lifeless body of Mr. Gordon. "SHIT!" Steve shouted in frustration. Nonetheless, he went at it again and this time found a nice normal return of darker blood for the subclavian vein. He placed the guide wire and floated the Swan without a hitch.

The situation remained troublesome. "Oh, shit!" yelled Steve. "The wedge pressure is only two! This guy is dry! Totally volume depleted, let's get a move on those fluids! Squeeze another liter of LR through the cordis! And someone get x-ray up here for a stat chest x-ray."

"I'm very impressed, Dr. Carmichael. How many of those have you done?" asked a very curious Agusta.

Steve looked Agusta straight in the eye and said, "I have placed three central lines and helped float two Swan's before-"

Just then, Dr. Rosberg burst through the ICU doors. "What the hell is happening, Carmichael? Where the hell is Douglas? That shithead is in deep shit!"

Steve hurried to fill Dr. Rosberg in with all the details. Right as he was finishing, a nurse shouted, "Vfib! Vfib!" Steve looked at Dr. Rosberg for anything: some reassurance, some ideas, anything to help Steve out. But instead, Steve saw Rosberg step back.

Steve cursed in his mind but continued, "Okay, let's get the paddles out and charge to 200. Agusta, start compressions.

And let's push a 100 of Lido. CLEAR!"

The machine jolted energy through the patient's body.

"Nothing!" shouted a nurse.

"Alright, charge at 360. CLEAR!"

"Still nothing," reported the same nurse.

"Maybe the Dopamine is over stimulating the heart," Steve considered out loud. "Let's stop that for a minute. Charge at 360 again!"

Steve was freaking out, but he quickly shot a glance at Rosberg. He saw him raise his eyebrows and nod his head up and down toward Agusta as if to say *I am very impressed with this intern.* Steve smiled and kept going.

Within a few seconds, the patient's pulse came back, and his blood pressure bounced back to 125 over 88.

"Good job, Carmichael! Nice save."

However, just as Rosberg was giving credit to Steve, the monitor alarms went off.

Steve quickly looked at the monitors to see a flat line. "Asystole! Shit. Go ahead and give one amp of Epi and one of Atropine. Charge the paddles to 360 again!" Steve was getting ready to shock the patient when he felt a warm secure hand reach across his back.

"You did a great job, Carmichael," said Dr. Rosberg. "But this guy came in behind the eight ball. After having his entire blood volume bleed out and be replenished a few days ago, I think he is trying to tell us something. I am going to call it. Time of death: ten thirty."

Steve just stared at him.

Dr. Rosberg continued, "Steve, you did a superb job. You have nothing to be ashamed of, young man. Let me go talk to the family, and I'll be right back. Good job! Agusta was right."

Steve was very proud of himself. He conquered the most frightening aspect of his internship: running a code. Just as he sat down to dictate the death summary, he heard a familiar shout.

"What the HELL is going on here, Carmichael?" shrieked Jake.

Steve wanted to crawl under a rock and hide, but there was nothing big enough to hide from Jake. Steve knew that Dr. Rosberg was impressed, but that wasn't going to make life with Jake Douglas any easier. One would think that after doing a good job at something you would get some kind of reward or positive acknowledgement, but not in surgery residency.

Jake stomped over to Steve demanding an explanation, "What the HELL! What the hell happened here, Carmichael?"

Steve paused for a thoughtful moment. He wondered if he should explain that after a person loses five liters of blood from a liver injury and then doesn't go on antibiotics, then he just might get septic and die. But Steve felt that would not be the proper explanation at this particular moment.

"I think he got septic and became hypotensive from that, and then he started swirling from a low blood pressure. Then he coded."

"Well, what stupid moron would-" Just as Jake was about to drill Steve, Dr. Rosberg returned.

"Jake, I want to see you in my office after rounds tonight, and don't make it late. My wife has plans for dinner. And Douglas, you should feel lucky that you have one of the best interns on your service. He did an outstanding job resuscitating Mr. Gordon."

Steve knew Rosberg was impressed, but Jake was not so happy about the entire episode. Jake made evening rounds difficult for everyone, especially for Steve. Every chance he could, Jake grilled Steve with questions, demeaning remarks, and generally speaking to him with a very condescending attitude. Jake made rude comments throughout rounds and tried to make Steve look stupid in front of patients and nurses by asking questions that had no answers. Fortunately, Jake had to meet with Dr. Rosberg, and so rounds were painful for only a short while. Before he left, Jake delegated the work that needed to be done for the night, which usually fell into the hands of the person on call. Tonight that was Steve.

After the work was listed for Steve, everybody else left, and Jake went to talk with Dr. Rosberg. Steve finally had a moment to himself to collect his thoughts and organize the work that he needed to do. Just then, his beeper went off. When he returned the call, Erica was on the other end of the phone.

"Hey, big surgery intern, the one who has mastered codes, would you like to grab a bite to eat?"

Steve glanced at the clock over the nurses' station and could not believe his eyes. "Seven thirty! Shit that went quick. Hey, how did you hear about the code?"

"Are you kidding?" asked Erica. "The entire hospital is talking about it. The brilliant surgery intern who can code anyone and do no wrong! I even heard two ward clerks talking about you."

"Shut up!" replied Steve.

"Why don't I meet you in the cafeteria?" asked Erica.

"That would be a great idea, if the cafeteria was still open."

"Yeah, I know, that's why I stopped and got some sandwiches for you. You see, your mother asked me to keep an eye out for you and make sure you don't wilt away to nothing."

Steve started to laugh. "Alright, thanks. I'll see you down there in two minutes."

When he got down to the cafeteria, it was empty except for Erica, who was putting some utensils on a table. "This is pretty nice of you."

Erica blushed. "Yeah, yeah, yeah. I just feel sorry for you surgery interns. You people work so hard."

"Oh, so then you do this for all the surgery interns?"

"That is not what I meant at all! I mean-"

"I know what you meant," interrupted Steve, "I just really appreciate your generosity."

They settled down to have dinner, but after only a few seconds, his pager went off. Steve and Erica looked at each other and smiled.

"That is how my entire day has gone," Steve said. "I get all of my scut and tasks done and finally sit down, and shit, the damn thing goes off again. Sorry, I will be right back." He walked over to a wall phone and spent a few minutes talking before returning to the table. "Well, that was easy. The nurses' station just wanted to clarify an order. I'm sure it will get worse as the night progresses."

"I'm sure," agreed Erica.

When Steve had a big mouthful of a turkey sandwich, Erica took the liberty to ask a few questions. "So how is it working with Dr. Jake 'the shit head' Douglas? I mean, is he as much of an asshole as the rumors predict him to be?"

Steve, trying to finish his sandwich before his next page, nodded yes with his mouth full. "He certainly has not impressed me with his four years of surgical experience. Besides being a jerk, he really is not a very good surgeon. The way I see it, Sally is really the one who keeps the patients alive. If she's late for rounds, the patients really suffer. Jake does not make very wise decisions."

Erica's curiosity got the best of her, "Do you think that is because of stupidity, or do you think he is moonlighting on the side, maybe doing something else?"

Steve looked at her with confusion. "What do you mean?"

"Well, I thought maybe if he is really tired or involved with doing other things, then he might not be as efficient. I mean, he has been a resident for four years, so you would think he would be able to take care of his patients a little better. I don't know, I was just thinking."

Steve was attempting to understand her direction of questioning and where it was leading when that all too familiar sound came from his waist. "Shit, there it goes again. Well, at least I got to eat something. Thanks a lot for the sandwich! I owe you."

Erica smiled and said, "I'll take you up on that and look forward to it."

Steve looked down at his pager, "Oh, shit, another trauma

code! I have to go. Thanks again for the dinner!"

"I hope your call shift goes well."

"It doesn't look like it. I have this feeling this is just the beginning of a busy night."

"Well," Erica replied, "Maybe you'll get to do an appendectomy later."

Steve laughed. "I doubt it. Jake is pretty pissed about the code this afternoon. I will have to put that wish on hold for a while. Hey, thanks again. I'll see you soon." He grabbed his white coat and disappeared through the cafeteria door.

Chapter 12

Steve dragged himself to the cafeteria where he could grab one more cup of coffee before he hit the road. After nearly forty hours in the hospital, he was ecstatic to get home. He certainly learned many things while on call, but he could no longer comprehend what his residents were telling him. Jake finally insisted he go home after he began falling asleep while they were discussing a patient on evening rounds.

He filled a cup with hot java, grabbed a bagel, and then made the long journey back to his car. He looked at the clock on the way out and saw that it read 10:10. He started to laugh when he realized that he had arrived at the hospital almost two days ago. The worst part was that he barely slept during the night. First it was the ICU patients, and then it was the ER consults. Steve would never forget Mr. Gordon. Every time he tried to go to his call room, his pager would go off. He finally did make it to his call room some time after four in the morning, but he only laid in bed with his shoes and socks on, waiting for the next trauma call or a code in the ICU.

He finally fell asleep around five o'clock, only to be awakened by the hospital operator at 5:30. He had requested a call at this time in order to make pre-rounds before the rest of the team returned. The day started off great, but by about 2:00 PM, Steve was having difficulty staying awake. He had one cup of coffee after another, but it didn't seem to make much difference. He just got more and more tired. *If I were an internal medicine resident,* he thought, *then I probably would go home after a call night until the next day.* But he wasn't. He chose to be a surgery resident.

Steve spotted his car and made a mad dash to get home faster. During the drive, he remembered when as a student he heard about a resident who died in a crash while driving after a night on call. He now understood how that could happen. He felt himself doze on more than one occasion on the way home. His eyes would get heavy and begin to fall shut. Then he would say to himself, "I'll just rest my eyelids for a minute..." *That's probably what that resident said to himself right before he died in the car accident.* So Steve did everything he could think of to stay awake. He rolled the window down and turned the radio on loud. He slapped himself in the face a few times and pinched his arm on occasion. He didn't care if these tactics were amusing to others: he made it home in one piece.

Walking up the stairs to his apartment was miserable, but he did it. Pudge started barking loud enough to wake not only the neighbors but also the entire neighborhood. Steve walked into his apartment, and it seemed like a foreign place to him. It was like he was visiting a friend. Even the smell of the apartment seemed foreign. Pudge's odor seemed strange too, but Steve did perceive that Pudge needed to go out badly. Steve had told his landlord that he would probably be home around dinnertime on his post-call days, not at 10:45 like this.

The dog was hungry, had a full bladder, and missed his master terribly. Steve let the dog out and put some food in his bowl. Steve seemed to move about his apartment in a non-purposeful manner. He was just too tired to concentrate on anything for more than twenty seconds. He threw a TV dinner into the microwave and sat on the couch. He tried to formulate a plan for the night in order to organize what needed to get done. As always, he wanted to read from his surgery text and to talk to Sweetpea to tell her about his first call night. His laundry and grocery shopping would have to wait for the weekend.

The dog started to bark outside, so Steve pulled himself up

to let him in. As he passed the clock, he became numb. In only five short hours, he would have to wake and begin another day. At least he wasn't on call, but five hours of sleep doesn't make up for two sleepless nights. He began roaming the apartment again in an unfocused manner until the microwave timer went off.

He decided that he would have to skip reading tonight. Besides, he probably would not comprehend or remember anything that he would read tonight. With that decision, he took his dinner to the computer and signed online. He figured that he could eat and talk to Sweetpea at the same time. This way he could get both of these necessities out of the way.

It took three tries but Steve was finally able to get into their favorite chatroom. Once they located each other, they moved to their private room.

"You must be totally exhausted!" typed Sweetpea. "They should give you guys a break after your call days. How do they expect you to safely take care of patients after a call day? I mean, what happens if you forget a simple thing that ends up killing a person? Now I know why they made those laws in New York."

Steve responded, "I think if you talk with the residents in New York and ask what their hours are like, they would tell you the same horrifying stories about long hours and lack of sleep. They just don't publicize it like most places because the public thinks the problem of long hours for residents is solved because there is a law against it. But like for any other law, it is sometimes broken." Steve continued, "Actually I didn't mind the call night. I learned a lot. The real problem was post-call. For the first few hours in the morning, I did fine. The problem started after taking a break after writing some chart notes. A few of us went down for a cup of coffee and that was it. I really couldn't get enough energy after sitting down for a while."

"That's too bad," consoled Sweetpea. "Tell me how the rest of your week went. I barely talked to you this week."

Steve told her about his first seven days in the hospital. There was so much to talk about. He told her about the canceled appy lecture and how most of the interns were disappointed. "We all want to do appys in the worst way, but instead we practiced placing IVs into each other. More than likely, this was because some nimrod never learned how to place them in med school. So here we were, poking ourselves until we got lucky with an IV. My friend Dennis and I were able to get them in right away and saved ourselves the misery of making several attempts on each other."

"That's cool," said Sweetpea. "Why don't you guy's practice appendectomies on each other? I mean if you did such an outstanding performance with the IVs, think what you could do with a knife!"

Steve replied, "I'll bring up that idea to Dennis and see what he thinks. Of course, there will be the operating room expense not to mention the time off from work for recovery, but maybe we can plan to do it on vacation."

Even as he typed, Steve began to fall asleep at the computer. He thought how nice it was that they were online and that she couldn't see him dozing. He figured if she did know that his head was nodding from lack of sleep while they were talking, that would definitely be the fuel for a disagreement.

Sweetpea asked, "So how was your first night on call?"

"Where do you want me to begin? The day started off ok but then one of our sick trauma patients coded. Basically, I had to take care of a patient who was terribly mismanaged by the chief resident. The doofus stopped his antibiotics way too soon and the guy went into septic shock. The patient then decided to code while I was on call and everyone else was in the operating room. It really sucked."

"So how did the guy do?"

Steve answered, "After a bunch of electrical shocks to his body and some pharmaceutical assistance, he pulled out of it for about thirty seconds or so, but then he crashed and died."

"That's really too bad. So where was the chief when all this was happening? I mean, isn't he supposed to help you out in tough situations like those? After all, he is the doctor ultimately responsible for the patient, right?"

Steve hesitated before continuing. It was obvious she had no clue what surgery residency was all about. "Yeah, you would think so, but you have to understand the residency system. It's set up like a stupid hierarchy. You really shouldn't bother the general unless… unless there is a major problem. Kind of like today. But when you do bother them with an emergency then they are pissed that there was an emergency, like it was you who created the situation. And in fact, this time the problem really evolved because the general screwed up. Jake did show up, eventually, after the guy was pronounced dead!"

Sweetpea started to seem more interested in learning about Jake. "So does this stupid chief have any life outside the hospital?"

Steve thought for a second, "I really don't know much about his personal life, and frankly I don't really care, and why would you care?"

"Well, I don't know, he just sounded like a complete shithead and…and…well, I don't know. So what happened the rest of your day?"

Steve realized she quickly changed the subject but he was too tired to care. He told her about the events during the night that kept him from sleeping, like all the phone calls from the floor nurses for pain medications or sleeping pills. "And then just after eating or rather swallowing dinner, I got a trauma code call from the ER. Unfortunately, the gentleman did not make it, but they brought him in after a single vehicle rollover. We tried for thirty minutes or so, but he was basically dead when they brought him into the ER."

Sweetpea was quite impressed. "A single vehicle rollover, huh? That sounds professional. Is that the same thing as a bad car accident? You must be really tired, so I'll let you go, but maybe we can talk tomorrow night."

"Yeah, I am exhausted," said Steve. "But I feel terrible. I didn't even ask how your day was or for that matter how your week went."

"That's ok. Some night when you have more time on your hands maybe we can have some conversations that last more than ten minutes."

Steve added, "…if you don't mind waiting five years or so."

They both said their goodbyes and Steve signed off. He was so tired he didn't even turn off the lights. He just dragged himself to the bed and collapsed.

Chapter 13

While Steve was saying goodnight to Sweetpea, Jake Douglas was across town in a smoke filled bar. He was waiting, waiting, waiting for the guy to show up to discuss his future endeavors, endeavors that were guaranteed to change his life forever, changes that would erase his financial troubles.

The dive bar did not seem like it was a place to discuss a situation in which one could make a lot of money. Jake also knew that this conversation was not the typical interview for a real staff surgeon job, but he was very curious. He wanted to know how he could make enough money to pay off all his debt and then some.

He had questioned the entire situation when the guy came to talk to him in the hospital. He demanded to know how he got Jake's name, and he had wanted to know more about this job that would change his life. But the man was very cautious about providing Jake with too much information. The man stressed that he and Jake needed to meet privately to discuss the job offer in more detail. It sounded interesting, so Jake agreed to show up. Now Jake was sitting in a bar, waiting for a guy he hardly knew to discuss his future.

When Jake walked into the bar, it was obvious he didn't belong. He wasn't the best dresser, but compared to the rest of the crowd in the bar, he was sharp as could be. He walked over to the bar and asked for a drink. The bartender gave him the beer on tap and then pointed to a table in the corner of the bar. Jake turned around, saw the empty table, and then glanced at the bartender with a puzzled look on his face.

"That table is reserved for you, Dr. Douglas," said the bartender.

Jake stared at the bartender for ten seconds and then said, "*Excuse me*?"

The bartender replied, "We have been expecting you, doctor. Please have a seat, and your acquaintance will be with you soon."

Jake slowly walked over to the table, but every fourth step, he slowly looked back to examine the bartender. He wondered if the man was a patient of his in the past, but nothing really registered. Jake finally reached the table, and he chose to sit facing the entire bar so could scope out the place.

Jake studied everybody to make sure he didn't recognize anyone from some past hospital experience. The closest table had two people who definitely didn't register with him as past patients. There was one man who had long gray hair with a leather jacket on his chair and leather pants to match. He displayed a large tattoo on his left arm of a woman stretching, and the right biceps had the Harley-Davidson logo inscribe into his skin. His muscles appeared rather large as they bulged out from his short sleeve shirt. His mustache was yellow from too much tobacco abuse. His companion was an exemplary biker chick. She too modeled several tattoos. The first that jumped out was a small colorful rose on her left breast. Her leather vest revealed most of her breasts but not all. Jake could make out two other tattoos on her shoulders. Jake could not see any others, but he suspected more hid beneath her leather attire.

The two of them appeared to be enjoying themselves as they drank beer. The man told joke after joke and leaned into her as they both laughed. Jake wasn't sure if the man was testing new material for comedy or just trying to peek down at her breasts for a better look at that tattoo. She didn't seem to have much to offer with respect to the conversation but looked comfortable listening to his jokes. A half basket of peanuts was on the table, empty shells on the floor. The ashtray had about fifteen butts, and both of them were chain smoking.

The music in the bar was from a jukebox in the corner next to the bartender. It wasn't too loud but did have a country western twang to it. Jake wanted to review the selections.

The entire bar seemed to become instantly quiet as he got up. Jake felt like all eyes were focused on him. However, by the time he got to the jukebox and had an excuse to offhandedly look up, he could see that no one was looking his way.

He was pleased to see that there were other music categories besides country. He placed a couple of dollars into the machine and selected a few songs. As he walked away from the jukebox, he looked at his watch and saw that it was nearly 10:45. He was supposed to have met with this unknown man at about 10:30. He started to think that this was just some joke from Dr. Rosberg or one of the other staff surgeons.

As he sat down at his designated table, he heard a loud crash come from the near the bar. He quickly looked over to notice two big guys ready to duke it out. "Come on, you little shit," said one of the guys, "I've had enough of your bull shit tonight." He threw a punch at the other guy, but the guy ducked just in time. The other man took his beer bottle and swung it at the guy. Then all of a sudden, the two of them were on the floor throwing punches at each other. The bartender quickly slapped a red button on the wall next to a line of bottles of alcohol. Then he jumped over the bar and jumped on one of the guys to try to break up the fight. The three of them struggled for a few minutes until sirens approached outside. Then one of the guys got up and bolted out the door. The bartender did his best to restrain the other man, but as the sirens became louder, the man overpowered him and dashed through the door too. A few seconds later, the police entered. They talked to the bartender for a few minutes, wrote some notes on a little pad of paper, and left.

Jake was thinking to himself that if it were some joke, this would be a good time to leave. He then reminded himself of the promise from the man that the job would more than pay off all of his loans. Jake forced himself to stay for a few more minutes, especially since all the commotion had ended.

The other patrons in the bar had barely noticed the fight. A few looked over their shoulders and then back to their conversations and drinks. The couple in front of him never even glanced up until the cops arrived.

The music on the jukebox finally began to play the selections Jake had picked. As he was reconsidering leaving, a waitress walked over with a bottle of Heineken.

"Hi. This is for you."

"I'm sorry," Jake replied. "You must have the wrong table. I didn't order a beer."

"Yeah, I know, but the lady sitting up at the bar thought you looked like a guy who drinks Heinies."

Jake glanced over to the bar and saw a very attractive woman sitting at the bar smiling in a somewhat shy way.

"I see," said Jake. "That will be just fine. She guessed right. Would that nice girl have a name to her?"

The waitress placed the beer on the table and acted as if she didn't hear him. "Would you like a glass with that?"

Jake took out a five and offered it to the waitress.

She didn't take it. "That's ok. This is already taken care of."

Jake smiled and said, "I know."

He grabbed his beer and stood up. Just as he started to walk toward woman with no name, the door to the bar opened, and in walked the man that had found Jake at the hospital. *Damn,* thought Jake. *What bad timing.* He fell back into his chair and raised his beer to the lady at the bar as if to say thank you.

Jake studied the man as he walked through the bar. He tried to figure out what this guy was all about. For whom did he work? How did he find Jake's name? Was he some weird guy gone crazy? Was the whole idea some illegal matter? There were many questions Jake had but knew he needed to wait for the right time to pursue them. He wasn't even sure about the meeting in the first place. He did need money, but certainly didn't want to jeopardize his five years of training as a surgeon for some illegal operation.

The man was dressed the same as he had been at the hospital. He wore a dark suit that seemed outdated under a long black overcoat. He was moderately overweight with a double chin. His teeth were stained yellow, implying a long history of smoking. He also had a mustache that showed signs of tobacco use.

The man walked over to Jake's table and pulled out a chair. "Good evening, I'm glad you could make it."

"You kidding? I wouldn't dream of missing a night out at this lovely establishment. I mean, the terrific clientele, the exciting bar fights, the wonderful ambience, what more could a guy ask for on a night out?"

The man didn't seem amused.

When the man started to take off his coat, Jake was surprised. "I thought that didn't come off, like maybe it was attached or-"

"Very funny," replied the man. "I thought you were more serious about this opportunity. I'm sure I could inquire about other applicants if you are not interested."

"Hey, sorry, it's just that you look unchanged since I last saw you."

Finally, the man sat down. "If you want to be a clothing

critic, that's fine. If you want to earn enough money to take care of your bills, loans, and ex-wife, then you better shut up and spend a little more time listening!"

Jake was paralyzed briefly, "How did you know about my wife?"

"I'll be more than happy to explain, that is, if your comedy routine is over?"

"Fine, fine, fine, I'll be quite. I'm all ears," said Jake. He sat back and folded his arms as if to give the gentleman his undivided attention. As the man finished taking off his coat, Jake saw the gun harnessed under his suit. Jake felt a lump in his throat. He looked at the people by the bar. He started to think that maybe this was not the way he wanted to make extra money. He had no clue who this guy was, but he sure did know a lot about Jake. What kind of guy walks around with a revolver next to his heart and hangs out at a dump like this? Not to mention the flashy overcoat.

This was more than Jake had bargained for. "You know, I'm really sorry to mislead you, but I don't think I have much of an interest in helping you out or making any extra money. I'm having a change of heart."

The man had perceived Jake's apprehension upon seeing the gun. The man looked down at his weapon and smiled. "Before you run off, give me a few minutes to explain. You came all the way to this part of town for a reason, so just let me explain." In fact, the man was concerned that Jake had already had too much exposure. If Jake wanted out now, he would have to be kept quiet. It would get too complicated if Jake backed out now. If Jake left at this point, he might be at major risk for exposing the entire operation. The man would have to get him on board.

The man reached into his pocket of his suit and pulled out a wallet.

Jake asked, “Are you going to pay me up front?”

“Just relax, young man. My name is Thomas, Agent Bill Thomas of the Central Intelligence Agency.” He opened his leather wallet to display a CIA badge with his picture.

“The CIA?” shrieked Jake. He grabbed the wallet to examine the identification more closely. Of course, Jake never had examined a CIA ID before. It wasn’t like he was examining a possible appendicitis case. He had no idea what to look for, but it seemed to be authentic.

He looked up at Agent Thomas and appeared perplexed. “I’m not sure I understand what you want with me.” Jake began to fidget with his hands under the table. His mind raced through all the things that an intelligence agency could question him about.

Agent Thomas was talking, but Jake’s mind was a million miles away. First, he thought about his ex-wife. Maybe she had set him up for this investigation. She certainly would have a motive to see him sweat with the authorities. Of course, there were numerous people who would like to see him sweat out an investigation: all the surgery residents and medical students of the past three or four years who he had embarrassed, tormented, and spoken condescendingly to. Then there was the entire nursing staff, not to mention all the staff surgeons to whom he was rude and disrespectful though they all deserved otherwise. The list could go on and on and on.

“Dr. Douglas? Dr. Douglas! Are you listening to a word I’m saying? Where are you?” demanded Agent Thomas.

“I’m so sorry, sir. I, uh, I was thinking about a patient of mine in the ICU who is very sick, and I think I should get back to review, uh, to review his labs,” Jake said frantically.

“Why don’t you just call the ICU and get the labs? Won’t

that be more expedient?"

Jake felt beads of perspiration form on his forehead. He tried to figure out how he could wipe his forehead without attracting too much attention to himself. By now his armpits were soaked, and every time he moved he could feel just how wet his arms were. Perhaps he could supplement his income by advertising for Brut, but lord knows that his stick bar wasn't working at the moment.

Agent Thomas had expected this reaction. In fact, all three people he had considered would have had the same reaction. They had the same features in common: they failed to show any morals, they had serious financial troubles, they were either divorced or cheating on their wives, their peers hated them, and basically they were losers. Jake was certainly no exception. Thomas had finally decided to recruit Jake because he was so screwed up. He thought Jake would rush to this opportunity with arms wide open. Jake certainly had the worst financial problems, the least amount of morals, and most importantly, the most gullibility and stupidity. He would never even think of questioning the mission when the CIA was involved. He would be so scared of what they could do to him that he would do whatever without asking questions, especially about the money involved.

"Dr. Douglas, just relax. We're not here to interrogate you. I'm here to see if you could help us out. Honestly, we had to go through a long list of applicants, and your name was the one that continuously came up as the one most likely to succeed in completing our mission successfully. Now just relax and let me explain. And if you would like, please feel free to wipe your forehead." He handed Jake a napkin from the table.

"The CIA has reason to believe that there is highly confidential material entering the United States from foreign territory," started Agent Thomas. "We think there is an international organization that is using human messengers as a means to bring in this material."

Jake interrupted, "That's fine and dandy, but what does this have to do with me?"

"That's a good question. We have reason to suspect that the next delivery to the US will be made somewhere in the Midwest. Our agency has been instructed to contact hospitals responsible for indigent care to be on the lookout for possible delivery sites. It may be Minneapolis, Chicago, or even Detroit. Other agents are making contacts with hospitals in these cities."

Jake continued to dig. "I still don't understand what you want with me. Why not let the proper authorities know of the situation, like the administrators?"

Agent Thomas replied, "First, we discussed this issue for some time and debated how to deal with the problem. We feel that if we contact too many people in high places, this mission would be scrapped because it would probably become public. You see, if we were to inform the administrators about this issue, they would need to contact their lawyers to discuss the situation and so on. So we decided that, before we announce it to the proper channels, we should make contact with the doctors that would be interacting with these human messengers first. Second, there has been a trend to send information within these human messengers. I mean literally inside them. That's where you surgeons come into play. These people appear at hospitals with severe abdominal pain and get operated on before they reach their contacts.

"Before they reach their contacts," repeated Jake. "What do they do once they reach their contacts?"

"We believe they are sacrificed and the package that is inside them is delivered to their contacts in the United States by someone else. We feel that there is information that may be threatening to our national security. We are not certain, but we need to intercept one of these packages to determine exactly what information is being imported. We are contacting several surgeons to discuss this highly sensitive situation. We will be in contact with our international agents, and as soon as we know the packages are coming and where, we will contact the appropriate surgeon in that city. We will kindly reimburse you for your surgical skills if you are involved with retrieving the package."

"This is a little more involved than what I really care for," said Jake nervously. "I don't think I really need the money that badly. I mean, I don't know these characters, but they sound pretty serious, and if I screw up their plans, I can only expect them to screw with me, and that's not worth the trouble of a few bucks."

Thomas hadn't expected Jake to be negative about this situation, but he knew too much at this point. Thomas knew that his colleagues would surely kill Jake if he backed out now. Not that Thomas felt close enough to Jake to really care, but Agent Thomas was getting tired of the recruitment phase of this project.

Agent Thomas tried to convince him. "I think you should really think about this opportunity, Dr. Douglas. Your role is very small, and for your troubles I will speak for the agency that not only will you be reimbursed well, we will make sure you receive adequate protection for a substantial period of time." Agent Thomas could see on Jake's face that he was not sold on the idea, so he decided to play dirty. He pulled out some papers from his coat pocket. "Let's see here. Your debt now is a little over three hundred thousand dollars. Not to mention your credit is shit, just pure shit. And for you to get good credit might be very difficult." Thomas looked straight into Jake's eyes and repeated, "Very very difficult." He glanced down at the papers and continued. "Now, I know the expense of medical training is quite a bit these days, but I don't believe the cost of prostitutes or drugs are included in the calculated expense of a medical budget. If I'm not mistaken, most medical boards might disfavor these activities. I'm also sure that any potential employer would question the use of cocaine while doing surgery."

Jake wildly tried to grab the papers from Agent Thomas.

Thomas quickly pulled the papers out of reach.

"Give them here, you little shit," pleaded Jake.

"You see, Dr. Douglas, there are much greater advantages to work with us versus against us. Despite all this negative information I mentioned, the CIA is still willing to reimburse you very handsomely for your efforts if indeed this patient does arrive at your hospital. There is no guarantee that the messenger will even arrive in Minneapolis or, for that matter, at your hospital, but the CIA needs to be prepared well in advance before the messenger enters US territory. If the messenger does not choose your facility, then the previously mentioned information will be disregarded, and your file will be removed permanently from our system. However, if the messenger does show up on your doorsteps, then we would greatly appreciate your surgical expertise and hand delivery of the package to us."

Jake was completely disgusted with the situation. "What if this dumb shit does come my way? How do I get in contact with you if he does indeed have this so called package?"

"Dr. Douglas, don't forget who you are dealing with. Our agents will notify us of the messenger and his destination, and the appropriate people will be contacted. At that time, if necessary, I will contact you and discuss the plan for delivery of the package, if it does indeed exist. Then arrangements will be made for proper reimbursement for your surgical skill and professional time committed to the mission."

Agent Thomas concluded in a very relaxed manner. "So Dr. Douglas, do we have your commitment to this mission?"

Jake stared hard at Agent Thomas with frustration. "It doesn't look like I have much of a choice. How much do I get paid?"

"The CIA has agreed to pay off the financial debt for the surgeon whose services are utilized. And in great appreciation for this sensitive and highly irregular activity, we will pay a five hundred thousand dollar stipend. This is, I'm sure, much greater than what is reimbursed from the insurance companies for a drainage of an intraabdominal abscess?"

Jake appeared more forgiving after hearing how much they were willing to pay him, but he was still pissed. "Great. I guess I'll just wait for your cue."

"I'm glad you agreed to accept this unusual opportunity, Dr. Douglas. Could I provide you with a ride home?" asked Agent Thomas.

"No, that won't be necessary," said Jake. "I think I've spent enough quality time with you tonight." He stood up abruptly to leave.

"Dr. Douglas, it was a pleasure to chat with you tonight," Agent Thomas said. He extended out his hand as if to make up for details brought up during their conversation.

Jake looked at the Thomas' hand, up at his face, and then back at the hand. Without returning the gesture, Jake slowly turned around and continued toward the door.

Chapter 14

Steve was slowly adapting to his new lifestyle as a surgical resident. The long hours and the lack of sleep were no longer a real bother for him. What really was getting him down was the lack of time spent with his friends. He felt as if he didn't have *any* since his residency began. He would spend so much time at the hospital that he would just be exhausted by the time he got home. And if it wasn't exhaustion that took him away from his extracurricular activities, it was the time spent studying surgery. His friends were surprised that he still needed to study despite having finished four grueling years of medical school, but he felt that a great deal of information had never been taught.

Medical school had been a chance to learn a little about everything in medicine, the basics about the human body. Residency was the means to augment that building block of knowledge. Every doctor needed to know some anatomy before finishing med school, but a doctor who selected neurosurgery would need to know a lot about the central nervous system and not really be concerned about the gallbladder or colon. Thus, residency was the time to specialize in your field of choice.

Steve had no regrets – yet – about picking surgery as his field of choice. Still there were days when he wished he had elected to enter a less demanding career. Tonight, for example, he was finally home at a decent hour. It was 9:30, and he felt like he had all night to goof around and get things done.

Despite the fact this was the earliest he had gotten home in the last three weeks, he was exhausted. He thought about all the chores around the house that could get done, like washing his clothes, washing his dishes, or picking up the house. He thought about calling a few lost friends like Deagan and Mary but figured it was too late to think about going out. So instead, he decided to read for a while and maybe go to bed before midnight for a change.

He fixed something to eat and then sat down with his surgery bible. He had been good about reading every day. Most of the residents were surprised that he continued to read every day and were jealous of his discipline. They all made similar promises about studying surgery, but too often they found reasons or excuses to miss a night here and there. Steve, however, continued studying a little every day – no matter what. Post-call he would push himself to read until he fell asleep. This only ended up being a few pages at a time, but at least it was something.

However, tonight as Steve started to read, he thought he should be doing something more relaxing, like going to a movie. He looked at the clock and realized that if he were to go to any of the late movies, he would probably not get back home until midnight. After a few minutes of debating this with himself, he chose to stay home and just watch some TV. He had been in residency for almost a month and hadn't had enough time to even sit and watch TV.

The time was near ten o'clock, and so Steve decided to watch the news. He plopped on the couch and turned to the local newscast. It seemed like months since he had heard the news. He didn't even recognize the newscasters. He sat back and listened to a woman discuss the events that happened in Minneapolis during the day.

After a few depressing stories, a male newscaster spoke up.

"And now for the national news: There is increasing concern in Washington about a terrorist group that is making threats to attack within the United States. For further details and the most up to date information, Jack Middlebury is in our nation's capital. Jack, what is the latest news concerning these terrorists?"

"Well, there are some serious concerns here. The latest information from the White House is that there is increasing security in all of the embassies worldwide. It's not just for US embassies either. The Canadian embassies have been increasing their security as well. But still the biggest concern is that, if the embassy in Great Britain can be attacked despite its new security system, then terrorist can probably get access to any of the other embassies." The screen showed a shot of the British embassy before cutting back to Jack Middlebury. "Most experts feel the real threat is to US Embassies and possible US cities. Other nations have been on alert, but the real focus has been on US property since so many of the recent attacks have been directed at US embassies."

The local newscaster stepped in again. "Jack, you mentioned US cities. Is there some real concern about access into US territory, and does the Department of Homeland Security think that is feasible?"

"Absolutely. There has been growing concern that the security in several US cities needs to be increased. There have been reports from undisclosed sources that some terrorist groups have targeted specific American cities. This information has not been available to the public until recently. We are not sure of the validity of these statements but will continue to provide information as it becomes available."

The newscaster again interrupted. "I understand the reason not to have any further discussions on this topic, but Jack do you know if this information has been available to White House officials longer and just not publicized until now?"

Jack replied, "I appreciate your question, but we just don't know. There are no officials at this point willing to discuss this highly sensitive issue. We are hoping that the White House will release a statement or conduct a press conference this week so additional questions can be answered and speculations cleared."

The female newscaster began asking questions. "Hello, Jack, this is Marty. I'm sure our viewers want to know if there is any real threat to our Twin Cities. I understand the White House does not want to start a wave of overwhelming fear, but are there particular cities targeted at this point?"

"Well, Marty," said Jack, "I will tell you there is only speculation at this point. Most of the officials that have given comments up to this point have not had their information validated by the White House. Consequently, their statements appear to be only their opinions. They have not had access to the information that White House officials have available."

"But Jack, what about the Twin Cities? Is there any real concern here?"

"Marty, I think right now the biggest concerns are the major cities, such as New York, Los Angeles, Chicago, Atlanta, or even Dallas. I don't think there is as much of a concern for Minneapolis and St. Paul as these larger cities. I will tell you there are unofficial statements that these cities have tightened security at their airports and other major transportation facilities. We don't want to start pandemonium, but certainly the public should be aware that these terrorists groups are moving closer to US soil. Officials in Washington have not been willing to make a statement, but I think the public deserves to hear what the White House knows. Otherwise, the speculation and unofficial statements will continue to be made and probably cause fear for many people…"

The reporters were still talking about these possible terrorists attacks when Steve's phone rang. He picked it up, but the person on the other end realized that a wrong number was dialed, apologized, and hung up. Steve rubbed his eyes and tried to return his focus to the newscast, but he was becoming too tired. He thought about getting ready for bed but wanted to hear more about this threat by terrorists groups. He couldn't believe that there was even a hint that terrorists could successfully get into the US for attacks. However, there had been the attack in New York at the World Trade Center as well as the attacks caused by domestic terrorists in Oklahoma and possibly Atlanta. It might be a plausible idea that terrorist attacks could happen in the US after all. Steve tried to follow the rest of the conversation before he fell asleep.

"…And Marty, one more thing. I don't think there is any alarm at this point for attacks in the near future, but the public deserves to know why those larger cities are beefing up their security. If the proper authorities don't inform the public as well as the media, I think speculation will begin to cause problems."

Marty replied, "Thank you, Jack, for this enlightening information. We all will be waiting anxiously for further details from Washington in the next few days. Thank you, again. Jack Middlebury, reporting live from our nation's capital."

The news report continued, but Steve was no longer listening. He was thinking about when life was much simpler and safer, a time when people didn't have so many worries, when kids went to school and didn't have to worry if their worst enemy was going to kill them or blow up their school, a time where mothers sent their kids to play outside without worrying if some stranger was going to abduct them, a time when people could go on a car trip and stop at a rest stops without watching for somebody to attack or rob them. Steve just could not believe the news these days. He never recalled such terrible stories from his childhood.

When he was a child he played in the streets without his

parents staring out the windows, he walked to the local convenience store without his parents tagging along, and it just seemed that life was so much safer. Steve thought about terrorists in the United States and what a frightening concept it was. Sure, there were terrorists abroad, causing trouble and fright for many people living in foreign countries, but that wasn't supposed to happen here in the great U.S. It just didn't seem like that would ever be a domestic problem, but after listening to the news tonight that might be the next thing parents will worry about.

Steve dragged himself up to get ready for bed, turned off the television, and locked up his house. As he crawled into bed, he could not stop thinking about the news and the concern for possible terrorists attacks in the United States. He remembered his trauma experience from his surgery rotation in medical school. There would be all sorts of violent injuries that came through the emergency room. Most of the penetrating injuries from gun and knife attacks were gang related. It was like clockwork: on a Saturday night, there would be three or four gunshot wounds and a few stab injuries. It never failed. Every Saturday some sort of trauma like this would come in. As a med student, Steve could not wait for a Saturday call night so that he could see a bunch of trauma and take care of serious injuries. If you played your cards right with a good chief resident, you might have been able to scrub in on a few cases and even repair some holes in the bowel after a gun blast.

Now as a resident, Steve wondered if it would be gang-bangers causing all the traumatic injuries or some screwed up terrorist attacking the local airport or whatever. He envisioned a Saturday night on call. "*Dr. Carmichael, Dr. Carmichael, stat to the ER!" When he got to the ER, he could see the nurses running around collecting equipment and getting ready for a trauma code. He would walk up to one of the nurses and ask, "What's coming in?" The nurses would turn around and look at him squarely in the eye and stare at him like he was from the planet X. "You mean you haven't heard? Where have you been the last hour?! There was an attack at the Governor's Mansion. At least two bombs went off, and they are bringing at least six patients here."*

Steve thought about this scenario and others as he drifted off to sleep. Oh how the world had changed. When he was growing up, the biggest worries he had to deal with was what he and his friends were going to do on a Friday night, but now kids might have to wonder where to take shelter when a bomb threat is announced. What a different world.

Chapter 15

Four weeks had passed since Steve and his intern cohorts had started residency. It seemed like a lifetime ago that he plunged into this hell they call residency. Similar to the other surgery interns, he had been working like a dog for a month without a single opportunity to do any surgery. Not that they expected to, but after working so many long hours and taking so much bullshit from chief residents, all of the interns thought they should have earned the privilege of at least an appendectomy. Steve was no exception.

Steve believed that he had to deal with the most bullshit since he had to answer to Jake Douglas each day. Jake had a special reputation amongst the residents, and for that matter, the surgery staff as well. No one liked him, no one respected him, and no one cared to be around him. It was considered terribly bad luck if you got stuck on Dr. Douglas's service. No one envied Steve, Sally, and Tom, the unfortunate souls on Jake's service for the first three months of the year.

Steve was hopeful that today would be the changing point. Today's lecture series promised to be interesting. It was the lecture that was cancelled in the beginning of the internship: the formal training session to complete an appy.

Most of the interns already knew how to do the procedure. In fact, it was the first thing they studied when they start their residency, knowing it was usually the first procedure they would be allowed to do in the operating room. Although most of them knew how to remove an appendix, the staff would not allow any of them to do the surgery until the lecture was completed.

The day started like any other day for Steve: rounds with

Jake and the rest of his team. As usual, the rounds were quick, appropriately nicknamed 'lightning rounds.' Jake flew through the ICU to briefly see the patients. He never really had much to say to the patients, and for the most part, they didn't care to spend too much time with him either. Jake was just as rude to his patients as he was to the residents. While he quickly reviewed labs and vitals for each patient, he would shout out orders to the person writing the daily note and then move speedily on to the next patient.

Everyone knew that Jake expected Sally to review the management issues of each patient since she was the next most senior on the service. Steve would often bring an abnormal lab value or culture result to the attention of Sally instead of Jake. It was not only easier to bring it to the attention of Sally but also safer because she usually didn't bite off his head for problems with patients. In fact, she was a very intelligent doctor, and if there were a problem with a patient's post-operative course, she would study the situation carefully and devise an effective plan to correct the problem.

After the team finished rounds, they went to the cafeteria for the usual cup of coffee and something to eat. Jake announced his plans for delegation of duties for the day. "...and Carmichael, you will scrub with me on the esophageal resection."

"But Dr. Douglas, we have the intern lecture today at ten, and I don't know if we'll be done by then." Steve tried to be very political about it. "Dr. Rosberg has told us over and over again that he expects all surgery interns to be at those lectures. He doesn't care what excuses we have, he just wants us there and on time. I'm sure you remember his concern for attendance to those lectures."

Jake remembered all too well the times when he had missed

the lectures and then got bitched at by Rosberg in front of all the other residents and interns. "Yeah, I remember how demanding he is when it comes to the lecture series. Just scrub in until it's time to take off for the lecture. What's it on today?"

Steve replied, "Appendectomies."

Jake laughed. "Oh, *that's* why you want out so bad. Don't assume that when you're done with the lecture you can run off and get the next available appy."

Steve wasn't sure if Jake was joking or not, but he was going to hope for that very opportunity anyway.

Jake continued, "Make sure you get all the details down so you can teach me the latest technique in appendectomies. I'm sure there will be a few appys along the way this year."

Steve stared at Jake and then at Sally. He wasn't sure what to make of Jake's friendly behavior. He was waiting for a bomb to drop, but one never did.

Sally finally interjected and asked the question that most of the team was wondering. "Jake, are you feeling okay? I know you've been under a lot of stress lately. Maybe we can give you a few days off so you can get some rest and-"

"I'll be fine," replied Jake. "I think it would be a good idea to work it out that each resident get a day off a week. There is no need for all of us to come in and round each day of the weekend. Perhaps one of us or even two should take a day or two off each weekend. I'll have to look at the schedule and see what I can arrange."

Tom, Sally, and Steve looked at each other and then at Jake.

Sally appeared as though she had seen a ghost. She leaned back in her chair and put her hands to her head in disbelief. "What have you done with Jake Douglas? We demand that you tell us what you did with him!"

Jake started to laugh and finished going over the plan for

the day. He paid no particular attention to her or the others as they sat in total shock. They were stunned from meeting this side of Jake Douglas.

Jake finished, "…and Carmichael, I'll see you in the OR, and bring your choice of medical student with you to the case." Jake stood up and left the cafeteria.

After Jake was out of earshot, the group at the table buzzed about Jake's abnormal behavior. For anyone else, it would be considered a pleasant attitude and normal behavior, but for Jake Douglas, it was definitely abnormal. Sally thought that maybe his ex-wife had called and wanted to get back together, but they agreed that would be ridiculous.

"If you had a chance to leave Douglas and *did*, why in the hell would you want to go back?" questioned Tom.

"Well, maybe his kids were missing their dad, and she felt they would be better off with a dad versus without a dad," suggested one of the students.

Tom told the student that Jake was barely ever home, and when he was, they would always fight. "The kids probably have enjoyed some peace and quiet since Jake left."

Steve added his two cents. "Maybe he just got lucky last night." As the words were coming out of his mouth, he remembered how close Sally and Jake had been the last few weeks and began to turn red. "But who knows. Well, I guess I better head over to the OR. See ya, guys." He kicked himself for being so stupid in front of Sally. He didn't know for sure about Sally and Jake but still left the cafeteria feeling a little embarrassed.

Steve was still thinking about what he had said as he made his way to the operating room. He was pulled from his guilty thoughts by a deep voice.

"Carmichael, what the hell are you doing here? Aren't you

supposed to be at a lecture today? Damn it, I hate when you and all the interns ignore those lectures. You think you know it all, and then bam, you're placed in the situation and what do you know, you guys screw up. Then you realize that you *don't* know it all!"

"Dr. Rosberg, Dr. Douglas asked me to help out on a case until the lecture. Sir, I reminded him about the appy lecture, and he assured me that I will be excused on time to attend."

"Carmichael, if you're late for that lecture, so help me I will make sure your internship is spent with Douglas the entire year. And maybe I'll have you repeat your intern year again just to be sure you don't forget about the lectures! Do you understand, Carmichael?"

"Yes, sir, I will remind Dr. Douglas again. Thank you, sir."

Steve was shaking as he finished putting on his scrubs. That was all he needed to do to screw up his residency – piss off Dr. Rosberg. Now the problem was not to piss off Jake while reminding him that he had to leave the esophagectomy early. Steve was thinking to himself and organizing a plan in his head as he walked through the locker room on his way to the operating room. He was so deep in thought that he didn't even see Jake on the other side of his locker.

"Hey, Steve," yelled Jake. "I can't find anybody else to scrub with me on this case so you are going to have to miss the lecture today. Sorry!"

"What?! Didn't you just hear my conversation with Dr. Rosberg?" Steve whispered frantically. "If I miss that lecture, my ass will be toast."

Jake replied in a husky voice, "Do you mean, Carmichael, that if you don't make that lecture, you will have to spend your entire intern year with me, the terrible Jake Douglas?"

Steve glared at Jake. "You asshole." He walked away as

Jake and another chief resident broke out in laughter.

Steve did not talk with Jake for the first thirty minutes of the esophagectomy. Finally, Jake pleaded with Steve to let up. "Hey, Carmichael, it was just a joke. Relax. Nobody heard it except Gary and me. It was no big deal. You've got to relax a little more. Otherwise, your residency will take a toll on you. I mean, you've got to joke every once in a while or this business will get you down. When you are taking care of sick little kids or dying people with cancer or AIDS, you will need to break from reality occasionally or you'll just lose it."

Steve didn't reply, but he thought about what Jake was saying. He realized that Jake was right about chilling out because there are many serious issues that could bring a person down. Still, Steve didn't appreciate being the butt of the jokes.

He remembered a medical student who was taking care of a little boy with AIDS and how upsetting that whole rotation was for her. The student felt like the child didn't have a chance: not only did he have AIDS, but his parents – or at least his mother – left him at the doorsteps of an emergency room with a note to help the child. She just left him there in a bassinet. Steve knew the student only from afar; he had never talked to her, but he heard that she had to receive counseling for the trauma she suffered during that rotation.

While Steve thought about his poor colleague, Jake continued yapping. "Hey, listen, Carmichael. I promise I won't do that again, so just get over it. All right? Besides, like I said, no one heard it, so stop sweating."

"Heard what?" demanded Dr. Rosberg as he walked into the operating room. He loomed behind Jake.

"Uh, nothing sir," lied Jake. "We were just talking about something a patient had said."

"Really? Now, why in the world would a patient want to go

to a surgery intern lecture about appys? Unless, of course, that patient was planning to attend our delightful surgery residency program here in our distinguished hospital. Otherwise, I've never met many patients who would be concerned about learning to do appendectomies, have you, Jake?"

Silence filled the room. Jake was turning red. The surgical mask hid his face, but his forehead below his surgical cap was beaming a bright rose color.

"You know, Douglas, I don't think I have such a husky voice. Of course, I really never hear my own voice. Maybe I should listen to you more often so I can appreciate the way I sound. What do you think, Douglas?"

"I'm sorry, Dr. Rosberg. I can explain."

"Do you mean you can explain like what that patient was talking about, or are you plotting some other bullshit lie, Douglas?"

The room remained silent but for the ventilator breathing for the patient. Dr. Rosberg took advantage of the situation to give Jake a little of his own medicine. "Sure is quiet in here, huh, Jake? Is that your stomach rumbling, or do you need to excuse yourself for a few minutes from my case?"

"Uh, no, sir. That won't be necessary, sir."

As Jake was answering Dr. Rosberg, the nurses giggled from the corner of the room.

Dr. Rosberg glanced at the nurses and then back at Jake.

"Oh, Douglas, don't worry about everyone laughing at you for having a bowel movement in your shorts. Just relax and chill out. I mean, taking care of patients can be pretty difficult at times, and we all need to laugh every once in a while."

With that, the nurses and the anesthesiologist began laughing loudly.

"Steve, why don't you let Dr. Douglas and me finish the

case today? I think Dr. Douglas could use some practice in retracting while I do the procedure, and I know you want to be on time for that lecture. Is that okay with you, Dr. Shithead Douglas?"

Jake didn't respond, but Steve took the cue and stepped back from the table without another word.

Steve grabbed his white lab coat and headed toward the conference room for the lecture. As he turned a corner, he ran smack into Erica. "Hi! Sorry, I didn't mean to run you over," he said.

"Hey, that's okay. So what have you been up to lately?"

"I just got out of the OR with Rosberg and Douglas."

"That sounds entertaining."

"Actually, I think the majority of fun is yet to come.

Jake was imitating Dr. Rosberg in the locker room, obviously not knowing he was there."

"It sounds like Jake pulled another dufus move. You think that idiot would learn sometime," said Erica.

There was a moment of silence, one of those awkward moments where both people have a ton to say but don't know how to get started. Then they both started at the same time.

"How about-"

"I was wondering-"

They both giggled.

Steve nervously asked, "How would you like to get together for dinner sometime? I mean a real dinner, not in the hospital."

Erica smiled. "Like a date?"

Steve turned red. "Uh, yes, I guess that's what I mean."

"That sounds terrific!"

"Great," said Steve. "That's great. I need to get to that lecture, but I'll get ahold of you soon."

"Good." Erica flashed another smile. "I look forward to

hearing from you."

Steve hurried to the conference room, grinning from ear to ear. He reached the lecture without bumping into anyone else. He took a seat next to Dennis Burrows.

Dennis took one look at Steve and joked, "Are you that excited about the appy lecture or are you just happy to see me?"

"Neither." Steve leaned back and smiled as he waited for the lecture to start. He wound up missing the first half of the lecture daydreaming about Erica and dinner with her.

Dennis nudged him in the shoulder. "Hey, wake up! Pay attention or it'll look as if we don't care about appys.

Where are you anyway?"

"Oh, I'm just thinking about something."

"It looks more like you are thinking about some*one*, not something."

Steve just smiled at Dennis and turned toward the lecturer. He was so absorbed by planning his date that he hadn't even realized that the lecturer was Sally. She must have been covering for Jake while he did his esophagectomy.

Steve forced himself to focus on Sally's voice.

"At this point, you need to either tie the base of the appendix or staple across the base. Whether it is an endo GIA stapler or a TA stapler doesn't really make a difference. Of course, if the base of the appendix or the entire cecum is necrotic and gangrenous, then a TA 55 or 90 might be the best choice. However, for the majority of cases, a simple tie is all one needs to close off the appendix. If the appendiceal stump leaks or the ties fall off, you can get some serious peritonitis and sometimes even a fistula between the colon and skin."

"What about burying the stump?" asked one of the interns from the back of the room. "Does this provide extra protection against stump leaks?"

"That is a great question," Sally replied. "Some surgeons will place a purse string around the stump and then bury it, but the most important thing to do is to make sure the stump is completely tied off. Otherwise it will leak."

Sally continued to share her ideas on the best way to complete an appendectomy and answer questions from the interns. Meanwhile, Steve went back to thinking about when to schedule his date with Erica. Since he was not on call this next weekend, he thought one of those days would be a good time to get together. Then he had to decide what to do and where to go and what time to pick her up and on and on. As he was thinking about this, he heard Dennis again.

"Carmichael, are you going to sit there all day or what?"

Steve looked up and saw that the auditorium was empty except for Dennis and himself. He'd had no idea that the lecture had ended. "Sorry, I was thinking about something or someone or whatever."

The two of them walked to the cafeteria to grab lunch.

On the way, Dennis tried to get the scoop on Steve and who was on his mind. Turning the corner into the cafeteria, Dennis ran right into Erica. "Oops, sorry about that."

"Hey, Erica," greeted Steve. "This is a friend, Dennis Burrows. Dennis, this is Erica."

"Nice to meet you," acknowledged Dennis with a big smile of approval toward Steve.

Erica and Steve started talking about something unimportant, and Dennis took the cue to excuse himself. "Nice to meet you, Erica."

After Erica waved at Dennis, Steve asked, "So what are you doing this weekend? I finally have some time off for us to get together. I mean, if you still want to." He hoped she wouldn't notice the boyish waver in his voice. "We could go and see a movie, and maybe drinks afterwards?"

"If we start off with dinner, we could probably consider it a real date. What do you think?"

Steve just smiled.

"Actually, that sounds great, Steve. I live in the North View condos, number 172."

"Great! I know where that is. I'll pick you up about five on Friday."

"Good. But now it's my turn to get some place. I have to get to afternoon rounds now, so I'll see you later."

Steve caught up with Dennis in the cafeteria. "Sorry about that. What's for lunch?"

Dennis just smiled and said, "Now I know what was distracting you during the appy lecture."

They laughed and dug into the buffet.

Chapter 16

Steve got home and did what he always did: he let Pudge out and started to plan a small meal. But after he let the dog out, he heard a familiar beep come from his computer to let him know that he had new e-mail. He figured it would be either Sweetpea or a friend from medical school. While the message loaded, he went in search of something to eat. He scurried around the chip drawer and brought a bag of pretzels to the computer. It must have been a busy time of night because he had to wait a few minutes to get online.

Once online, he found that Sweetpea had been the one to leave him an e-mail. Her note let him know that she wanted to chat at 9:00 that night. He looked at his watch and noted he had another hour to get things done.

He started by killing a few minutes with thoughts about dinner, about things he needed to do, and, of most significance, about Erica. He barely knew her, but he felt a certain attraction to her. The fact that her beautiful eyes matched her nearly perfect figure would have any normal man taking a second look at her, but there was something more that attracted him. He couldn't really pinpoint it yet, but there was something special. It was as though they had known each other for a long time. He had a weird sense of attraction that was more than physical. It didn't hurt that she was beautiful, but the comfort level between them was as though they had been friends for ages. The ease with which they spoke and joked with each other seemed unique. Steve had friends who were girls and girls he had dated in the past, but none of those relationships felt so at ease. He was relaxed with her. It felt like more than just friends, but maybe that was just because Steve wanted it that way. He wasn't sure how she really felt.

As he sat thinking about Erica, Steve heard his dog bark and his stomach growl. He figured he better take care of the dog first. Pudge ran in after the door opened and nearly attacked Steve. He slobbered Steve with enough saliva to fill a pail. Steve played a few minutes with Pudge before filling the dog dish. He then fed himself something quick. By the time both stomachs were filled, Steve looked at the clock and was surprised to find it was almost nine.

Soon he was online and catching up with Sweetpea in their private chatroom. Steve discussed in grueling detail the appy lecture. He didn't mention that he had been daydreaming about another woman but explained, basically, how to complete an appendectomy. Sweetpea asked a few questions about the operation and when he would be able to complete his first appendectomy. After those questions had been satisfied, she started to ask more specifically about his residency and coworkers again.

"Hey, didn't we go over all these details a few weeks ago?" Steve typed.

"I can't remember," replied Sweetpea. "Sometimes it seems like we haven't talked in so long that maybe something changed. And quite frankly, that asshole chief resident sounds interesting. I mean, we could just talk about him forever. It seems he always gets himself into some sort of trouble. I just figure there would be some new story you could share about him or some of the other surgeons you work with. From what I can figure, you always have some good story to tell me about one of the different surgeons you work with."

"Alright," said Steve. "I see your point. It just so happens there is a good story I can fill you in on."

"See, what did I tell you? I just knew it. And it probably

has to do with that jerk chief you have that… Dr. Douglas, right? I bet I'm right!"

Steve started right in. "Alright, miss smarty pants. I do have a great one for you, and you're right, it does pertain to Jake Douglas. Jake had told me to help scrub on a big esophageal case today, but I was a little torn because I had to be at the lecture for appys. I didn't want to act like I didn't care about the case, but Dr. Rosberg gets pissed when the interns don't show up at those lectures. So anyway, I was in the locker room, and from behind a few lockers, Jake pretended to be Dr. Rosberg and started to scold me for being in the operating room on a lecture day. He pretended to give me shit and threatened my butt if I didn't make it to the lecture. Well, it turned out that the real Dr. Rosberg was in the locker room the entire time and heard the conversation! He let Jake have it in the operating room, made him look like the true dufus he is. Most everyone silently applauded Dr. Rosberg. Well, that was my Jake story for the day."

"I just can't believe that asshole," replied Sweetpea. "You would think he would get it after a while. But when you're that stupid, I guess you can't help it. So have you seen him talking to any more creepy characters?"

"Not really. Fortunately, I have not been doing much with Jake. Since Sally and Jake have developed this sick relationship, or what I presume to be, I really have not been interacting with Jake much. That's just fine with me. He sometimes has this aura about him that makes him almost scary. It's not the condescending attitude either. It's just that he has some really different ideas or morals. Now, I know all surgeons are a little different," joked Steve, "but this is not that. This is deeper into his personality, and I don't care to figure it out." He paused before typing, "So enough about my work and me. How is life in your neck of the woods? Do you think we will ever get together? I feel as if I know you already, but I would like to meet you and put a face to the conversations, if you know what I mean. I get a few weeks of vacation this year and thought it would be fun to see you. I promise I'm not a sort of weird freak who would hurt you or whatever. I just thought it would be nice to know you in person. What do you think?"

Steve waited patiently for a reply but noticed it was taking a little longer than usual for Sweetpea's response. He started to wonder if he had pissed her off or offended her in some way. After all, there were all sorts of strange stories about people meeting on the Internet and then finding in real life that the person they had been conversing with all that time was in fact twelve years old or an abductor or worse.

After a few more minutes, a reply started to show up. "I'm not sure how to respond to the magnificent suggestion. There have been a few times I thought I would make the same offer, but I didn't want to be too forward. Now that *you* have made the move, I'm not sure how to respond. I truly believe that you are sincere and honest and would not hurt me in anyway, but then there are those crazy stories in the news. I mean, there are good stories too like people falling in love over the Internet but not meeting each other in person for years and then they end up getting married and so on. But what if, by some weird chance, you are one of those creeps who would rape me or do whatever? I think I would rather just talk for a little while longer on the net, and then maybe we can make some arrangements to meet. How does that sound? I do really want to meet you in person, and I think that will happen sooner than you think, but for now I would like to hold off. Ok?"

Steve understood why it took her so long to answer him in the first place. Now *he* didn't know how to reply. He typed a careful response because he didn't want to say anything that would jeopardize their relationship or offend her in anyway. "That sounds like a reasonable thing. Hey, you could hurt me in some way too, so for the time being we can just talk online. And when we do get together, we should find some neutral place so neither one of us feels threatened or uncomfortable. That sounds just fine to me. On that note, I really need to get going, but I will talk to you later. Take care." Steve signed off.

He thought to himself, *That was strange.* He understood Sweetpea's concerns but felt they'd just had a misunderstanding like people do in person. He knew that he was taking a chance asking her, but then it was nice to know that she'd had the same thoughts about getting together. How did she know that they were going to get together sometime soon? Weird.

Steve did a few chores around his apartment and then took out his surgery text. He started to read and soon feel asleep with the book on his chest.

Chapter 17

The week went well for Steve, but he spent a great deal of time distracted by thoughts about Erica. He barely knew her, nothing outside their hallway conversations, but they seemed to get along great when they interacted. She gave the impression of a laid-back person. That was a difficult characteristic to find in the medical field. Everyone else in residency had too much stress going on to show their true side, and when their true colors did show, they were usually too anal about life and medicine. Erica, on the other hand, seemed to be quite calm and in control of her life.

Steve contemplated what they should do on their date while he drove home. He had been on-call last night for the last time for three whole days. He was looking forward to his wonderful weekend off. It didn't occur often that a surgical resident got an entire weekend off, but Steve had a fortunate call schedule. Without being expected to take call over the weekend, Jake had decided to give Steve the entire weekend off. The intern wasn't sure if that decision had to do with any of the conversation Jake had shared with Dr. Rosberg, but Steve was in no way going to argue about it.

The drive home from the hospital passed in a blur as per usual the days after taking call. Tonight was especially blurry with Steve so deep in thought. He didn't even remember turning on the highway, and now he was pulling into his driveway. He turned off the car and left the keys jiggling in the ignition. He glanced at his watch and then placed his hands on the steering wheel, resting his head across his hands. He let his weary eyelids close and started planning his night.

He needed to shower and change first. Last night was a

rough night for call with three trauma codes in the ER. With the stress of each code, he sweated like a pig and then didn't have time to change his clothes or shower during the day. Without a doubt, the first thing to do was a shower. He continued to keep his eyes shut, planning where to go for dinner with Erica and how nice or casual the place should be. He thought about the movie and where to go afterward for drinks.

Steve smiled to himself, thinking about all the planning that had to be done including reservations. *Oh shit*, he thought to himself *Reservations!* He had forgotten to make reservations at a restaurant. He jerked himself up in the car and made his way to his apartment as quickly as possible. How could he find a nice place to eat on Friday evening without reservations? He ran through his place trying to find a phonebook. He flipped through the Yellow Pages: Mexican, Chinese, Italian, Indian, whatever. He paused thoughtfully and then decided that Mexican would be a nice dinner. Most places were not too formal but just right to grab a drink and dinner before a movie. He turned to the section for Mexican restaurants and reviewed the places to which he had been before. He had not realized there were so many Mexican restaurants in town. Finally, he saw a familiar place: "La Cantina." He had been there as a student with some friends after one of the many tests they had in medical school. He remembered it being a nice place and dialed the number. As he spoke with the receptionist, he let Pudge outside.

The receptionist laughed when he asked for a reservation. "I don't think calling two hours ahead of time on a Friday night would give you much of a chance for a table, but let me go through the list real quickly. Could you please hold the line?"

"Sure" responded Steve. While waiting, he poured Pudge his dinner, another helping of wonderful dog food. He let the dog in and went back to the bedroom to sort out the clothing situation.

"You're in luck, sir. I have a table for two that is available at seven. Would that work for you?"

"Absolutely! That will be perfect. I can't thank you enough!"

Lucky, lucky, lucky, thought Steve. Nothing bad about being lucky. He glanced at the time on his way to the shower. Realizing it was already fifteen minutes to five, in addition to the fact that reservations were a little behind schedule, he thought he owed Erica a call.

"Hi, Erica, Steve here. How're you doing?"

"Just fine," she answered. "Let's see. A surgical resident calling fifteen minutes before he's supposed to pick me up. Let me guess: you're a little late?"

"Wow," said Steve. "You're good. But I'm not only late with you; I kind of forgot to make the reservation for dinner. But not to worry! I was able to get a reservation at seven at La Cantina."

There was a short pause on the other end of the phone. "Uh, great, Steve. There is one small problem. I really don't like Mexican food."

How could someone not like Mexican food? Steve thought, but he said, "Oh shit, I'm sorry. I really didn't know. We could go someplace else. What kind of food *do* you like?"

"Hey, Steve, settle down," laughed Erica. "I was just joking. That sounds great. I actually love Mexican. When should I expect you?"

Relieved, Steve replied, "You little shit! You got me good. I'll remember that. Let's say I'll be there in about one hour, maybe 5:45."

"Great, Steve. Why don't I just meet you down in the lobby?

I'll be looking for you. Scc ya then."

Steve hung up the phone and laughed to himself. *What a shithead,* he thought, but Erica had a great sense of humor. She really seemed quite different from other people he had dated. She was so much more confident and secure with herself, and because of that, she didn't hold much in. Of course, there could be disadvantages to that as well, but he continued to think fondly about her while he rushed to get ready.

Steve hadn't had any serious relationships over the last few years, but something about Erica made him consider the possibility. He found himself thinking about her all the time, like a kid in high school with some puppy love girlfriend. He would catch himself daydreaming about her during rounds, hoping that their paths would cross in the hallways. He constantly watched for her at lunch times. He didn't doubt that a few of the residents had noticed moments when he had been aloof. They probably wondered if he was burned out on the residency like so many others who left the program due to the long hours and the grueling schedule. Steve would assure them that everything was ok, but still they would wonder.

Steve was still thinking about their date as he stepped into the shower. The warm water felt good after a long day. The intern didn't have too many days off, but he had learned to enjoy the free time when he did. Since starting residency, he had missed his long showers. Medical life never allowed time for those luxurious, self-indulgent activities such as washing at a relaxed pace. With the reservation made for seven, he took time to unwind.

Steve made sure to pick up Erica on time. When he arrived at her complex, she was waiting outside. He was amazed by her beauty as he drove up. She had a pair of blue jeans on with a white blouse and dark blazer. She let her hair down, something

Steve had never seen at the hospital. As he got closer, she flashed a simple yet gorgeous smile that glowed. He noticed her lipstick and makeup. Never did she ever have this on at the hospital. Steve thought she was very attractive at the hospital with her everyday appearance, but he realized he was not going on a date with Erica the Internal Medicine resident, but rather Erica the beautiful young woman.

Erica gracefully slid into the car and never was there a silent moment. "So you finally made it here," laughed Erica as she shut the car door. "I thought maybe I should just stay near my phone for any other important calls, like your car won't start or your dog ran off with your keys or all four tires are flat or-"

"Alright, alright I get it. I really am sorry for the delay, but I'm sure this won't ever happen again."

"Again?! Are you kidding? You think I would go through this again. Next time you probably would just stand me up."

Steve wasn't sure where to go with this. She had every right to be upset.

"Carmichael, just relax. I was just joking. I mean I would never let myself get set up like that again. Next time I would just turn you down from the beginning."

Steve looked down guiltily and continued to drive.

Erica reached over to grab his hand. "Hey, seriously, I really did look forward to this date. I'm just trying to break the ice, but maybe I should take it easy on you. After all, you are a very sensitive and caring surgical resident- or wait, do they even exist?"

They both laughed but continued to harass each other on the way to La Cantina. Erica gave Steve grief for being late, and he returned the favor by amusing himself with internal medicine residents. After a few minutes of joking about, the mood simmered down. They were much more relaxed by the time they arrived at the restaurant.

The restaurant was as busy as Steve had remembered. Waiters and waitresses were running in all directions. Bus boys moved through quickly with trays balanced above their heads with dirty plates and glassware. Young girls with cantina garb were trying to seat the most impatient customers.

Despite this hustle and bustle of the cantina, the place maintained the same pleasant vibe. The authentic nature of La Cantina was superb, transporting diners from Minnesota to Mexico. The aroma of Mexican food was everywhere. The sweet smell of sizzling fajitas was tremendous.

Just as Steve was about to comment to Erica about the place, a waiter dashed through with margaritas.

"I have never been here before, but so far it seems like a great place!" remarked Erica. "And I could really use a few of those." She pointed to the drinks.

Steve motioned to grab the margaritas from the waiter's tray, but Erica slapped his hand. He smiled at her as they tried to make their way to the hostess. "Hi. Steve Carmichael, I have a reservation for two."

The girl scanned her seating chart. "Oh, yes. Mr. Carmichael, your table is ready for you. Won't you please follow me?"

Steve turned to smile at Erica. "See? No problem. I told you that I had a reservation."

"Yeah, and by the looks of how busy this place is, you were pretty lucky too."

A basket of chips and a bowl of salsa were placed on the table as they were seated. "Enjoy your meal," said the hostess as she turned around joyfully and made her way back to the front entrance.

"This is quite the cantina, huh?" mumbled Erica.

They both had their menus in hand, but neither opened them. They quietly observed the crowd instead to soak in the atmosphere. They continued to look around until a waiter came by and offered to take their drink orders. "Anything from the bar tonight for you two?"

Erica didn't hesitate. "I'll have a margarita."

"Make that two, please," said Steve.

The two of them spent the first thirty minutes of dinner sipping on their drinks and learning about each other.

"Well if that waiter comes by one more time and we're not ready to order, I think he will call out the menu police," said Erica, pointing out that neither had glanced at the menu.

Steve looked up from his menu after a minute and caught Erica gazing at him. It was an awkward moment. They both silently turned red but slowly smiled as they went back studying the menu. Despite his embarrassment, Steve felt a warm feeling rush through his body. Before that moment, he was not sure if his feelings toward Erica were mutual, but now there was no question.

"What are you going to order to please that patient but empty stomach?" asked Steve.

Erica giggled. "I'm not sure, but I think the chicken enchiladas look good."

"They are, but their fajitas are the best. They must have a special recipe because the taste is so different from any other fajita I've ever tried."

"Wow, a real-life fajita connoisseur. I have never met one before, but I've heard stories about them. I do feel privileged to finally have met one. Would it be possible for you to kindly sign my menu? I mean, for my kids, of course."

Steve replied, "Sorry, I don't sign menus. Is there a picture or something else that I could sign? Menus tend to get misplaced and then there you have it, my signature would be lost and probably in the hands of a young person who would never appreciate the worth of that menu and signature." They both giggled as the waiter approached. Despite his apparent frustration with Steve and Erica, he asked to take their orders.

"I wonder if we will ever see our dinner tonight. You really seemed to piss off that waiter!" Erica teased.

"Me!" exclaimed Steve. "What about you? You were like a third grader with the giggles. You know, if we keep this up, he may have to split us up."

"If he does, I will still enjoy my meal while thinking of you."

Steve was left speechless as he considered what she had said.

Erica stood up and brushed her hand over his shoulders as she made her way in the direction of the ladies' room. "If we are going to share dinner together, then there are a few things you will come to know about me. One is that my bladder is very small, and the other is that I'm a lightweight when it comes to alcohol." As she leaned down and whispered into his ear, "So please don't take advantage of me." She smiled as she walked away.

Steve smiled too, but he wasn't sure what to say or do. He looked around quickly to make sure nobody had seen or heard what Erica had said, but everybody around him was involved in personal conversations.

Steve felt completely off-balance. Usually he would find himself in a position to initiate some sort of intimacy on a date. Erica had turned the table on him, and he was unsure where to go with it. It wasn't that he didn't appreciate the affection that she had showed, but he wasn't sure if he was reading the right signals. He surely didn't want to be too aggressive and upset her, but maybe that kind of energy was what she wanted. He just wasn't sure.

There was one thing that was for sure: he didn't want to screw up and ruin their chemistry.

"Hey." Her sweet voice regained his attention. "I'm really sorry. I probably said a few things that were out of line, at least for now." She giggled a little. "I'm really a lightweight, and I guess I didn't feel how strong those margaritas were until I got up."

"That's okay," said Steve. "I can feel the tequila, too. Maybe until we have some food in our stomach we should have some Pepsi or something."

"Caffeine!" yelled Erica. "I drink caffeine all day at the hospital in order to get the work done. No, this is a night out, and I am going to treat it like that. I'm just apologizing and warning you now that I get a little goofy when I drink, whether there is food in my stomach or not." With that, she held up her glass and motioned to the waiter for another.

They continued to talk throughout dinner. Between the serious comments, they found things to giggle about. As the time went by, they spent more and more time giggling rather than earnestly discussing work.

The waiter was clearing the last of their plates, and Erica was laughing. "So your dad made you do mouth-to-mouth at the young age of ten? That's funny. That would have been a turn off for me to enter the medical field. I still get grossed out doing codes and CPR. The nice thing about doing the codes in the hospital is that you can at least use an ambu bag. I still freak about putting my lips to some stranger's and blowing hot air. There is only one situation I want my lips on someone else's, and it better not be a stranger. Otherwise my mother would be very disappointed."

Steve laughed. "So what about you, Erica? Why did you decide to get into medicine?"

"Well, it's kind of a sad story. My dad died when I was eighteen, and my mom still had four young kids at home, so I thought I would get a job to help support the household. Twelve years later, I'm finally ready to get a job to help my mom. The only problem is that all the kids are grown up and out of the house, and my mom remarried a rich guy, so I did all this shit for nothing."

Steve listened intently, but was looking at her for a hint to tell if she was giving him the truth or bullshit.

She recognized his curious look and giggled. "Okay, I'm messing with you again. I can't help it! It's that you're so gullible. But I will say my dad did die when I was leaving for college. I saw him suffer with his cancer for a long time, and I decided then to help people who are afflicted with cancer as much as I can."

"I'm sorry to hear about your dad, but I can see how that would influence anyone in that situation. And I think that will make you a better doctor. I mean, to be perceptive of other people's emotional wellbeing while taking care of their medical and physical issues. That's excellent. So are you going to complete an oncology fellowship?"

"Nah, I don't think so. I want to take care of people and all, but I don't want to limit my practice to just cancer patients. You know what I mean?"

"Oh, sure," replied Steve. "I can understand. But you are so great with your patients and you are so humorous. I just think you could make the most difficult situation more comfortable for really sick patients."

"That's nice of you, Steve, but you haven't even seen me with my patients. I'm pretty serious and anal about their care.

It's just when I get around cute surgery residents that I get so nervous I can't stay serious. And besides it's so easy to give you shit I just can't help myself."

"Thanks, I guess." Steve grinned.

Erica glanced at her watch. "Whoops. I guess we'll have to make a movie next time. That is, if you want to get together again?"

Steve looked at his watch too and saw the time in disbelief. "Ten-thirty. Shit, where did the time go? I'm sorry about the movie, but next time sounds great."

"Well, Steve, not all of us are as fortunate as you to have a weekend off. See, Internal Medicine residents are a little more hardcore than you surgeons. We don't believe in taking weekends off, so I think I should get home sometime soon 'cause I'm on call tomorrow."

"Sure, that sounds fine," said Steve.

As if the waiter were eavesdropping, he came by just then and dropped off the bill.

Steve glanced at the ticket briefly before reaching into his pocket and pulling out a wad of money. He placed three twenties on the table and then motioned to Erica's chair. "May I help you, ma'am? I mean, with all that alcohol tonight..."

They both laughed as Steve reached over to help Erica up. They continued to giggle as they leaned on each other to walk out.

Steve noticed that barely anybody was left in the restaurant. "I guess we're closing the place tonight."

"Maybe the restaurant, but not the cantina," said Erica.

Steve heard the loud music and laughter as they passed the entryway to the bar. He motioned to Erica to go into the bar for a drink, but she just shook her head no.

"Sorry, tomorrow's a school day." They both laughed. "Well,

okay since you're twisting my arm, just one more."

They sat in a corner for a nightcap. They talked and talked, never really noticing the people around them. After another hour, Erica went to the bathroom again, and then they left. As they walked out, Erica leaned her slim body against Steve, smiled up at him, and grabbed his hand. They were mutually content.

The drive home was somewhat quiet. Steve wasn't sure where to go with all these non-verbal signals, but Erica was about to pass out. When they pulled up to her building, he got out and hurried to the passenger side to help her out. When he opened the door, she jerked up as if to wake.

"Sorry, I guess I feel asleep. I'm so embarrassed! Sorry."

"That's okay, but let's get you inside so you can get some real sleep before tomorrow."

"Tomorrow. Shit, that's right, I've got to work. Sometimes I hate working." Erica giggled to herself as they made it to the front door.

They both stopped to face each other at the doorway. Steve felt a little awkward as they gazed into one another's eyes, but he slowly reached over to hold her hands, and Erica let him. They both smiled and he slowly moved toward her for a kiss.

When their lips met, he closed his eyes to enjoy her kiss. After a few perfect seconds, he slowly leaned back.

"Well, that was nice," said Erica. "I look forward to the movie next time." She smiled.

Steve took the cue. "I guess I'll see you Monday."

"Ok," Erica responded, still smiling.

Steve started to turn toward his car, but Erica was still holding onto his hands. She pulled him back close to her. She gently put both her hands on either side of his soft, shaven face. With a slow but deliberate motion, she gently brought his face close to hers. She sensually touched his lips with a finger and then placed her lips on his and kissed him.

After one last sensual kiss, she touched his face and said goodnight.

Chapter 18

Kandahar, Afghanistan

The room was a picture of poverty. The cement walls had paint peeling from the edges along the corners. The windows were small, square, and above everyone's eyesight. The depth of the glass only allowed a fraction of light to penetrate, giving the room a permanent appearance of dark gloom. The vertical bars on the windows gave a feeling of imprisonment. A musty smell seeped from the walls of cement and the dampness of the building. Only one light hung from the ceiling, a large round lamp with a single light bulb surrounded by a reflective material. Directly beneath the light was a wobbly wooden table the shape of a medical exam table.

Atop the table was a young man with torn pants that were a little too short and very dirty. His shirt had been removed, and he lay motionless on the table. His breathing was short and shallow. A plastic mask lay over his mouth and nose, and a small thin tube went from the mask to a canister with peeling green paint. On the side of the canister was written OXYGEN. An IV connected his left hand to a glass bottle of clear fluid. A man near the bottle intermittently injected medicine into the IV tubing from a syringe.

A white sheet with a hole in the center was draped over the young man's right lower abdomen. Red stains from the boy's blood framed the hole in the sheet. Inside the hole was a moderate size cut on the young man's skin. Within the small cut, the beginning of his colon with a thin tubular structure arising from the surface could be seen. No redness surrounded this tubular structure, nor was there any inflammation, pus or swelling associated with it.

Standing alongside the table was an older man with a pair of plastic gloves and a paper mask covering his mouth and nose. He wore no hat or gown. He was quietly moving instruments around in the wound. He worked swiftly because the young man was heavily sedated but not under a general anesthetic.

"Dr. Mohammad, please," said a man who stood behind the man with the mask. "My friend, we have been through this many times. It must be done my way."

"I know, but this poor man needs to travel to the United States," pleaded the doctor. "If I don't tie off the base of his appendix, he will surely die before he arrives at his destination."

"Just the contrary, doctor. I will remind you that young Ziamuddin is very aware of the risks of this mission. He has given his body and soul for the cause. Let's not take that away from him. When he wakes up, he plans to carry out his part of the mission. We need to assure ourselves that Ziamuddin does make it to his destination. Once there, he will visit with a doctor who will discover the problem and make him feel better. But in order to see that doctor, he must be sick, very sick. So please, Ahmed, don't tie off the appendiceal stump. Do it for me, do it for the cause, and most importantly do it for your daughter. I believe she still lives in Kabul?"

"WHAT?" exclaimed Dr. Mohammad. "Abbas, you guaranteed to leave my family out of this. You must leave them alone. I beg you, please leave my family alone!"

"Ahmed, do it my way, and no harm will come to your family."

The doctor continued to work. The appendix was free except where it was attached directly to the colon. Dr. Mohammad glanced up at a window and stared for a minute before he took a knife and cut the appendix off flush with the outside of the colon. He picked up a suture. "Abbas, let me just dunk the stump and bury it into the colon. I'm sure he will still get sick for you, for us, for the cause."

The man who stood behind him placed his hand firmly on Dr. Mohammad's right forearm. Gently the man pushed his hand down. "Please, my friend, this young boy Ziamuddin has to carry out this mission that he so graciously has volunteered for. Let him fulfill his commitment to the cause. Otherwise, he will be terribly disappointed. Let's not disappoint him."

Dr. Mohammad again glanced out the tiny window toward the sky. He spent another moment contemplating his dilemma and then gently pushed the colon back into the abdomen and under the wound. He grabbed a plastic clear bag of white powder. The bag was securely closed, but the doctor rechecked it one more time before gently pushing it through the incision. The bag was quite large for the relatively small incision, but he gently pushed and squeezed the contents until the bag slid in. The doctor inspected the bag one more time to make sure it had no defects. He gently laid it alongside the colon near where the appendix had been. He hesitantly sewed the layers of tissue together and closed the abdominal incision. When the surgery was done, he tore off his gloves and turned around to face Abbas.

"I'm through with this dirty work for you. It has gone on far too long. We have not made any progress with our mission, but we still put our youth at great risk. For what? To make a point? No one listens, Abbas. No one! I'm tired. You must let me live my life now. I must go. I must go, and please don't bother me again. Please leave my family alone. You promised to leave them out of this; I have great confidence that you will stand by your word. Ziamuddin will wake soon. He will be in much pain." The doctor held up a bottle of pills. "These will help his pain. Please let him at least take these with so he can have some relief while he travels and searches for this doctor in the United States." He slammed the bottle on the edge of the table and walked out.

The man who had been injecting medicine into the IV tubing looked at Abbas. Abbas returned the look but shook his head no. "He will be back again when we need him. He is just a little frustrated now, but that will pass. Otherwise he knows the consequences."

Ziamuddin started to turn from side to side on the table and moan in pain. His hands quickly grabbed his side as he rolled to and fro. "Uhh. The pain is very bad. Oh, please is there anything I can take? Please, Abbas. Is there anything at all?"

Abbas looked down at the bottle of pills, at the boy, and at the man near the IV tubing. "Please, my friend, take two of these, and then we must get going. We need to catch a plane to Kabul." He gave the young man the medicine with a cup of water. He turned to the other man. "Is the transportation ready?"

"Yes," replied the man. "There is an Airbus to take him to the capital, and from there he will leave for the United States. Here are the tickets. There are two tickets for the Airbus as you requested." He handed over a manila envelope.

The young man suddenly sat up and vomited onto the floor. The two other men quickly jumped back as a reflex reaction.

"That will make you feel better," lied Abbas. "Now we must get going. We need to get on that Airbus. Let's go, my friend. I will remind you of the plan that we had discussed last night on the plane."

Young Ziamuddin slowly attempted to get off the table, but he collapsed to the floor.

"Please, Abbas, let this poor soul take a moment to recover from the surgery. You have enough time to catch the Airbus.

Besides, there is another after that, and you will still get to Kabul in time for his flight to the United States," warned the other man.

"Fine, fine, we will wait a few minutes, but I want to leave in thirty minutes and no longer. Do you understand, my friend?"

"Yes, of course, Abbas. That should be sufficient time to allow him to recover. I'm sure you can still make your flight without any problems."

Abbas helped the man get the young surgical patient back onto the table. Abbas motioned the other man to clean the mess and made his way to a narrow wooden door. He opened it and squinted at the daylight. After his eyes acclimated to the bright light from the dark gloom of the room, he watched the car of Dr. Mohammad race away. The car sprayed dirt and sand as it made its way back to the main road. The car had disappeared from view after a few moments, but the cloud of dust was still visible. It became hazier with time, and the dust eventually settled back down to the ground.

Abbas still did not move. He watched the sun begin to fall and studied the land in front of him. He thought about what Ahmed said about the mission. He, like many others, have given up the cause and moved on in their lives. But Abbas thought about the courageous Ziamuddin and his peers who still believed. Abbas reminisced about the promise he made to his father as he lay in his arms dying. His father had blood all over him from four bullet holes. "Abbas," he said, "you must keep up the fight. You must move forward with our mission. We will prevail. You must, my son…" As his father finished his final words, the young Abbas held his dying father in his arms and promised, "I will, my papa. I will."

"Abbas!" called a voice from inside. "Our friend is better now. We can safely move him to the car. Let me take you two to your plane, and I will come back to clean this mess."

"Fine, that will be good." Abbas reached over to hug the other man. "You have been a good friend and a true comrade with unyielding support to the cause. My father would have been so proud." He released his grip on the man's shoulders and shook his hand firmly.

The two older men helped young Ziamuddin to the car. It was a rusty black vehicle with paint peeling and dents in the hood and on the sides. A taillight was missing, and none of the tires had hubcaps.

These faults were unimportant to the men. All that mattered was that the key went into the ignition, turned, and started the car.

The three men were very somber on the journey to the airport. The young man slept most of the way, and Abbas and his friend stayed quiet. When they arrived at the airport, the car pulled up to a curb to let Abbas and Ziamuddin out. Neither had any luggage. None was needed.

Abbas again shook the driver's hand. "Thank you again, my friend," he said, "I will contact you soon."

The man replied, "Good luck to both of you."

The sky was nearly dark by the time the small airplane took off. Abbas and the young man sat next to each other. Once the doors were closed and the plane started to move on the runway, Abbas looked nonchalantly forward and backward to make sure the seats around them were free of any passengers. The seats across the aisle were also empty. He was pleased but not surprised. The plan was to purchase all the seats around them so he could discuss the plan without unwanted ears listening.

By the time the plane had taken off on its way to the capital, Ziamuddin was awake and alert. Abbas leaned over to him and spoke in the kind soft voice that Ziamuddin had heard many times before. “Are you feeling better, my friend?”

“Yes, a little sore down on the right, but I will be fine, Abbas.”

“Good. That sounds good. Well, we have just a short time here, so let me go over things with you quickly, and then you may ask questions."

Abbas continued. “Your flight takes you to the Hubert Humphrey International Airport in Minneapolis, Minnesota. No one will meet you. You must find a way to make contact with our comrades there on your own. If you are feeling well, you must contact a Bill Thomas. He has all the information about you and is aware of our cause. He has agreed to help get the package to our other comrades in the United States.” Abbas briefly looked over at Ziamuddin to make sure he was still awake and listening.

The young man glanced up at the older man. “What? Is there a problem, Abbas? Why do you stop with the instructions?”

“I want to make sure you were feeling okay. Are the pills working?”

Ziamuddin smiled back. “I am fine. Please continue. I can hear you fine, and I am still awake and listening.”

Abbas smiled with great pride in the integrity and bravery of this young man. “As I was saying, Mr. Thomas will be the primary contact. I have his number in this package. You must memorize the number and return it to me on this flight. The authorities in the United States must not know that you have his name and number in case you pass out. If that were to happen, someone would surely go through your few belongings and notice his name and number. This would expose him, and the entire mission would be endangered. Do you understand, Ziamuddin?”

The young man nodded his head yes.

"Fine. There is another name in the package you must know. He is the doctor who will help you and retrieve the package from you. His name is Jake Douglas. He works at the University Hospital. He has agreed to do this for a price. However, he does not know the extent of our mission or the cause. Please do not discuss our plans with him or anyone else except Mr. Thomas."

The older man leaned closer to whisper, "Now, Ziamuddin, if you get sick and feel like you cannot get in contact with Mr. Thomas, take some transportation to the University Hospital. The other material in the package is money in United States currency. There is enough for you to use if you must." Abbas now placed his hand on the man's forearm and looked him in the eye. "There is a green pill in the package. Ziamuddin, if you feel the pain or sickness is too much and you cannot make it to one of our contacts, take the pill." Abbas sighed. "The package must not fall into the wrong hands or our plans will be exposed. We cannot let this happen. We have come too far and many of our comrades, *your* comrades, are counting on us. But if the package falls into the wrong hands, then everything is lost. All of our hard work will be destroyed. Do you understand, my friend? Do you?"

Ziamuddin again nodded his head yes.

"The pill will assure us that the package stays with us. The pull…the pill will kill you, my friend."

Again the young man, without showing any fear, nodded his head yes.

Abbas smiled and squeezed Ziamuddin's forearm. The young man courageously smiled in return. Both of them leaned back into their seats. No more conversation fell between them for the remainder of the flight.

FOREIGN THREAT

Ziamuddin looked through the contents of the package. He put the money and the pill in his pocket. He then looked at the pieces of paper in the package. He studied the information and then closed his eyes in great concentration, repeating this until he had everything memorized.

Chapter 19

Kabul, Afghanistan

As the plane approached the gate, the two men gathered their belongings. Before they exited the plane, the two men shook hands and embraced silently. Abbas then walked with the other passengers off the plane. Ziamuddin slid back into his seat, resting comfortably. He leaned his head back on the seat and closed his eyes. After a short few minutes, he slowly got up and joined the remaining passengers' slow departure off the plane.

As the young man walked through the airport, there was no sign of Abbas. Ziamuddin walked toward an airline employee and obtained some information about his international flight and departure. She waved her hands in different directions and pointed to the west side of the airport. Ziamuddin nodded his head with gratitude and understanding. He began to make his way to the next flight.

He determined that if he walked slowly, the pain was minimal, but if as he turned from side to side, he could feel some pulling and sharp pain. He stopped by a drinking fountain and pulled out the bottles of pain pills. He took two with some water and continued on his journey to the gate.

The walk started off fine, but as the distance became greater, he began to feel weaker. He never felt like he had a fever or was going to vomit again, but he knew that he was getting sick and those symptoms were inevitable. He knew that he might become so sick that he would become delusional. At that point, he would need to take the suicidal medication that Abbas had given him.

After a few more minutes of walking, he arrived at his destination. Two people were behind the counter, one male and one female. He approached the female and presented his ticket for her to inspect. She arranged a seat for him on the flight, and he took a seat in the waiting area to close his eyes.

Ziamuddin felt as if he had been there for just a few minutes, but nearly one hour after he arrived, an announcement initiated the boarding for his flight to the United States. He reviewed his seating arrangements and waited for his row to be called to the gate. The little nap seemed to help him feel stronger and less uncomfortable. While waiting, he placed his hand over his abdomen and gently pushed as if to make sure the package was still there. It was.

His row was called, and he approached the gate. He was three people from the flight attendant when he felt a strong grip rest on his shoulder. His breathing stopped abruptly, and his heart rate raced wildly. He felt sweat appear on his temples, and his body became very warm. He cautiously turned around to see who was there.

An old man stood in his view. He shook his head in disgust and apologized, "I am terribly sorry for bothering you, but from behind you look like my son. I am sorry to bother you, young man. Have a good and safe journey."

Ziamuddin was still in shock when the flight attendant asked for his ticket. "Excuse me, sir. Do you have a ticket for this flight to the United States?"

"Uhh, yes I do. Here it is." Ziamuddin handed over his ticket and boarding information. His pulse was still racing as he walked along the ramp. He looked over his shoulder several imes, but he didn't see that man again, nor did he witness any other suspicious characters studying his moves.

He found his seat without too much difficulty, but as he

lowered himself into his seat, he felt a sharp pain in the lower abdomen. He was not sure how much worse this was going to get, but he experienced a moment of concern as the pain was the worst thus far, causing him to double over for a minute.

"Are you ok, young man?" a woman sitting along the aisle asked.

Ziamuddin lied, "Yes, I'm fine. I will be ok. Thank you for your concern." He leaned over in his seat to connect the seatbelt and was hit by another wave of pain. He attempted not to be so obvious this time. He grimaced a little but settled into his seat with the seatbelt securely fastened.

The passenger closed his eyes. He could hear all the noises in the plane. He could hear someone wrestling with luggage in the compartment above the seats. He heard a woman asking her husband about all of their luggage and complaining that they should have checked in more luggage at the ticket counter; the man responded by saying he didn't trust these people. Ziamuddin just smiled.

He hoped the man would sit next to him so they could have a heart-to-heart conversation about western capitalization and terrorism. He opened his eyes to see who had the foreign paranoia, but the man had already taken a seat. Ziamuddin was not able to decide for sure who it had been. He felt too weak to walk around in search of the couple, but he was tempted.

He started to feel more pain in his abdomen and looked at the bottle of pills. There were only about ten left, and he needed to make it to through this flight. He shut his eyes and thought about all the things Abbas told him. He thought about his mission and about the green pill. He focused on a number of distractions until his mind gave out and he fell into a deep sleep.

Ziamuddin was jerked awake by what felt like a sudden drop in the plane. He suspected severe turbulence, but he wasn't sure. As he sat in his seat, there was another significant drop. This time many passengers let out whimpers of concern. There were cries of fear from a few children, and Ziamuddin saw a little boy across from him with huge tears running from his eyes. His mother held him tight and whispered into his ear. The boy tried to stop his tears, but they still ran down his cheeks. Ziamuddin felt sorry for the little boy, but fortunately, there were no other episodes of turbulence.

The pilot spoke on the intercom, telling people to keep their seatbelts fastened despite the worst being over. He assured them that the airspace would be without any further turbulence for a long period of time.

Ziamuddin looked at the mother and little boy. The mother was coddling him and again whispered into his ear. Gradually the boy seemed more content and less scared.

Ziamuddin glanced at his watch and briefly looked around in search of any intruders. He then closed his eyes and fell back asleep.

No other turbulent activity interrupted the flight. Ziamuddin slept for nearly the remainder of the flight. He opened his eyes as the plane started its descent. He noticed that most of the passengers were smiling and talking about the flight and the scare they'd had. They all seemed happy, especially since the flight was nearing its end.

Ziamuddin again reviewed the plan in his head. He had been through it many times since he and Abbas had discussed it, but now it seemed a little different. It seemed real. There was no room for error. He straightened in his seat but quickly felt pain throughout his abdomen. He got dizzy but did everything possible to not faint. He acted as if he were picking up a carryon item from the floor, though he had none, to place his head well below his knees. In addition to creating more blood flow to his brain, bending down caused more pain. Ziamuddin straightened and promised himself not to do that again.

Just as the pain was subsiding, the plane hit a turbulent pocket of air. It jerked up and down quickly for about five seconds. The sudden motion caused Ziamuddin excruciating pain all over again. This time he developed a severe feeling of nausea, but he was able to control himself and resist throwing up in front of everyone. He was afraid that would attract too much attention.

Fortunately, the plane had no further episodes prior to landing. The landing itself did seem to bother Ziamuddin a little but not as much as the up and down motion of the turbulence. Once at the gate, he waited until everyone else was off the plane before he even moved. The pain was getting worse, and he didn't want people inquiring about his health. He took two more pills and got up slowly. He still felt lightheaded, and the nausea returned quickly. Without warning, he threw up in the aisle.

A flight attendant quickly came up to him to offer assistance.

Ziamuddin shook his head and said in his Middle Eastern accent, "I guess the flight got a little too long, especially with all the turbulence and stuff."

The flight attendant nodded in agreement.

"I think I'll be fine now."

"Maybe we should get you a wheel chair," the flight attendant offered. "That way it would be easier for you to move about in the airport. It's quite large."

He acknowledged her suggestion but said, "Thank you so much for your thoughts. I think I just need some fresh air, then I'll be fine. Thank you again."

Ziamuddin walked toward the front of the plane. He slowly moved one leg in front of the other and smiled as he passed the flight crew. He continued gingerly along the ramp up to the terminal. He passed the door to the terminal and moved slowly to a seat near the ticket counter. He sat to recover from the long walk. He had sweat running down his face, so he used the back of his sleeve to wipe it off. All of a sudden, a deep chill set in, and he started to shake uncontrollably. It wasn't like a seizure convulsion but rather muscle spasms that were fortunately not so obvious to others.

Ziamuddin felt terrible, and he looked terrible, too. He didn't want to attract attention to himself, but his appearance alone would make anyone stare. Rather than looking like an international traveler, he looked as if he had been living on the streets for a few months. His hair was a mess, complete with a three-day beard. It was wavy black hair, but had not been combed for a few days, and sleeping on it for the last several hours made it look even rattier. The sweats he had experienced during the flight made the waves terribly greasy.

This physical appearance combined with his torn clothes made him stick out like a sore thumb. If this wasn't enough, his body odor was unreal and could be detected twenty feet away. Without realizing it, he was drawing all sorts of attention to himself.

Ziamuddin realized he was starting to get sicker and needed to make contact with Bill Thomas. He painstakingly pulled himself up and out of the chair in search for a phone. As he walked, he felt dizzy and slightly faint, but he kept on moving. He had to call his contact.

He placed his hand in his pants pocket and felt the green pill. He stopped for a moment and wondered if he should take it right away. But he still had his senses about him and felt clear. Yes, he felt and looked lousy, but that was not a reason to abort the mission. That was not a reason to take his life…yet.

Chapter 20

Minneapolis, Minnesota, the United States

The phone rang. It was much too early for anyone to call, but then he really had no friends. It was either work or his contact abroad, neither of whom he really cared to speak with at this time. He rolled over to look at the time: 5:30 A.M. *Shit,* he thought to himself. *What a shit time to get this stupid ass phone call.* He patted his bedside table to find the phone but couldn't feel the correct structure. He resorted to turning on a light and illuminating the entire room. Once the light came on, though, he was sure to be up for another two or three hours trying to fall back to sleep.

The light showed clothes all over the place. A dress shirt from the day before was draped over a chair. His pants were on the floor in a crumpled pile. His tie was near the bathroom door. The floor was barely visible with old socks and underwear. His overcoat lay across the foot of his bed. The room was in shambles as usual.

He dragged himself from the warm, comfortable bed to search for the phone. He listened carefully to each ring, moving toward the sound. It was like playing a game with a kid. As he got closer to the ringing noise, he would tell himself, "Warm, warm, warmer…hot." Finally, he found the phone and answered. "Hello?" he said in a very tired, hoarse voice.

He heard a woman's voice with a Middle Eastern accent. "I'll connect you now."

"My friend, the package you requested has been sent."

There was a click from the other end, but Bill Thomas sat for several minutes with the phone to his ear.

He was not ready for this. He hadn't made plans for travel out of the country. He was not sure how closely he was being followed. For that matter, they had probably heard that phone conversation. He was not entirely sure that Jake Douglas would come through for him. There were too many unresolved issues. He just was not ready for that package to be delivered.

Only one thing was for sure: the mission was a go, and the pressure was on. There would be no room for error or he would surely be busted.

The first thing he needed to do was contact Douglas. The doctor had to be aware that his expertise would definitely be used. Thomas also had to arrange for the doctor's payoff. There were too many things to do. Thomas wanted to call Abbas back and ask more specific questions, like when did the package leave? What flight was he coming in on? What did the guy look like? Could he speak English? But he was on his own now.

He still held the phone in his hand. He stared out the window in a panicked gaze. He didn't blink, and he didn't move. He was just paralyzed with the thought that it was time and he was not ready. It was no longer a little business adventure in order to get some extra cash. If he were to get busted, he would surely be convicted, and instead of spending his remaining years on a beautiful beach with gorgeous women all around, he would be locked in a small cell with no beach and no women.

He needed to get busy. First, he tried to figure out if the phone call was intercepted. He had scanned his phone and his beeper and his clothes, not to mention his entire living quarters, multiple times and never came up with a bug. Nonetheless, he disassembled his phone and rechecked it. He found no evidence of tampering, and the scan was negative as well. Still, he knew he had to get in contact with Jake Douglas without taking the chance that any line was connected to a bug. He needed a payphone.

He stumbled around his bedroom for clothes and made his way to the kitchen. While having a cup of coffee, he thought about where to go. He'd had it all set up in his mind but hadn't made any final plans because he didn't think they would be moving that fast. But it was time: while he was out calling Dr. Douglas, he would make travel plans to Brazil.

Not only would flight arrangements need to be made, but he would also have to arrange for his money and local accounts to be changed to an account in Brazil or somewhere in South America. He thought about packing, and he thought about leaving his friends and family, but he realized that right now he needed to focus on the mission. He could plan his escape later.

The coffee had cooled as he thought about all that needed to be done, Realizing that he was daydreaming instead of getting ready, he took one last gulp of cold coffee and jumped in the shower. He got dressed, but before putting on his overcoat, he secured his gun harness and put the gun inside. He walked to the windows and discreetly glanced out through the blinds. No cars or vans were in sight, and no people walking around the entrance of his apartment. Since the time he was spotted at his old residence, they had yet to locate him. He suspected that the scans were all negative because they had not found his new residence.

Although nobody was visible, he didn't want to take a chance. The mission was a go. He couldn't make any mistakes at this time. He decided to use the emergency escape route to ensure that he was not followed. He left his fourth-floor apartment via the front door but walked swiftly to an apartment door on the other side of the hallway. He unlocked the door and walked in. With a quick glance over his shoulder, he closed the door.

He stared out the peephole in the door for several minutes without noticing any suspicious activity. Finally, he walked through the empty apartment to the window in the back bedroom. He propped open the glass with a spare piece of wood, the only thing stowed in the apartment.

Outside the window was a cable wire that went across to the adjacent apartment building. It was attached to the next building near a window on that third floor so there was a slight slope downward. He had portrayed himself as a cable man before he lived there. He selected wires with strength and placed them with care so he could slide down to the next building and escape from two blocks away if ever he needed to.

Although this was not an emergency, Thomas felt the phone call to Douglas and his own travel arrangements needed to be completed with the utmost security. He slipped his legs through a body harness that was in the bedroom. He carefully stepped up on the window ledge and secured the harness to the cable with a mountaineering rig. With a gentle push, he was on his way to the next building. He always left that window open just in case. As a result, when he arrived now, he was not at all surprised to see bird markings and smelled mildew from recent rainstorms. He spent little time in the apartment, so he really didn't care. He unhooked himself from the harness and glanced down at the alley to make sure there was not any unusual activity. It was incredibly quiet, but as he started to make a move toward the door, he heard some garbage cans clang together. He quickly leaned out the window to evaluate.

There was no visible movement below. This made Thomas quite anxious. He could see no dogs, cats, or other animals scurrying around causing mischief. He stared out the window for several moments until he saw a cat jump out of a garbage can that was lying down. Apparently, that was the commotion. Now the cat was done scrambling for food. Thomas still watched for a few minutes, but the lack of other activity left him comfortable to continue with his morning plans.

He crossed the filthy bedroom, opened the door, and entered a much cleaner living room. He left through the front door and took the stairs outside. He hailed a taxi and asked the driver to take him to a phone booth about eight blocks away at Tenth and Lapont Street.

They came across a Stop-N-Go, and he then got out. He handed the driver a twenty to persuade him to stay. Thomas quietly walked over to the phone and called the University Hospital. He paged Jake Douglas.

An unfamiliar voice answered the phone. “Hello, this is Nurse Anders. I am answering a page for Dr. Douglas. He is currently in surgery, but I would be more than happy to take a name and phone message.”

“No, that won’t be necessary,” replied Thomas. “Do you have any idea how long this case will take him to complete?”

The nurse replied, “One moment, please.” Thomas could hear the phone being muffled by her hand as she asked how long he was going to be. “Dr. Douglas should be done in about two hours.”

Disgusted, Thomas replied, “Thanks. I will call him back later.”

He returned to the taxi and had the driver return him back to his apartment. He decided to get ready for work and not bother Douglas until later in the day. It would be nice to let the doctor know immediately that a man would be coming to the hospital seeking his assistance, but Thomas didn’t want to leave a verbal message. It was too important to have someone leave a message or bring another person in contact with the whole process.

When Bill Thomas arrived back at his home, he found a message on the answering machine. He tried to see where the call came from on the caller ID, but it was an unfamiliar number. He quickly played the message, thinking that Douglas might have taken a moment to call him back.

Instead of the doctor's voice, the only thing he could hear on the machine was a man breathing deeply. This lasted for fifteen seconds, and then a soft whisper said in a foreign accent, "Oh shit." A click sounded, and the message ended.

That was the contact. The man was smart enough not to leave a message and not to stay on the line too long. However, Thomas had no way to reconnect with him.

Chapter 21

The OR crew didn't take long to respond to the stat call. Within ten minutes, the whole team was at the hospital getting ready for emergency surgery. Jake had ordered some labs in the mean time but realized that whatever the labs were, surgery still needed to be preformed. He realized that this was serious business. Whatever this Ziamuddin character had inside him would certainly shock the OR staff. He couldn't begin to imagine the impact it would have for the CIA and nationally. He wondered if the thing inside was a bomb and Thomas had gotten the whole thing mixed up. It could detonate while Jake was taking it out. What if the guy died before the surgery, what would Thomas do then? A host of questions and scenarios were playing in Jake's mind when he heard a familiar voice.

"Well, Jake, for what did you bring us in tonight? Maybe a ruptured abdominal aortic aneurysm or another pancreatic case?"

Jake looked up from his deep thoughts and saw A.J. standing above him. A.J. was a great anesthetist who was hoping to retire soon. He had been doing call and anesthesia for years and was tired of it. He was only in his fifties but ready for a less hectic life.

Jake responded with a smile. "I see they brought in the cavalry for this one! Well A.J., you better hang on tight to the reins because this one is sure to give you a rough ride. He is totally dehydrated, his electrolytes are all screwed up, and I'm sure his white count is sky high. We just don't have time to wait or he'll die."

A.J. became more serious and asked some questions about the patient. Jake offered most of what he knew about

Ziamuddin's health issues but left out the fact that the man had something intentionally planted in his belly.

"Alright, Jake. We'll get this guy straightened out and set for surgery in a few minutes. Not that I was looking for a challenge tonight, but since you found one for us, we'll go for it."

As A.J. walked over to the gurney to ask Ziamuddin some questions, Jake felt two delicate hands on his shoulders.

"Well Dr. Douglas, what did the cat bring in?"

Jake looked back to find Karla, the scrub nurse, massaging his shoulders. Karla was in her late thirties, divorced with two kids, and determined to find a doctor to take home. Take home permanently. She was so desperate that even Jake Douglas was a target. Jake and most of the doctors knew what Karla was up to, but Jake was still trying to piece his complicated life together. He didn't need extra baggage at this point.

"So you didn't have anything else going on either tonight?" he teased. "It's so nice we could all be together on this happy occasion."

"Frankly, Jake, after that shit case today, I was kind of hoping for a reprieve, but I guess not," replied Karla. She turned to begin the wonderful job of completing paperwork in which only lawyers were ever interested after surgery.

A.J. returned to the desk with the patient's chart and handed it to Karla. "Knock yourself out, kid. I'm ready when you are. I'll see you two in the OR."

Karla gathered some papers and put them with the chart. "If you're ready, I'll take him over?"

Jake replied, "That sounds great, Karla. I'm going to pick up a sandwich on the way over, and I'll meet you in the OR. Don't get started without me," he joked.

Karla smiled and offered a polite but fake laugh.

Meanwhile, Steve was begging Agusta in the ICU not to blow his chance to go to the OR. "Come on, Agusta. Both Jake and I will be right over in the OR, and Roger, who happens to be one of the best medical students ever – at least since me – will be right here the entire time I'm gone. If you need anything, I will run back just as quick as you could call Rosberg. *Please*, Agusta. I'll do anything for you, I promise."

"I can't stand it when a grown man whines. It is so sickening. But I tell you, a third year medical student doesn't really count for jack shit when the patient is coding!"

Steve began to plead his case again when the station clerk answered the phone and relayed that the ER patient was on his way to the OR. Steve looked at Agusta, gently blinking his eyes until she gave in.

"Fine! Fine, Dr. Carmichael, but if you turn into a Jake Douglas by the time you're a chief resident, I will remember this moment and make your life pure hell. Do you understand, young man?"

"Yes ma'am, thank you so much!"

Agusta walked over to Steve and gave him a big motherly hug. "Go enjoy yourself and learn a lot. You certainly have earned the right to the OR tonight." She patted him on his back and released her grip. As he walked out of the unit, she shouted, "Don't forget my warning, Dr. Carmichael!"

Steve smiled over his shoulder and waved his hand.

Steve kept a steady pace as he walked toward the OR.

He was not particularly looking forward to working with Jake, but he was excited to operate again. Besides, Jake seemed to be beaten down after Dr. Rosberg's lecture, so he might be much more congenial tonight. Either the beating by Rosberg had him down, or that very stressful case all day left him just plain tired. Whatever it was, Steve didn't really care. He knew that he was on his way to the OR for surgery. It didn't even matter to Steve what the case was.

Steve and Jake arrived at the entrance to the OR at almost exactly the same time. The automatic door opened, and they walked in.

Steve asked excitedly, "So what is the plan of attack for this guy?"

"Well, Steve, you didn't get a chance to see this guy, but he already has a McBurney incision, so I suspect that he had an appy recently and that he developed an abscess. We don't have any information on him, so as far as we know, he could have had a perforated appendix with abscess intraperitonealy. We'll just have to wait and see."

They were already in scrubs, but each grabbed a surgery cap and mask. They quickly walked to OR 2 where A.J. was putting Ziamuddin off to sleep. Karla was standing next to the patient both to calm any anxiety the patient may have had as well as to assist A.J. with the breathing tube. Jake was always impressed with how sensitive the OR nurses were with the patients, despite knowing nothing about them. The nurses would try to relax the patient as they came into the room and would make a strong effort to calm any fears. Some patients would often ignore their fears.

Ziamuddin was like this. He was stoic as he entered the operating room and remained so as A.J. put the black oxygen mask over his face.

Sue, the scrub tech on call tonight, was busy organizing her table with surgical instruments as the patient drifted off to sleep. Sue was the most inexperienced in the group, having only worked there for two years. She was in her twenties: vivacious, cute, and innocent. She grew up in a small town and continued to have a small-town personality. She trusted everybody and was very gullible when people were telling stories. Nonetheless, she won the heart of most everyone she worked with, especially the medical students. She wasn't searching the way Karla was for a husband, but she didn't think it was right the way medical students and interns would get hassled by chief residents and staff. She would often stand up for a student who was getting abused. Consequently, she knew Jake very well.

"Hi, Sue." Jake waved from the door.

"Hi, Dr. Douglas. Are you going to be nice tonight, or do I have to set you straight from the get go?"

"I think I'm too tired to do much except get this case done and get home."

"That sounds like a great plan," Sue replied.

A.J. motioned Jake and Steve to scrub. "Jake, this guy is septic, big time. His WBC is nearly 28,000. We're talking a major left shift with a bandemia of about twenty percent. Not to mention the fact that despite the volume you gave him, his blood pressure was still only in the 90's and his pulse, the 130's. I think we should have a foley for this case, and maybe when you are done, either you or Steve should put a central line in for him. Why don't you two move it so we can get this septic foci out of him before his septic shock is out of control."

"Alright, we'll be right in."

While they scrubbed, Jake spoke. "Steve, there are certain times when you shouldn't do the full ten-minute scrub, and I think this is one of those times. I trust A.J., and if he says move it, then we need to move it." With that, Jake washed his hands as one would do before dinner. He opened up a scrub brush and lathered his hands for about thirty seconds before rinsing. "Let's go, Steve. He has the tube in. This guy will be prepped and with a foley in about a minute. Let's not waste any time. Your scrub is over, man."

Steve followed Jake into the OR suite as they dried their hands.

"Since this guy probably has an intraabdominal abscess," Jake continued, "I think you should make a midline incision. That way we can get a good look at everything to make sure we know what we're dealing with."

Steve was surprised but pleased to hear that he was going to make the incision. "That sounds like a good plan, Jake. By the way, did you have a chance to call staff in on this one?"

"Oh, shit," whined Jake. "I totally forgot. Thanks, Steve. Karla, would you please call whoever is on call for staff? I'll talk to them."

"That would-be Dr. Rosberg tonight. Aren't you feeling lucky, Douglas?"

"Shit," whispered Jake under his breath. "Well, call him anyway, and I'll talk to him when he's on the line."

After she tied their gowns, she dialed Dr. Rosberg's number. "Hello? Hi, Dr. Rosberg. This is Karla from the OR. Jake Douglas asked me to call you. Hang on one minute please." She held the phone to Jake's ear.

"Hi, Dr. Rosberg. I have this unusual situation." It was more than unusual. "There is this young foreign man who looks as if he recently had an appy. He comes in tonight septic with a great deal of rebound and belly tenderness. He had a major left shift with a bandemia. I called in the OR crew immediately and plan to do an exp lap with Steve."

Dr. Rosberg responded, "Go right ahead, Jake. If you encounter any problems, please give me a call right away. I can be back in three minutes."

"Alright, that sounds fine." Jake turned as Karla hung up the phone. "Thanks, Carmichael. I would have forgotten to call Rosberg. I owe you for this one."

Karla then quickly washed Ziamuddin's abdomen and then stepped back as Jake and Steve draped the sterile field. Next came the suction device, followed by the electrocautery. After everything was set up, Sue brought up the scalpel.

Steve stared, unsure if he should grab it or not.

"This would be the time to get going," ordered Jake. "Otherwise I'll start for you, Dr. Carmichael."

"No, no, that will be fine. I just wasn't sure if you wanted me to start or- I don't know." Steve's voice was barely audible as he reached forward.

As Steve took the scalpel from Sue, Jake drew an imaginary line from above the umbilicus to about six centimeters below. "Let's do it, Carmichael!"

Steve was a little anxious but he knew this was his chance to operate. That's why he put up with all the bullshit: to operate.

He made a generous incision and watched the blood ooze from the fatty tissue under the skin. He used the electrocautery to control the bleeding. The electrical current created a small cloud of smoke above the patient's belly as it burned the blood vessels. The smell of burnt tissue crept in the masks of everyone in the operating room, but it didn't faze anyone.

Steve continued to carefully burn tissue as he went deeper into the caverns of Ziamuddin's belly. Finally, the fascia was visible. Steve continued until the thin layer of tissue that covered the abdominal contents was protruding through the incision. Then he looked up at Jake as if to ask, "Should I keep going?"

Jake motioned impatiently for Steve to continue.

Steve sharply entered the peritoneum and opened it with a pair of fine scissors.

A flood of stool contents mixed with pus erupted from the incision as the thin layer of tissue was cut. A fowl stream of vapor reached everyone's mask, no longer the familiar cautery smoke.

Steve called out for a culturette, a small Q-tip that could be used to swab the pus and test it on separate culture plates in a special incubator found in the lab.

"Very good, Carmichael," commended Jake.

Next Steve asked for a pool tip suction, which was a long device that could be placed into an area blindly to suction out the contents.

Before the suction device was placed in the abdomen, Jake halted the surgery. He was afraid Steve was going to ram the device into whatever might be tucked away in Ziamuddin's belly. He quickly shouted, "No, Carmichael! What the hell do you think you are doing? We have no idea as to what is going on there. What happens if you slam the suction into his aorta or liver? You need to see where you are putting things or you will be asking for big trouble." Jake was saying whatever it took to keep Steve from damaging whatever was in this guy's abdomen. "What I would do in this situation, since I didn't do the initial surgery, would be to place my hand in his abdomen like this, and then protect abdominal structures with your hand while you are suctioning out the fluid, pus, and stool."

Jake demonstrated exactly what he meant. In doing so, Jake had the opportunity to have his hand in the abdomen first. He could not see much with all the stool that was in the cavity, but he quickly explored down in the pelvis and felt a soft but large mass.

He briefly closed his eyes in case it was a bomb. Nothing happened, so he continued to feel it and tried to figure out what it could be.

"What the hell" shouted Jake. "There is something growing inside this guy's belly. Steve, why don't you take a feel? But be gentle, I don't want to disrupt this thing. He is from abroad, so for all we know, this could be a huge parasitic cyst. Let's be careful."

Steve gently reached his hand into the patient's abdomen and felt around. As he got toward the pelvis, he too felt the mass and said, "Oh, shit. This thing is huge."

Steve was still moving his hand around inside when Jake motioned for him to stop.

"Alright, that is enough there, fellow. Let's get this thing out, ship it over to Path, and head home."

"That sounds like a winner to me," cheered A.J.

Steve didn't mind relinquishing responsibility for the surgery. He'd had the chance to open up and feel the abdominal contents. That was the most he had done yet in the OR, and he was ecstatic.

"Steve, why don't you take this Richardson retractor and pull up?" Jake placed the retractor inside the abdomen via the incision and under the muscle. He then pulled up as if to show Steve what he wanted him to do. "There you go, Carmichael. Now just keep that exposure, and we'll try to get this mass out."

Jake placed both hands in the cavity and palpated around this mass. He continued to move his fingers around it in order to free it from any attachments that might have been made in the short while inside the body. Jake wanted to see the mass, so he did what no surgeon should do: he placed his head directly over the incision. The mass appeared to have a thick fibrinous layer of tissue covering it, so the doctor still could not tell what it actually was.

Jake's interest in identifying the mass was waning. He just wanted to collect the money and be done with it.

After getting a good view of the thing, he then leaned back to his original position and again started to dissect the mass. Just as the mass was freed, he placed his left hand behind it and started to push it forward as if to get it out into the field and out of the abdomen. As he did so, he felt his index finger enter the mass.

At first, he didn't want to think it had really happened. He wasn't sure what Thomas would think, but most likely, it would not be something that he was expecting. Jake reminded himself quickly that the most important thing right now was not to attract any attention to the hole. He squeezed his fingers together on that hand to occlude any material from escaping from the mass. He could feel his finger inside the mass. It felt like a soft material contained in a plastic bag, but he could not make out for sure what it was. He became paralyzed by the frightening thought of what it might be. He felt sweat eveloping on his forehead. The room started to spin around, and he was growing nauseous.

"Dr. Douglas? Dr. Douglas! Are you alright?" Sue asked as she noticed Jake starting to sway.

He didn't reply, so Steve asked again, but louder, "Jake! Hey, are you okay in there? Is anybody home?"

Jake glanced at Steve and then at Sue. "I think I had better take this over to Pathology myself. I'm not sure if anyone else should handle this." As he was speaking, he pulled the mass out of the abdomen ever so slowly.

Steve thought that Jake was having a difficult time with getting it out. "Here, let me help you-"

"NO! Don't touch it! I'm just fine. Don't touch this thing. I am doing good. I just need to get it out carefully, and then I'll walk it over to Path."

Sue wanted to protect the innocent as usual. "Alright, Jake. Let's just take it easy on Steve. He was just trying to help out." Everyone else froze. No one wanted to piss off Jake, thinking this was another moment when he might start acting like a complete asshole.

"SHUT UP, SUE!" screamed Jake. "Just give me a moment, then you all can speak afterwards."

Sue was shocked. Jake Douglas almost always listened to her.

The others stared at each other as if to question the abrupt change in Jake's demeanor.

Jake continued to slowly pull the mass toward himself and out of the field. He asked Sue for a basin to carry it.

She hesitantly held the basin near the wound for him, still upset that he had been so rude to her and everyone in the room.

When the object was free, Jake clamped his fingers even tighter so no one could see that his finger was inside the mass. He gently placed the specimen in the container, leaving his hand attached. Without changing gloves, he placed his right hand under the basin in order to stabilize the specimen inside the container. He turned around and quickly headed toward the door.

Everyone else in the room held still for fear of the wrath of Jake Douglas. They waited silently for Jake to remove that thing.

Steve had glanced down at the wound as the specimen was being meticulously removed. He thought he saw a trace of white powder trail behind the specimen. He wasn't sure if his eyes were playing tricks on him, so he blinked twice and looked again at the wound. The phantom white substance had disappeared. As the specimen came out, a wave of blood filled the cavity.

Jake was almost through the doors when he looked up at Steve and said, "Carmichael, pack the wound. I'll be back in a moment, and we'll look for an appendicial stump leak."

Everyone remained quiet after Jake departed. The doctor always had a way of creating a mood, and it was difficult to break.

Steve grabbed a few lap pads from Sue and began packing the wound. Soon the blood stopped welling up in the wound.

Finally, Sue broke the silence. “What an asshole.”

Chapter 22

Steve had a horrendous day on the floor taking care of patients. The work never seemed to stop: first a blood draw for cultures on a woman who developed fevers the night before, then a central line in an older man who had part of his colon removed for diverticulitis and needed intravenous nutrition, and then a young girl who'd had her appendix removed three days ago and was ready to go home but needed discharge planning to be completed. The list continued. Steve never had a boring day at the hospital, but he yearned for the day that his service was light enough to go to the library and read from his surgery text.

Despite the great amount of work on this particular morning, Steve was able to keep up with the schedule. As always, Dr. Douglas was in surgery with a resident. Today he picked Sally to go to the operating room with him. Steve had determined that no one really bothered them with questions or gossip. The problem he had recently was that Jake hardly picked him to go to the OR. Since their encounter in the locker room and Jake getting in trouble with Dr. Rosberg, Steve hadn't been invited back to the OR. Instead, he was responsible for all the scut work on the floor. He had to take care of all the admissions, all the discharges, and all the patient management. Steve reminded himself to use this to his advantage, learning about all the different issues surrounding his patients.

Steve grew used to referring to the patients on the floor as *his* patients. After all, they were in his total care. Jake never bothered with many questions on rounds as long as the patients were flourishing. Steve took a great sense of personal satisfaction if his patients did well and would be just as disappointed if there were a problem that would develop with one of them. Jake evidently realized this pride that Steve had with his care of patients. The senior doctor would take advantage of this, knowing that Steve would take good care of the patients.

Neither Jake nor Steve realized that Dr. Rosberg and the other attending staff also noticed the major accomplishments and excellent patient care that Steve was providing. Steve was always on the floor when a staff surgeon would come by to check on a patient. The comment would be, "Oh, Dr. Carmichael, are you out of the OR again? Weren't you on the floor yesterday, too? Doesn't Jake ever let you operate as part of your surgery residency?" Steve would just smile and shrug his shoulders. Then he would provide all the pertinent details to the staff about their patients, including morning lab values, events that occurred during the night, and the overall progress of them. The more Steve gathered information on complications like post-op pneumonia and atelectasis or deep vein thrombosis, the more the staff sensed his knowledge base and commitment to patient care. This built the staff surgeons' trust in Dr. Carmichael to manage their patients. It would translate into more surgery time in the future as an upper level resident. The more a staff doctor trusted him with patients, the more he would get to do in the operating room. Retracting would be a thing of the past.

It was nearly 3:30 in the afternoon before Steve finished the floor work. All of the patients who were supposed to be discharged had been discharged, and all the staff doctors had come by to do their rounds. Steve still had not heard from Jake or anyone else from the OR, so he took the opportunity to get some lunch. He knew it might be the only chance he had to eat for a while since he was on call overnight again. One of the first things he had learned as a surgery intern was that if you have a chance to eat, do it; you never knew what lurked ahead. You could only eat at reasonable hours for meals if you were at home on a day off or if you were attending a noon hour lecture with lunch provided.

No sooner did Steve sit down with a cold sandwich from the refrigerator than his beeper went off. He swallowed the sandwich in just a few bites and grabbed his soda on his way to the nearest phone to answer his page. He knew it was not a true emergency, because as Erica had told him, the nurses would have paged him overhead to get his attention for something serious.

He dialed the number and then heard the voice on the other end. "Uh huh…yep…okay. I'll be right up." Jake was done with surgery, finally, and wanted to make afternoon rounds.

Sally was the one who had called Steve. From her tone in her voice, she sounded exhausted. On the way up to the ICU, Steve was thinking that the surgery took a long time and maybe there was a problem with the patient during surgery. He ought to know since he was on call and expected to manage the patient during the night. He arrived in the ICU to find the rest of his team in Room 4 going over Jake and Sally's new post-op.

Nurse Agusta Johnson was in the room admitting the patient to the ICU. She was busy trying to untangle several loops of IV tubing. "Well, Dr. Carmichael, looks as if we will be getting to know each other quite well tonight." She was referring to how critical the post-op course would be during the night for the patient laying in the bed.

Dr. Rosberg was standing nearby. "Not to disagree with you, Agusta, but I would rather you get to know Dr. Douglas tonight. Mr. Conrad will require a great deal of attention and TLC." Dr. Rosberg looked over toward Steve. "Not that I don't think you can handle managing this patient, Carmichael, because I know you can. I've seen what you do on the floor, but being on call for surgery as an intern will get you pulled in all sorts of different directions. Mr. Conrad needs a little more attention tonight, and it will be good for Jake to do some ICU monitoring and management with his patient. Isn't that right, Dr. Douglas?"

Jake looked down at his feet. "Yes, sir."

You see Dr. Carmichael," Dr. Rosberg continued, "Drs. Douglas and Jenson were going to do a simple gastric ulcer resection for a persistent gastric ulcer. Unfortunately, no one seemed to think about getting some pertinent lab work such as white cell count or an amylase. So what was supposed to be a simple hour-long case turned out to be an eight-hour pancreticoduodenctomy. The pancreatic tumor appeared to be a stomach ulcer because it had eroded through the stomach wall. Steve, are you familiar with a Whipple procedure?"

"Kind of," he replied. "It's when the pancreas, stomach, and duodenum are removed for a tumor in the head of the pancreas gland."

"Very good, Dr. Carmichael. Post operatively, these patients require a lot of attention. They have drains, feeding tubes, and gastrostomy tubes. Mr. Conrad will also need to be on the ventilator for a while as the case lasted a little longer than Dr. Douglas anticipated. Isn't that right, Jake, my boy?"

Jake kept his eyes aimed at the floor without responding Apparently Dr. Rosberg had already had a few words with Jake.

Dr. Rosberg finished reviewing the initial vitals and then glanced at the labs. "Alright, Dr. Douglas, I expect you to stay around a few hours to make sure this patient is rock stable before you leave. Agusta, if Steve gets called away for a significant period of time during the night, please call Jake in, no matter what time it is, okay?"

Agusta smiled devilishly. "That will be no problem, sir."

Rounds continued as painful as any other time that Jake had been in trouble. Dr. Douglas would make a concerted effort to be a know-it-all about every patient. However, Steve had become practiced in knowing most everything about all of his patients. He knew their history, past medical history and surgeries, their medications before surgery and their meds in the hospital, as well as any post-op problems and their complete lab work. He carried a notebook with everything written down to be sure he never failed. Jake would ask and ask, and Steve would answer with few hesitations.

Rounds were almost done when Jake suggested that the whole team review the complete x-rays of every patient on their surgical service in the x-ray department. The doctors shook their heads in disgust but followed their leader to x-ray.

On the way, Steve leaned over to Sally and asked, "Got in a lot of trouble today, huh?"

Sally made sure to whisper so Jake would not hear. "Dr. Rosberg has reached his limit of tolerance for Jake. This case was the last straw. After finding out intraoperatively that we were dealing with a complete mess and had not been prepared for it, Jake had to confess to Rosberg that the preoperative work up was neither complete nor satisfactory. When Rosberg saw this tumor and reviewed the chart, he nearly strangled Jake. Then, well, you know: eight hours is a long time, so Rosberg began quizzing Jake on all the patients as if he were an intern again. Unfortunately, Jake didn't know much about many of the patients, and it was obvious that he really didn't pay too much attention on rounds. Then he made the idiotic mistake of trying to bullshit Rosberg about some lab values on one of his patients.

Rosberg knew right away what Jake was doing and toyed him along for a few more lies. By then, Jake was swimming alone in shark-infested waters. Rosberg started to take bites out of him. First, they were small and painful, but then they got bigger and bigger. There was no sign of any rescue. I kind of think Rosberg enjoyed himself. Whatever. By the end of the attack, Rosberg threatened to ax Jake if he doesn't get his shit together, and he meant it. I think that really scared Jake."

Steve stared at Sally with a dumbfounded expression. What a disappointment that would be to spend five to six years training and then to have it all pulled out from under you. *It couldn't happen to a nicer guy*. Steve smiled to himself.

When Jake was done going over every x-ray on every patient, he sent everyone home except for Roger. "You get to take call with Steve." It was a common practice for med students to have the option to take call on surgery, but Jake had not enforced that before tonight. Jake, Steve and Roger went back up to the ICU and checked on Mr. Conrad. "Alright, Carmichael, why don't you and Roger go and get dinner before the cafeteria closes? Check in with me when you're done."

Steve looked with confusion at Roger and then back again at Jake, but he didn't argue. They left the unit without another word.

They returned to the ICU about an hour later. Jake was in Mr. Conrad's room looking over vitals and checking his urine output.

"Sorry, Jake, we got paged during dinner, and then I had to go to the ER for a perirectal abscess."

"That sounds yummy. I hope you had a chance to eat before you drained the abscess."

Just then, Steve was paged overhead for a trauma code in the ER. He and Roger glanced at each other and left Jake in the dust.

After Steve finished what felt like a late-night rush at a restaurant, he and Roger returned from the ER to the ICU. They found Jake sleeping in Mr. Conrad's room.

Steve nudged Jake. "Hey, wake up. It's almost ten. Why don't you head home now? I think things have slowed down for a while."

Jake groggily looked at his watch and then at Mr. Conrad and the ventilator. "Alright, I'll head out, but don't hesitate to call me."

Agusta leaned into the room and said, "Oh, don't you worry about a silly little thing like that, Dr. Douglas. I'll be sure to call you if we need you." As she walked away, she whispered, "And even if I don't."

Steve tried not to look at Jake after he heard that, but he saw Jake smile wryly.

Just as Jake stood, his pager went off. He looked at the number. "Shit, the ER. Don't they know I'm not on call?" He grabbed the phone off the wall and spoke to one of the doctors in the ER.

The guy had such a loud voice Steve could hear the conversation across the room.

"Sorry, Jake. I know you're not on call, but there is this interesting looking guy with a funny accent who just came in with some pretty serious belly pain. He looks like shit but refuses to see anybody but you."

Jake looked like he had just seen a ghost. His face turned pale, and beads of sweat started to collect on his forehead. He looked down at his pager to review the last several pages.

The ER doctor continued, "Apparently this guy came in several hours ago looking for you. The nurses said he had pretty serious abdominal pain, but he found out you were in surgery and said he would come back. Some kids just found him unconscious two blocks away, and EMS brought him back in. He woke up after a liter of LR, but he's still terribly dehydrated with significant rebound. His belly is rock hard, probably perforated something. It looks as if he had recent surgery, but he says that was done elsewhere so we won't have any records of his surgery. He refuses to see anyone else but you. Quite the following you have here, Jake. Already building up your private practice?"

Jake was paralyzed.

"Douglas, are you coming down or what?"

The ER doctor repeated himself three times before Jake said quietly, "Yeah, I'll be right there."

Without saying another word, Jake turned and headed out of the ICU. He kept flipping through pages as he walked, noting several pages with numbers that he hadn't recognize or bothered to call back. He noticed now that all but one was the same number. Jake thought to himself, *Bill Thomas*.

Jake looked through the ER windows at the guy sitting on a gurney. He had black hair, was unshaven, and wore torn pants. He looked like he had been repeatedly run over by a truck. Before Jake approached the patient, he stopped by a desk to call the unknown number that appeared the most on his pager.

A deep male voice answered, "Hello."

"Thomas, is this you?" asked Jake.

"No, you dumb shit. It's Snow White! Don't you ever answer your shit ass pages? What kind of neglect is that from a nice doctor?"

"Listen, I can answer that, but if I spend the next ten minutes explaining myself to you, this guy over here will probably die. So maybe we'll discuss it later. I have not seen him yet, I mean formally, but I am looking at him right now, and he looks like shit."

"Alright, alright. This is what we need to do, Douglas. Conduct your surgery, and get the specimen. Walk it over to pathology yourself. A lab person is there 24 hours a day. I'll be down the hall between the operating rooms and pathology. Deliver the specimen to me, and I will place your package in your locker."

"But- my lock?"

"Jake, I have that covered, but don't take all the gifts home at once. It will be too obvious, sparking too many questions. You must not tell anyone about this, and don't try to contact me. You should have no worries or questions. I will leave all that you need in your locker. I'll see you in a bit."

The phone clicked. Jake slowly put the receiver in the cradle.

He slowly walked to the man on the gurney and picked up his chart, moving as if in slow motion. Jake looked up at the man as if he were a familiar face but realized he didn't know anything about him except there was something in his belly that needed to come out.

The stench from the man was horrendous. He had the smell of body odor combined with vomit. His clothes were in shambles, and his face was unshaven and drawn out like somebody who was extremely dehydrated. Jake noticed the IV tubing and saw an empty bag of LR that was disconnected. He saw the present bag almost empty as well.

Jake reached out his hand and slowly but quietly introduced himself. "Hi. I'm Dr. Douglas. I was told you have some belly pain."

The man nodded in pain and shook his hand. "I'm Ziamuddin."

Jake slowly but carefully felt the man's abdomen. Indeed it

was tight as a drum and exquisitely tender throughout. The man moved about squirming beneath the exam. Jake leaned over and said, "I think you need to have surgery to see what is going on inside. I'll give you some antibiotics and Morphine right now. That should make you feel much better."

The man nodded again.

Jake slowly backed away from the man, maintaining eye contact. He continued to walk backward until he bumped into the nurse's desk.

"Dr. Douglas, are you okay?" one of the nurses asked. "It looks as if you have had a tough long day. Maybe we should get one of the other surgeons to take a look at that man for you. I don't think you are in any shape to do surgery tonight."

"Uh, that's okay, Margret. I'll be okay. Maybe I'll get a bite to eat while you all call in the OR crew. That should make me feel better."

"That sounds like a good idea," the nurse agreed.

All the while Jake could not stop looking at the man.

Steve and Roger burst into the ER to see what the excitement was all about. "Jake!" they shouted.

"What?!"

"We thought you might have an appy or something," Steve said. "Maybe after I do the History and Physical on him, could Roger and I scrub on the case?"

Jake turned around slowly and looked Steve right in the eyes. "Carmichael, I'll do the H and P. Why don't you get Mr. Conrad all straightened out?"

Steve was adamant. "Come on, Jake. It has been over a month since I started, and I'm probably the only intern that has not done an appy yet, not to mention that I haven't scrubbed for, I don't know, a couple of weeks or so."

Jake stared at Steve for a few seconds before reluctantly

giving in. "Alright. Go get Mr. Conrad tucked in and tell Agusta to give us a call if there is a problem. Have Roger sit up there with him until you get out. And Carmichael, you might want to sweet talk Agusta into not calling Rosberg in right now."

"Oh, yeah. Fine. Fine. Fine. I'll take care of it. Thanks, Jake!"

As Steve ran off to the ICU, Jake turned around and started to write a History and Physical on Ziamuddin. He glanced up to find Margret, the charge nurse in the ER.

"Margret!" he yelled.

"Yes, Dr. Douglas. What can I do for you?"

"I need to take this man down to the OR immediately. Make sure that the OR crew has been called in and that they know it is for a stat procedure. Then they won't dilly-dally. And give the patient another liter of Lactated Ringers, three grams of Unasyn and four of Morphine in his IV. Thanks."

Jake tried to write the preoperative notes and history but discovered that his hand was shaking and his heart was pounding. He wasn't sure what he was going to find, but there was no way to back out of it now. Even if he tried to give the case to someone else, the man on the gurney wouldn't tolerate a transfer to another facility. Jake had to do it, or the guy was going to die.

Chapter 23

Jake burst down the corridor of the OR toward the Path department. He was trying to move slowly in order not to attract too much attention but at the same time move quickly to get rid of whatever this thing was. He was in such deep concentration trying to stabilize the mass that he almost sped right past his contact.

Bill Thomas interrupted his concentration. "Where are you going in such a rush?"

Jake looked up franticly at the man and stared at him. "Uh, here you go, Mr. Thomas. Here is your prize as requested. But I have just one question-"

"I put the money in your locker. You are now a man without debt."

"That's great," replied Jake, "but that was not what I am concerned about. You see, I inadvertently slipped my finger through whatever this is. And since it happened, I've wondered if it might be dangerous shit. Could this be true?"

Now it was time for Bill Thomas to panic. He couldn't believe what he just heard. This would probably change everything. He wasn't even sure if his contact would even pick the package up after this.

Thomas grabbed Jake's shoulders and jerked him back and forth. "Did anyone else see you do this? Does anyone else know that you put a hole in this thing?"

Jake already felt a little better. If it were truly dangerous, there was no chance in hell Thomas would jolt it around like he was doing. "Hey, hey, settle down," he said with a sigh of relief. "I never even took my finger out of the hole. It's still in this piece of shit here." He lifted the package up with his left hand.

"Here is my little old finger stuck in this piece of shit. No one saw, and no one had a clue. So let's relax a bit."

Thomas wasn't as satisfied and kept jerking Jake around. This issue could jeopardize the entire project. As he reacted, he realized that Jake had no clue what this meant; the more attention Thomas created, the more trouble he might make. With that thought, he stopped jostling the other man. He was about to thank him for his duty when they both heard the overhead speaker.

"Dr. Jake Douglas, Dr. Jake Douglas, stat to the OR. Dr. Jake Douglas, Dr. Jake Douglas, stat to the Operating Room."

Jake thought out loud, "Shit. I bet that poor guy is totally septic and bottoming out his blood pressure." He glared at Thomas. "Well, it has been a real fuckin' pleasure working with you, and I hope our paths don't ever meet again. See ya." The doctor turned and ran to the OR, leaving his contact holding the specimen in the container with white powder spilled in the bottom of the basin.

Chapter 24

Jake barreled through the OR doors. He found Steve doing CPR and Karla running the crash cart over to the table. A.J. too was moving about quickly.

"What the hell is going on?" shouted Jake.

A.J. replied, "It is the damnedest thing, but about a minute after you left, this kid's blood pressure shot through the roof. His BP was 245 over 125. That is just nutty. I mean, I thought the guy would code but maybe from a hypovolemic or septic component. I initially gave him more inhalational anesthetic thinking that he was waking up, but that didn't help in the least. Now I have an Esmolol drip going, but he just went into Vtach, and his blood pressure just came crashing down. We can't get good femoral pulses, so we started CPR. I have given two boluses of Lido without any change. I'm not sure what the hell is going on, Jake, but you better get a hold of Rosberg before this patient crumbles. And he is about there now!"

Jake could not believe his eyes or ears. He knew that the patient had a good chance of becoming septic since his belly was filled with stool. He just didn't figure the guy would do the opposite and become hypertensive. Nonetheless, A.J. was right about getting in contact with Dr. Rosberg. Rosberg would not be happy but probably wouldn't trouble himself to come in for a homeless foreign patient about to die. Instead, he was likely to stay at home and figure out ways to pulverize Jake at the next Morbidity/Mortality Conference.

Jake quickly dialed the memorized phone number and told Dr. Rosberg what had happened. As expected, Dr. Rosberg didn't feel inclined to come in since the patient sounded as if he was about to die.

Jake asked, "Do you have any ideas about what the mechanism is here? He just is not responding to anything!"

After a moment of silence on the phone, Dr. Rosberg said, "I really don't know what the hell is going on, Douglas, but I don't think it was anything you guys did. We don't know this guy at all, but it sounds like he had a little too much cocaine this afternoon. Does he use, do you know?"

Jake quickly responded, "Not that I am aware of, but then I didn't really get a good chance to talk to him prior to surgery. He was so sick. I just wanted to get him down here and explore his belly as soon as I could."

"That was an excellent idea, but maybe there was something more to this story than meets the eye. Oh, well. You and A.J. give it your best, and I'll talk to you in the morning."

Jake could not believe how sympathetic Rosberg was, but maybe he had been fast asleep and didn't realize to whom he was talking. He did refer to him by name, so maybe he'd had a little cocktail and forgotten to be an ass while talking to him. Whatever the reason, it was nice that Jake was not placed on the defensive tonight. Without a doubt, he would be raked over the coals at M&M conference later this week.

After hanging up, he hurried back to the operating table and the patient. "What is his BP now?"

A.J. hollered back, "The last systolic I could get was about 60, but it's a thready pressure. I'm not sure if this guy can hang on much longer!"

Steve was busy doing chest compressions and thinking how badly he had wanted in on this case. Now he wished he were a million miles away. He thought to himself, *Poor case selection.* This was his first real case to scrub, and now he and Jake would have to defend their actions at the M/M conference. Fortunately, Steve would not get picked on much as the intern, but still there was the possibility of shark bites from the hungry staff surgeons who enjoyed watching their prey squirm before getting attacked.

Steve tried his best to focus on the moment and saving this guy's life. His surgical cap was becoming soaked with his sweat. He could barely feel his hands as they were clinched together to do CPR. However, there was no one else to relieve him as A.J. was busy running in meds, Sue was helping A.J., and Karla was monitoring the defibrillator. Steve glanced at Jake who was staring at the monitor. It was if Jake was waiting for the right moment to give up and call the code.

"How long have we been at this?" asked Jake.

"About eight minutes. It was shortly after you left the room that the guy started to get hypertensive and then went into Vtach," answered A.J.

"That's it!" yelled Steve as he bounced on the patient's chest. "I don't know what caused his high pressure, but once he went into Vtach, he lost his pressure. Let's treat his Vtach and disregard his Hypertensive episode."

"That sounds like as good as a plan as any," said A.J. "Karla, bring the defib unit over, and set us up for 360 joules. Sue, draw up five of Epi, and let's blast this guy with it."

Jake grabbed the paddles, and Karla placed the insulation pads on the chest.

"CLEAR!" yelled Jake, and everyone stepped back from the table. With the push of a red button, the doctor sent a strong shock through Ziamuddin's body.

Everyone looked up at the monitor. Instead of a flat line, there was almost a fine Vfib.

"That's a start," cheered A.J.

Jake took the reins. "Go ahead and charge me up, Karla. A.J., blast him with the Epi and then give him another 100 of

Lido. CLEAR!" He sent another jolt through the body of the young patient.

They all looked at the monitor again. After a moment of disbelief, they all cheered. The rhythm showed sinus tach at about 100 beats per minute.

"I can't believe it!" yelled A.J. "I would never have guessed that he would come back. His pressure is up to 105 over 70. Not bad, kids!"

Jake patted Steve on his back. "Way to go, Carmichael! I have to congratulate you on a job well done. I don't care what they say about you." They both laughed as Ziamuddin's heart rate continued to beat normally.

"Now let's not get too excited," said A.J. "We still have to get this guy closed and off the table."

"Right you are, A.J., my boy," chuckled Jake. "Let me wash my hands. Then we'll irrigate, leave a drain, and get out. Karla, let's put some strong antibiotics in the irrigation. Carmichael, I would advise you just get regowned and gloved. Sue, I guess you and I need to wash up. I'll wash you if you wash me."

"Shut up, Jake. This is not the place I was expecting a proposal to take place."

They all laughed.

Just as Jake and Sue reached the door, A.J. shrieked, "Shit, here we go again, Jake! He's back in Vtach. Oh shit, make that Vfib. PADDLES, NOW!"

Jake ran back to the table and looked at the monitor.

"Indeed, Watson. That is truly Vfib. Ah, shit. What is his pressure? Karla, charge me up to 360. Let's go gang!"

Karla was running in all different directions. She dashed to get the machine and, at the same time, threw A.J. another bag of LR. With an extra hand somewhere, she pushed the charge button on the defibrillator.

"CLEAR!" yelled Jake. "Another 100 of Lido and this time, A.J., let's get a drip going at two a minute. Karla, give him another amp of Epi!"

They knew that in the second round the patient had less chance of surviving. With the stimulation of electrical current that was intended just for his heart, Ziamuddin's whole body jumped into the air. His arms flopped up and down off the table. It looked as if he was having a short-lived seizure.

After the shock went through the young man's body, the whole team looked at the monitor with hope for a sinus rhythm. Despite their gallant efforts, the heart rate was still a fine ventricular fibrillation.

"Alright, gang, let's go through this exercise again. Charge me up, Karla. A.J., let's roll with another amp of epi. Let's do it, gang!" Jake shouted.

The crew continued the code for several minutes. Jake delivered shock after shock, and A.J. continued to administer the medication. Steve did chest compressions between the bolts of electricity, and Karla and Sue were watching intensely, hoping for a miraculous comeback.

After nearly twenty-five minutes, Jake looked up at the monitor and then at A.J. The rhythm on the monitor was flat line and had been for the last ten minutes. A.J. returned Jake's look and shook his head from side to side. Then he looked down in defeat.

Jake slowly motioned to stop the CPR. "Let's call it." He looked up at the monitor one last time and then at the clock. He turned to Karla, "Ten forty-two PM. Cause of death: septic shock." Jake bowed his head and walked out of the OR without another word.

A.J. started to clean up his mess near the head of the bed. They could still hear the respirator breathing for the young man.

Nonetheless, the monitor still displayed a flat line. A.J. continued to arrange his area but leaned over to the on/off switch and regretfully turned the machine off. The room became exceptionally quiet.

Steve recalled how just a few months ago, he was so scared about these codes because he was not sure what to do. Now he was fearful of these codes because many patients rarely survived.

Jake walked back into the room. “Steve, would you mind closing? By the way, you all did a great job. We were just behind the eight ball on this one.”

Jake turned around and was on his way out again when Steve had an idea. “Jake, do you think we should get a tox screen on him? It might show us that this wasn’t Sepsis but maybe drug induced. I mean-”

Jake quickly cut him off. “I don’t think so, Steve. The guy came in with a belly full of pus and septic. We didn’t create the situation, and we did the best we could do. I think you did a great job, Carmichael, but you need to move on from this one. You need to realize this will happen to you sometimes, and there is no simple way to deal with it. You just need to chalk it up to experience and learn from it.”

“Exactly,” said Steve. “I, uh, just wanted to, uh… Never mind. I’ll just close him up, Dr. Douglas.”

Jake walked out of the operating room, and Steve asked for closing suture.

“You are right, Dr. Carmichael,” said A.J. “This was not a typical septic arrest. Usually with sepsis the blood pressure just bottoms out.” A.J. continued to talk as he put things away on his anesthesia cart. “I mean, first the guy’s BP jumps sky high, and then we get this tachy arrhythmia. That just is not the way a guy with septic shock should act. I think something weird was going on."

Steve could tell that A.J. hadn't seen the white powder in the abdomen, but Steve wasn't sure if he had really seen it either. The abdomen was filled with pus and blood, and the exposure wasn't great. Still it sure looked as if the stuff at the base of the mass had a different appearance than the pus nearby.

Steve stalled for a minute as he thought. He glanced at the man's foley catheter and saw yellow urine. He looked up at Karla and didn't say a word. He just stared blankly at her. Finally, he said, "Karla, why don't you quickly send some urine for a tox screen? I mean, just for us here now. We don't need to share it with Jake unless there is a big problem." Steve went back to work sewing his belly shut without waiting for an answer.

A.J. agreed with the new recommendation. "I think that's a good idea, young Dr. Carmichael. If it comes back positive, we'll know that we were running up the wrong tree while trying to save this guy."

Steve didn't say anything but continued to sew. He knew that A.J. was probably right. The guy had more experience than he and Jake put together. But getting the lab test clearly went against Jake's wishes. If something came about from it, he would have to bring it to Jake's attention.

Of course, he could always say that it was A.J.'s idea. Steve knew Jake would never argue with A.J.

Steve was finished closing. The two women were softly talking while Karla was getting paper work ready. A.J. had most of his anesthesia cart put together and had turned the music back on.

Steve hadn't even noticed the song. He was still thinking about the code and that they would need to get in contact with this guy's family to let them know about the unfortunate event tonight. He was in deep concentration with his final stitches when he noticed Karla waving the lab sheet in front of his face.

He looked up and saw the report: Cocaine - positive.

Chapter 25

While Steve Carmichael closed the incision on the late Ziamuddin, Bill Thomas was driving in his car around town. He was not on his way to any particular place: he was just driving and thinking.

This was not the way it was supposed to turn out. The bag was not supposed to be punctured. There was not to be any breach in security. With the package damaged, the receiving party might not even want the contents. If that were the case, then all his efforts over the last several months would have been futile.

His job was already on the line. He had no doubt that he was being followed, his phone lines tapped. They were on to him, and they were just waiting for the right time to make their move. Then they would bust him. He knew how they worked. They were just watching and making notes of his actions, whereabouts, friends, visitors, and basically every movement. When the time was right, they would jump on him and bust the entire operation.

He knew because he was one of them. He made many a bust in the exact same way. Because he knew their every move, he felt like he could be one step ahead of them. That's why his ticket to Brazil would be the most important aspect of his escape. If he were able to get on the plane before they found him, he would be home free. Once in South America, they would not be able to target him or arrest him.

However, if he were unable to get the money for this job, he would not be able to retire in Brazil or anywhere exotic. So he was driving around town, determined to come up with a plan that would help him explain the hole in the package and allow him to exchange it for the guaranteed money.

He knew that, whatever excuse he offered, they would be reluctant to take the tampered package for security reasons. If they wouldn't take the package, then no money for him. It was not complicated, but he had to come up with the right plan to convince them that there had been no breach of security. He thought that maybe he could tell them that he entered the package after it was delivered and that no one else saw the contents. Or maybe during the drop off there was an inadvertent hole punctured into the bag and that it was not noticed until he got home.

Thomas spent hours driving around town trying to come up with a safe and plausible plan. By dawn, he still had not come up with a logical excuse that he could back up. He drove up to his apartment around five thirty in the morning. Despite the lack of sleep, he still was not tired. He was more worried about losing the millions that they had promised.

As he opened his door to his apartment, he heard the phone ringing. He thought to himself that it was too early for a friendly phone call. The only person this could be was Jake Douglas. He dashed to the phone, thinking there would be some news about the young courier. However, when he picked up the receiver he heard a more familiar voice.

"My friend, please meet me at 3rd and 10th in two minutes."

That was it. Thomas heard the click of the phone before he could even get a grunt out. It was nearly impossible to get over to 10th in just a few minutes, but since it meant millions of dollars, he had to find a way. He glanced at his watch, noted the time, and dashed out of his apartment. He figured that his lines were probably tapped, so he only had a few minutes before his followers picked up on his whereabouts. He knew a pay phone was located at 3rd and 10th but they would only have a minute to talk before the line might get picked up.

Thomas nearly knocked over a man on the stairs as he

quickly ran down the bottom flight and out the lobby door. He looked in all directions out of habit to make sure no one was staking out his apartment. There was nothing obvious, and he didn't have time to dawdle. Down the street to the left was a garbage truck going the opposite way and no cars at all in the other direction. He looked up to see if any lights were on in any of the other apartment windows above the front door. None. It wasn't a perfect scan, but Thomas didn't have time to waffle around. If he missed that phone call, he could kiss millions of dollars away.

The morning was clear, and the sun was just beginning to rise. He glanced at his watch again before starting his car. The trip down the stairs and into his car took twenty-five seconds. Too much time had been spent looking around. He sped down his street, keeping an eye out for police officers. If efficient people were on his case, they had already notified any officers in the area to just let Thomas speed as much as he needed to in order to make this meeting. The one thing they probably anticipate was that Thomas was rushing to make a phone call on a public line. It would still take them at least one minute to make the connection.

Since he was running late, he decided to take the most direct route to his destination. He nearly hit a dog on the street as he turned onto 3rd. He drove his car near the telephone booth. He slammed on the brakes and threw the gear into park. He jumped out of the car and glanced for any transmission parts on the street as he ran to the booth.

He could hear the phone ringing and knew one thing: if he missed this phone call, they might never attempt to contact him again. Just as he was about to pick up the phone, it seemed as if the ringing had stopped. He grabbed the receiver and placed it to his ear. "Hello, hello? Hey, anybody home?"

No one was on the other line.

"SHIT!" he muttered out loud. He glanced at his watch. He thought he had been on time, but his watched showed that he was about thirty seconds late. He couldn't know if that was the second or third time calling. The only certainty was that the phone was not ringing anymore.

He thought about just leaving, but he knew that this package was too important to them. If they really wanted it, they would try again. Of course, they could send another shipment with another courier, but then they would have to take a chance with all new blood and go through the entire plan with someone else. The biggest risk would be that the new contact would go to proper authorities and expose the entire plan.

He was thinking about all sorts of options of what could happen when the phone started ringing again. He didn't let it sound even one series through. "Hello?!"

The response was moment of silence as they identified his voice to make sure it was actually Bill Thomas. These people did not want to take any chances of talking to the wrong group of people and thus putting an end to their plan.

"Alright, my friend. We have thirty seconds. I'm glad you could make it on such short notice. I knew you wouldn't let us down. We selected you for your perseverance, not your punctuality. You should have received a package of mine by now. Have you not?"

"Yes, as a matter of-" Thomas was quickly interrupted.

"We do not have time for your little chit chat. I need you to deliver the item to a friend. I assume it is intact?"

Agent Thomas hesitated. This was the moment he spent all night trying to iron out. If he said the truth, they would surely call off the deal. If he lied and delivered the package opened, he would be killed. There had to be a way to outplay them. Maybe he could place the contents in another bag. *That's it!* he thought. He would just place all the contents in a new bag before delivering it to its destination. Even if they did figure it out, he would be long gone. He would be on a plane to South America, and no one would have a clue where he was.

"My friend, you hesitate. Please tell me the truth. I have no time for your bullshit."

"You see, the package came to me intact, but then I inadvertently punctured it with one of my keys as I was placing it in a safer container, and then I-"

Again, Thomas was interrupted. "My friend, you know the terms of this deal!" Another moment of silence followed.

Agent Thomas could not believe what he had done. In a matter of a few short seconds, he had lost out on millions of dollars, not to mention the safety of his life. He had quickly devised a great alternative to the problem, but he just didn't have the time to rehearse the correct way of hiding it from the appropriate party.

"My friend, this really screws this up, but we have come too far along this time to abort the mission. I don't believe your story, but even if it were true, there is only one way to continue forward. I need you to determine who witnessed the entire event and make sure they don't share that knowledge with anyone. When this is complete, please contact me. My associates and I will then verify your work. If you have been successful, then we will again move forward. I will grant you ten days. My friend, I must tell you I will keep an eye out for you, and if you make any attempts to channel this package to any other party than who it is intended, then I will take action. If I have not heard from you in ten days, I will be forced to take action as well. I will be watching you, my friend."

Click.

"My friend, my ass," muttered Thomas into the dead phone line. *What a shmuck.* But Thomas couldn't get too mad. He himself had screwed this up, but the old geezer gave him a second chance. He looked at his watch: less than a minute had passed. The guy was good.

Thomas walked back to his car and was about to enter it when he heard from down the street the noise of cars. He thought that was odd at this hour in this part of town. He looked around curiously.

Ten seconds later, he saw two black Ford Explorers roll past on Eighth Street and cross over Third Avenue. It appeared that Thomas' colleagues were well on to him, but he knew they would keep their distance until the package showed up and the delivery was made. Until then, it would be useless to bust him. They didn't have anything on him, and they wouldn't have the package. That was exactly why he placed the package in safekeeping.

Thomas slowly got into his car and shut the door. He sat with his head resting on the steering wheel. He thought about the entire conversation. 'Take action' only meant one thing: to clean up any potential leaks. If any links to this operation could be exposed, it would destroy not only the entire plan but also possibly the existence of their coalition.

He knew that if they wanted him dead, it could be accomplished with ease. He didn't think for a minute to sell the contents to a third party. For one thing, it would be too risky, but more importantly, the financial gains would not be comparable. If he wanted the money, he would have to do it their way, even if they were asking a lot.

They want him to identify everyone who was in the operating room that night with Jake Douglas and Ziamudin. Then Thomas would have to find a way to eliminate each of those potential leaks without attracting attention from the public. He would need to make sure everything was low key, lest his colleagues discover the coverup and bust the operation before the delivery was made.

He looked out the front window and shook his head. Ten days was not much time to devise a plan and to carry it out without a hitch. He would have to come up with different plans and the materials for each person. Normally it would not be a big deal. He usually would be able to go to the agency and get whatever supplies he needed without question. However, he would need to be more discrete because they were already on to him. If he made one bad move, they would be all over him.

He started his car and drove home. There was much work to be done little time to do it.

Chapter 26

It was another long night on call for Steve. After the code in the OR, several traumas came in. Close to 3:00 in the morning, he finally got to sleep. He slept for almost three hours without getting disturbed. That was usually unheard of for call, but Steve wasn't complaining. The hospital operator woke him up at 5:45 just as he requested.

Steve found his shoes near the bed and combed his hair with his hand. He rarely bothered with a real comb, but no one seemed to care about his appearance as long as he kept all the patients alive during the night and had all the lab numbers in the morning. When he first started taking call, he would bring his toothbrush with him. Soon he realized that he would only get to use it about half the time, so he decided instead to spend the post-call day with bad breath. That worked out quite well because it would serve two functions: he would not have to lug around a bulky toilet kit, and it usually kept people at great distance from him. That meant fewer interactions with people who would normally give him a thousand extra things to do.

Gradually he decided not to shave post-call either. This would never cut it at some prestigious residency program, but then he wasn't at one. It seemed to be a trend for residents not to bother with facial grooming after a night on call at this hospital. Most of the residents didn't have time anyway.

Steve had a few minutes this morning for a cup of coffee, necessary to start any day. In the cafeteria, he ran into Erica.

"Well, good morning, sunshine." She smiled. "Don't you look wonderful? Are you showing off that post-call look? You know that does wonders for you. I think you are so cute anyway, but when I see you with that manly facial hair and your hair in a mess like that, well that just turns me on. Why don't you get a little closer? Come over here, you hunk!" She grabbed Steve by the shoulders and leaned over to his face as if to give him a big smooch. "Ah, just as I expected: you didn't even brush your teeth. Oh, you don't know what you are doing to me, Carmichael. I can't stand it any longer. Come with me, you fool, I need you now." She tried to pull Steve's hand in the direction out of the cafeteria, but he pulled her into him instead. She was a little taken back by Steve's actions with her.

"If I have that kind of effect on you, then why not show the world how you feel?" With that, Steve pulled her even closer into his arms. Their faces were only a few inches from each other.

Erica was so shocked, she couldn't devise a quick come back.

Steve took full advantage of the moment and that he was without much sleep and uninhibited. He leaned forward and kissed her lips. He waited for her to push away, but she never did. Finally, he finished the kiss and gently let her go. "Well, good morning, beautiful, and I hope your day goes just as well as mine has started."

Without another word, Steve walked away to get his coffee and head toward the ICU for rounds. He turned around for a quick glance at Erica before he disappeared around a corner.

She had not moved an inch and was just staring at Steve.

He gave her a warm smile and walked on.

The day progressed on schedule. Jake was late for rounds, and Sally completed them. When Jake finally arrived, Sally and the team were just getting to the cafeteria for a quick bite before the OR day started.

Steve noticed that Jake was not any different than usual. He'd thought that the doctor might show a little remorse about the events from last night, but he was wrong.

Jake was himself as usual. "Well, Jenson, how did rounds

go? Anything I need to be aware of before the OR? How about the lady in room 203? Did she get through the night without too much trouble? I know Carmichael was on last night and that he probably put out any fires that started, but fill me in before I have to see Rosberg."

Steve listened to Jake ramble, but his mind was elsewhere. Obviously Jake didn't care about that young kid who had died the previous night. He probably didn't care to know about the cocaine in the patient's body. Steve debated about whether to share this information with him anyway. Jake didn't want to know last night and probably still didn't want to know this morning. But the cocaine had killed the man, not the sepsis.

Steve was just as interested in the specimen sent for pathology. He thought that it would perhaps shed light on the reason the young kid coded the way he did. However, there was no way the Pathology Department would have the slides made up yet. Twelve hours had not even passed, and there was not a chance in hell that a pathologist would be at the hospital this early.

Steve was wondering if the specimen would show cocaine or if the cocaine in his system was from drug use. The mass could have been just an abscess that collected after a severe appendicitis. It was not unusual to develop a collection of pus after a perforated appendicitis. Events occurred so quickly last night that Steve never had time to explore the abdomen, but the fact that there was so much stool in the abdomen meant there was a hole somewhere in the colon. Neither Steve nor Jake had time to explore the abdomen. Slowly, Steve realized that Jake went right away for this mass and never spent time exploring the abdomen.

As Jake continued to get caught up on all the patients from Sally, Steve continued to reexamine the details of the surgery. The hole in the colon could have been from a variety of causes.

One was that the appendiceal stump broke open and leaked stool. There could have been necrosis around the cecum, which would have caused a perforation. Another cause for the stool leak might have been an inadvertent injury to the bowel. Still, Steve was not sure why there was so much stool and why it even happened. He figured that the pathology report would answer some of his questions. He would check in with the Path Department later that day.

"Steve, Steve! Hey, Carmichael! Where the hell are you, sport?" Sally was trying to get Steve's attention while going over the day's plan.

"Sorry, Sally. I guess it was a long night. Where do you want me today?"

"Well, Steve, let's try doing what we have done for the last several weeks. That means the post call person gets to go to the OR. As far as I can remember, you were the one who was on call. Is any of this coming back to you now, or are you still sleeping?"

"Yeah, right," laughed Steve. "I am still a little tired after last night."

"So be it, Carmichael. I still need you to get your little ass over to the OR and scrub with your favorite chief resident."

Steve was half listening and half trying to replay the code last night. One thing was for sure: he didn't need to be alongside Jake for the next four or five hours as he tried to figure things out. "Dr. Jenson, I am just not feeling well right now. Maybe someone else could scrub in this morning. After all, scrubbing for cases is a reward we earn as interns, and if I choose to relinquish that reward, that shouldn't be a problem. I'm just too tired today."

"That's okay, Steve," joked Tom Formin. "We know surgery residency is tough and it's not for everyone. So if you need to go to Mommy's for some chicken noodle soup, well, that's okay."

Tom Formin, the other junior resident, usually didn't say much, but when he did, it was usually not very complimentary. He was rude to interns, students, and anybody who was underneath him on the totem pole. If an attending came by, however, he would shower them silly with admiration.

"Fuck you, Formin." Steve pulled out a tissue. "Here. Why don't you wipe your nose? You got a little something there. Oh, wait a minute. What is that smell? Oh, I see, Formin. That is just a little shit left over from this morning's session of kiss the attending's butt!"

The entire group laughed uncontrollably, including Sally. Even Tom smiled, but his face became redder and redder.

"Alright, you two," Sally said as she tried to regain her composure. "Tom, why don't you go to the OR today? Steve, there are three discharges and two admits so far. Here is the list. Why don't you give me a call when you have those done?"

Although Steve was tired, the real issue was not fatigue. He was too preoccupied with the case from last night. He felt awake, but he had spent almost every minute thus far in the day rattling his brain about the code and why the young man died.

Steve had the medical students go to the OR with Tom so he could get the work done and still try to figure out why the guy died last night. Work even went a little quicker without the burden of medical students asking questions about this and that.

By about 1:30, Steve was done with all the floor work, including the admissions and discharges. He strolled into the cafeteria soon thereafter to sit down for a bite to eat. The place was almost empty except for the few people finishing their lunches. Steve paid little attention to the surroundings. He bought a sandwich and a Pepsi and then sat down to eat. As he chewed his food slowly, he seemed to be mesmerized by the lightly blowing trees.

"Boo!" shouted Erica as Steve was looking off into outer space.

"SHIT! What the hell are you trying to do, give me a heart attack? You must be bored today if you're creating medical situations just so you can have a few more patients."

"Shut up, Carmichael. I'm far from being bored. But *you* look like either you are either bored or extra tired from last night." She grinned. "I'm beginning to like you even more when you are sleep deprived."

Steve looked up and realized she was referring to this morning. He felt a sense of pleasure to know that she responded in such an accepting manner. He let her know with a slight smile.

He leaned back and said, "Actually I'm not so much tired as I am puzzled as to why this young guy coded in the OR last night during surgery. He basically died as quickly as he arrived. I know he was sick prior to surgery, but he should have made it through surgery and even survived the code. Something doesn't fit. I mean, this guy comes in from who-knows-where with a belly full of pus and shit, and then he dies. His tox screen is positive for coke, but he didn't respond to anything last night."

"Yeah, I heard. It seems to be the talk of the day. You know what the medical fleas are saying about it, don't you?"

"Not really."

"Well, since you surgeons were having trouble with the medical code, you should have just called one of us. We probably could have help save the guy's life."

Steve looked at her and stared for about half a minute. Then he smiled and shook his head. "I'll remember that next time I code a guy with a belly full of pus and all coked up. Thanks for the talk, but I need to get a few things done before I leave." He stood up. "And about this morning, uh, I was really tired, but I think that definitely should be followed up with another dinner sometime."

Erica turned a deep shade of red and smiled. "That would be great."

Steve turned around with a satisfied look and left the cafeteria. Just before he was out the door, he glanced back at Erica and saw her still red and watching him. He smiled, waved to her, and headed to the surgical nurses station.

On the way, he thought about asking Sally if he could leave early. He wasn't so physically tired, but this preoccupation with the case had really worn him down. He figured she would have to OK it with Jake first, but after all that Steve had done last night, he hoped Jake would give him a break.

Steve reached the station and logged onto the computer system to look up the pathology from last night.

As he began working, Sally came up from behind him. "Boo!"

"What the hell! Does everybody have it out for me or what? That is the second time today that somebody nearly gave me a heart attack!"

"Sorry there, big boy. I didn't realize it was such a popular thing to do. Are you looking up some labs?"

"No. I already did that, and they all look fine. The guy in room 204 has a UTI and probably on his way to getting Urinary Septicemia. I put him on some Levaquin." Steve continued, "No, what I need is to find that Path specimen from last night and see what the hell that mass was."

Steve pulled out a card from his pocket and began typing in the ID number for Ziamuddin. He waited a few minutes while the computer searched his file. Finally, a screen came up. "That's really weird. There is all his lab work but no path specimen."

"Steve, you sound really tired. I asked Jake at lunch, and he said it would be okay for you to head home after all your work is done. So scram, man!"

Steve looked at Sally, wanting to give her a big hug. "Thanks a lot, Sally. I really appreciate that and will take you up on that offer. I'll just call Pathology to see when the report will be complete from last night."

"That's great, and then get some rest!" said Sally.

Sally walked off, and Steve was even more perplexed. He reviewed the ID number that belonged to Ziamuddin and tried again to get his report on the path specimen. After several tries, Steve finally just called the Path Department and asked the receptionist to locate the abdominal mass from last night.

After a few minutes away from the phone, she came back on and said they never received a specimen from this patient.

"That's impossible," Steve said. "I took that out myself last night, and then Dr. Douglas ran it to the department. He took it right during the case, and then-"

"I'm sorry, Dr. Carmichael, but I have no record of anything coming in last night."

"Maybe it came in late, but you must have it by now."

"I'm sorry again, doctor, but I do not have it on my in-shelf now, and there is no record of it coming in! You might want to check with Dr. Douglas himself."

"Alright, fine. Thanks a lot!" Steve couldn't help the sarcasm dripping from his voice.

He sat staring at the computer screen, trying to figure things out. He remembered without a doubt that Jake had walked out of the OR suite with the mass in his hands. After the guy coded and Steve was so busy, he didn't actually see Jake come through the doors back into the OR. He just heard his voice. Maybe Jake didn't have time to make it all the way to the Path Department. But as they were cleaning up after and closing the patient, Steve vividly remembered Jake leaving without any specimen.

This was getting too weird. The more Steve thought about

it, the more frustrated he got. Maybe Sally was right. Maybe he just needed some sleep. He signed himself out of the computer, collected his items from the call room, and left.

As he walked out of the hospital, he was in such a daze trying to piece this all together that he failed to hear Erica say goodbye to him. By the time she ran to the doors, he was already almost to the parking lot. She watched Steve get into his car and drive away.

Chapter 27

Steve arrived home feeling totally exhausted. He went through the motions as always: first, he let Pudge out, then he let Pudge back in, fed Pudge, and then collapsed on the couch. The remote for the TV, though nearby, was not within hands' reach and consequently too far away this time. Steve rested his head softly on the back of the couch and gazed up at the ceiling.

He reviewed the last twenty-four hours, starting with when he had begged Jake to allow him to scrub on the case. After much pleading, he found himself in the OR operating on a guy no one knew anything about except that he was terribly sick. Jake seemed to be rather preoccupied himself. Although always cocky, there had been something strange about Jake's demeanor last night. This mass inside a body that had recently had surgery made everything more confusing. Steve tried to remember exactly what the mass looked like. The events of the code seemed to mask everything else that happened prior to and after it.

Steve went back to the thoughts about the mass. It was soft and compressible, but as he recalled pushing on it, no pus had come out of the mass itself. He remembered that the mass was covered with a thick layer of pus and stool and that the odor was horrific. As he tried to feel more of it, Jake pushed his own hands into the wound to quickly extract the mass. After that, Jake held on to it as if it was a favorite toy that he didn't want to share with anyone else.

Steve continued to reflect on the events of the day until he fell asleep on the sofa. He went quickly into a deep sleep with Pudge by his side. He slept for several hours until a beeping noise woke him up. He reluctantly opened his eyes, forcing one eye open and then slowly opening the other. He heard a beep again. He recognized the noise but was not sure from where it came. He had definitely been in a deep sleep because he initially thought he was waking up in the morning to head back to the hospital.

When both eyes were opened and functioning, he noticed the clock in the kitchen. 12:30. Either he was very late or it was the middle of the night. As he lifted his body from the couch, he glanced out the window and saw a pitch-dark sky. With a sense of relief, he made his way to his computer. He finally recognized the beeping to be that from his email messenger.

He opened his message board and found about ten messages from Sweetpea, all of them just saying hello or wondering why he hadn't showed up for the daily chat in the last few days. That was odd, he thought, because they always communicated via a private chatroom. He didn't recall giving her his email address. He always thought it would be the easier way to communicate with her but felt somewhat uncomfortable giving a stranger access to torment him. After so much communication with her, they had discussed exchanging email addresses and communicating via that route. But he was so tired now that he could not remember if he had actually given her his address.

Nonetheless, he wrote back. "Sorry I have not talked to you for so long, but I have been really busy at work…as always. Last night I had this young guy die on the operating room table. It really has bothered me the entire day. I hope it will be the last time that ever happens to me again."

Sweetpea replied, "I'm so sorry about that. I'm sure that you did your best to help him out. That is all you can really expect of yourself. Don't forget that you are human just like the rest of us. Sometimes you will have good outcomes, and unfortunately sometimes they will not be so good, but as long as you do your best, no one can ever fault you."

Steve always appreciated the way she made him feel okay even after a terrible day. Maybe that is why he chose to write back in the middle of the night. However, he was surprised to see her respond so quickly. It was as if she was waiting right there online to get the message and write back. Either way, she seemed to always find the right words to make him feel better. "I appreciate your kind comments. You always make me feel better. I knew there was a reason why I decided to write back in the middle of the night."

"Thanks. I don't mind at all. Sounds as if your days are a little more stressed than mine. So was that jerk of a chief with you last night? If he was, I bet he didn't really help matters much."

"Actually he was there, well, kind of. You see, we took out this mass from this kid and then Jake, my chief resident, took full responsibility to get the specimen over to pathology. It was while he was gone that the shit hit the fan and the young kid coded. He was really sick with a bad infection in his body, something we call sepsis. And then I think he went into septic shock and coded. I paged Jake back immediately, but we were well into reviving him – or at least trying to – when Jake came slamming back into the room."

Sweetpea was very interested. "It seems like this chief resident of yours is always evading his responsibilities. So what kind of mass was this? Was it like a tumor or cancer?"

"I don't really think so. The guy'd had surgery just a short while ago, and it looked as if it was an appendectomy. He probably had a leak after his appy and spilled stool into his belly after surgery. Things happened so fast that night because he was so sick that we don't know where he had surgery or where he was from. He was foreign and didn't seem to speak too much

English. Anyway, I think it was an abscess. But Jake grabbed the thing as if it was his long lost favorite toy. He swept it away and ran off to the path department with it."

"That is kind of weird. What did it look like? I mean, was it hard or soft? Was there a lot of gunk on it?"

"I can tell that you are not medically literate: GUNK? But to answer your question, it seemed somewhat soft and did have a lot of pus around it. But Jake literally took over the case once I exposed it. He just darted his hands into the wound as if to get there first and then snatched it and ran off. I will say it was kind of weird. Right before the guy coded, I thought I saw white powder in the wound. But as quickly as I saw it, the blood and pus in the wound covered whatever was there. It was strange."

"That is *really* strange. Do you think it was just something from his stomach? I mean, if you thought there was a leak, then maybe that was just food particles, right?"

"Actually if he leaked from where the appendix usually is connected to the colon, the food that he ingested was already digested once it reached the colon, so what leaked out was stool. And that is exactly what was in the belly, shit and a lot of it." Steve continued typing. "But what was really odd is that after the guy coded and died, I was closing, and the anesthesiologist and I were talking about the cause of his death and why he didn't respond to anything. I mean, he didn't respond to fluids *or* to drugs. It was the strangest thing in the world. So I decided to get a tox screen even though Jake didn't want me to."

"Why didn't he want you to?"

"I don't really know, but A.J. and I thought it would help try to figure why this kid didn't respond to any of the therapy. And as it turned out, he was full of coke…and it wasn't diet either."

Sweetpea stressed her curiosity. "Well what did the path

show? Did that report come back yet? That would probably shed some light on the matter."

"Exactly, it would probably give us a lot of information. The only problem is that the specimen is missing!"

"WHAT?! Where did it go? How can you lose a large mass like that?"

Steve tried to explain in his reply message. "I don't recall the events after the code that well, but I know for a fact that Jake ran off with the specimen to the Path Department immediately after he got the mass out. Then all I remember is that he returned when the guy was coding. I don't remember if he brought the specimen back with him to the OR suite. I need to ask him tomorrow. I just didn't get a chance to ask him today. After I discovered the path specimen wasn't in the computer system, I quickly called the Path Department, but they had no idea what I was talking about. They had absolutely no record of the specimen."

"You're right. That entire situation is weird. I hate to be abrupt, but I forgot that I need to get up early in the AM, so I've gotta go. I hope you have a better day tomorrow. And if I were you, I would not approach your chief on this one. I mean, if he asked you not to get the tox screen, then you don't want to piss him off by showing your insubordination. Stay good, stay safe, and watch your back."

Steve frowned at his screen. "Watch my back?"

"I mean watch out for those fellow residents. You never know what they are up to. Hey, I need to go. See ya."

Steve looked at the screen to see if there were any other messages. He thought to himself, *Watch my back? What the hell did she mean by that?* And why was she in such a hurry to log off?

Steve turned off his computer as he pondered those thoughts

and got ready for bed. He made sure his alarm was set and then climbed beneath the sheets. Lying in bed, he thought about her last statement and how fast she wanted to get off. It was like she waited all night to talk to him and then signed off as quickly as she could. That was just as weird as the previous day. Steve went to sleep hoping tomorrow would be a little less weird.

Chapter 28

Steve yawned as he entered the locker room. He needed more sleep last night, but talking to Sweetpea had kept him up longer than he had wanted. He promised himself not to talk that late at night post-call. It didn't matter if it was Sweetpea or the Queen of England, post-call was just not the right time to chat in the middle of the night.

He put his backpack in his locker, grabbed his lab coat, and quickly left to get to the ICU for rounds. The locker room for all the surgery interns and residents was located in the OR, which made perfect sense as they all had to change before operating. As he dashed past the main OR desk to get up the stairs, he saw Karla crying at the desk. He wanted to joke and ask if she was scheduled to scrub with Jake again, but he decided that would not show much tact. He did wonder what was wrong but didn't have the time to ask questions. Probably a bad night or some family issue. Steve didn't give it a second thought as he made his way to rounds.

He walked through the doors of the ICU, and his jaw dropped. He quickly looked at his watch to check the time. He checked the clock over the nurse's station to confirm that he had the correct time. Both read 5:45.

What startled Steve was the presence of Jake Douglas. "Good morning, Dr. Douglas. What a surprise to see you bright and early. Couldn't sleep last night? Or are you just starting a new thing by rounding with your team?" Steve realized what he had said and began to turn red. "Uh, sorry, Dr. Douglas. It just slipped out."

Jake laughed. "I know all about having words slip out of one's mouth. I didn't realize, Carmichael, that you too can fit your foot in your mouth so easily. Welcome to the club." With that, Jake gave Steve a nice slap on the back as if to congratulate him on his initiation to the whoops-I-shouldn't-have-said-that club.

Jake went about his business, and Steve followed suit. He visited each of the three patients in the ICU that morning to go over their labs. He reviewed the events during the night and looked for temperature spikes or any changes in their vital signs. He briefly discussed with them how they felt and if there were any problems. It was nice to have this information prior to formal rounds. However, this morning it seemed fruitless as Jake was already there, making rounds and checking everyone over himself.

Even odder than Jake's early appearance was that Sally had not arrived yet. She was almost always the first resident in the ICU to start looking over the patients. She was particular about the details of her patients, and even though she was not the chief resident, she still pushed herself to know everything about the patients, not to impress an attending but just to take good care of the patients. She felt it was her responsibility to manage the patients and make sure they got the appropriate medical treatment for their surgical problem.

The rounds in the ICU were routine, with the students writing down the labs for the morning and the residents and interns going over the patients. What was not routine was to see Sally come into the ICU late for rounds without prerounding.

Not only was she late: she looked as if she had been through a sleepless night with a drinking binge. When she finally arrived, her eyes were blood shot, and the skin below her eyelids was dark as if she had not slept for days. One could see where her mascara had bled down her cheek. Her nose was red and runny, and her eyes were swollen as if she had been crying.

The students didn't dare say a word, and Steve didn't feel as if this was the time or place to inquire about her appearance. Jake, on the other hand, had no problem asking personal questions. "So what the hell happened to you?"

Despite his lack of tact, Sally would have answered him if there wasn't a crowd around. Instead, she put her hands to her mouth and whispered, "Later."

She started to whimper, and Jake decided to not be an insensitive shit. He must have realized there was something serious going on. Sally, who was usually pretty strong, would not be so upset over something small. Jake let it go and did what he rarely had done since he was a resident himself: he led rounds. "Alright, then, let's get done with it. Carmichael, why don't you start going over Mr. Bettles and have one of the students write the progress note so we can get this done and over with?"

Steve did as he was told, and so did the students. Although it was unusual to have Jake around for morning rounds, he sure did pick the right morning to show up, with Sally unable to take charge. Rounds in the unit went well and quick. Soon the team headed out of the ICU and off to the surgical floors to see other patients.

Jake fell behind when Tom Formin finally showed up and began to pick up the slack. He motioned to the others to follow. As they did, Jake and Sally slowed down to talk in private.

Steve was curious what was wrong. He tried to put the pieces of the puzzle together. First Karla and now Sally, upset and in tears. This couldn't be a coincidence. Steve never saw the two of them together for lunch or snacks and didn't believe they were close friends, so it was very strange that they were both upset this morning.

He slowed down to hear the conversation. At first, all he

could make out was Sally crying as she tried to talk to Jake. He continued to listen carefully and was able to pick up a few thoughts.

"Did you hear the awful news? I just can't believe it," exclaimed Sally.

"What? I didn't hear a thing."

"The OR called A.J. this morning because he was unusually late. His wife answered the phone and was totally hysterical. She had heard the alarm clock go off, but A.J. never turned it off. She just figured that he was sound asleep. So she rolled over him to turn the alarm off and he…" Sally whimpered a little and then cleared her throat as if to become stronger. "That's when she discovered his body was stiff as a board." Sally cried for a few seconds before finishing the story. "Apparently he had a heart attack during the night. Never felt a thing, he just went in his sleep."

Jake was shocked. "Shit! I just did a case with him the other night. Not once did he let us know that he was having any trouble. I can't believe that guy could have died! He was in great shape, not to mention that he was so young. I don't think he was past his mid-fifties. Well, at least he went in his sleep. That is definitely the way we all should die. I'm really sorry to hear about that, Sally. If you need to take the day off…"

Steve hurried ahead. He had heard enough. It made him sick to his stomach. That certainly explained all the tears in the OR this morning. He couldn't believe it either. A.J. was in great physical shape and never really complained about anything. Steve recalled a 36-year-old patient from his medicine rotation that needed cardiac bypass surgery, but that guy had terrible genes with lots of heart trouble in his family history, so he was doomed to have heart problems too. Maybe that was the trouble with A.J. He could have had high cholesterol or a family history of heart conditions. Steve wondered if that was why he was always working out and in such great shape. Either way, it was a terrible event that shook the entire OR Department and staff.

Steve caught up with the rest of his team by the time they reached the surgical floor. By the time they began reviewing the chart of the first patient, Jake had caught up with them as well. Sally was not with him.

They finished rounds in record time, and the students along with Steve and Tom Formin headed to the cafeteria for breakfast. Jake went on to the OR to check on the cases. He spoke a few minutes with Tom and then left. The others got their food and coffee and sat down. They started with small talk, but then one of the students asked where Jake and Sally were.

Tom had been on call last and was still too sleepy to pick up on anything, so Steve stepped up to inform them of the current events. "I don't know if this is supposed to be made public yet, but I'm sure it will get out sooner than later. Last night A.J., the anesthesiologist, died in his sleep. It has kind of freaked everyone out here. I guess Sally took it really hard, so Jake offered her the day off."

Tom had a total look of surprise and disbelief written on his face. He knew A.J. well, and they even had gone boating several times to enjoy a shared love of water skiing. "I can't believe it," Tom said. "That guy was in great shape. I never heard him complain at all about any angina or other problems." He sat back, shaking his head in denial.

Steve answered some other questions from the group as best he could. By the time he was finished, Jake walked solemnly up to the table. "I don't know if you guys have heard, but A.J. died last night unexpectedly. That has really set the OR and Anesthesia Departments into a tailspin. And because of that, the OR manager has decided to cancel all elective surgery cases.

What that means for you slugs is that we will have a sweet day."

Jake continued, "Tom, since you didn't get much sleep last night and you're post-call, why don't you take the day off? We will see you in the ICU for rounds in the A.M. Steve, I'll have you take care of the floor with the boys here." He waved at the two medical students. "At about three or four o'clock, make afternoon rounds. You can do that on your own since there won't be any fresh OR patients. If you have any questions, just contact me on my pager. I already sent Sally home because she was so distraught about the events of last night. Any questions?"

Steve chimed in, "What if new patients come in from the ER?"

"That shouldn't be an issue today because the other surgery service is taking call tonight."

Steve nodded. "Okay."

Tom scooted his chair backward and took off without further questions. Jake walked off too without adding anything else. Steve stayed with the students at a table, discussing morning rounds and delegating what needed to be done.

The three of them split up to get everything done. Steve told the others to check in with him when the work was done. If everything looked okay, he planned to send them home early. He could make evening rounds by himself.

The day went without a hitch. The students got their work done by two o'clock. They reported to Steve to discuss what they had done and any other issues that needed to be covered. As promised, Steve let them have the afternoon off. He took the opportunity to hit the medical library for some quiet reading. He didn't feel right about signing out the patients so early since usually they wouldn't sign out patients until eight or nine at night.

Steve rarely had time to just sit and read while at the hospital, so he took full advantage of this unfortunate event. As he settled in with a stack of books, he thought about A.J. and how he was just with him the other night doing the case with Jake. Steve had seen a number of people die since he had been an intern, but to lose someone you knew was a different feeling. Besides that, A.J. seemed so young and healthy. Steve wondered if A.J. had been having angina or if his cholesterol was elevated and not treated. He was searching for some logical explanation as to why A.J. had died so young.

Between wondering about A.J. and his death and trying to study, the free time flew by. Steve looked up at the time and found it was almost five o'clock. He felt that this would be a reasonable time to make rounds and leave. Rounds went flawlessly with no one for Steve to answer to. He wished it could be that easy every time. After rounds, he signed off his patients and left. It was a very strange day indeed.

Chapter 29

An unusual few days followed as everyone in surgery and anesthesiology were trying to get back on track. Life in the OR was solemn, but everybody did the best they could to get over the tragic sudden death of A.J. People greeted each other with a slight smile and nod of their heads. The nurses and scrub techs went through the motions of the day, but they really weren't there. Everyone was thinking about A.J., or thinking about their own lives: their children, their parents, their grandparents or their friends. The tragedy affected so many people that dealt with death and dying on a daily basis but now had an unfortunate chance to experience it firsthand.

Sally returned to the team after taking an extra day off to collect her thoughts. She looked well rested, but she didn't really speak unless spoken to. She didn't offer any smiles or hellos. She just saw her patients and reported to Jake. At breakfast in the cafeteria, when Sally would usually delegate the day's responsibilities, Jake stepped in and assigned duties to the students and interns. For the early days surrounding A.J.'s death, Sally and Tom would exclusively go to the OR, and no one questioned it.

Steve worked with the students on the floor, and if he had extra free time, he used it to his advantage for studying. All in all, things were slowly getting back to normal. A.J.'s wife decided to have his funeral the third day after his death. This seemed somewhat quick, but no one asked any questions. Steve didn't attend because he didn't really know A.J. that well, but Sally and Tom attended because they had worked with him longer.

The OR was shut down except for emergencies on the day

of his funeral. Steve and the students covered the service again, but the number of patients had been getting smaller. It was no big deal for the three of them to take care of all the work.

Steve was not sure if Jake was going to return to the hospital that night, but they were on call together. Although the chief residents were not required to spend the night in the hospital while on call, most of them did. In fact, Jake was the only chief on the staff who would take a chance and go home. If anything serious came in, he would rush into the hospital.

The night started off quietly for the surgery team on call. The mood seemed subdued, especially in the operating rooms. Steve had to see two patients with abdominal pains in the Emergency Room. He discussed these cases with Jake, and to no surprise, Jake elected to admit the patients and observe them. He would rarely operate on a possible appy or belly pain unless their white count was sky high or they had free air in their abdomen, which was usually a sign that there was a perforation somewhere in the abdomen. It was a quiet night until about midnight when a trauma code was announced over the loud speakers and over the pagers of the entire surgery call team, including Steve's.

When a trauma code was called, the complete surgery team on call would have to show up in the ER to help run the code and stabilize the patient. If necessary, they would take the patient up to the OR to complete surgery. For this reason, the OR team had to be on call from the hospital. An entire OR crew had to be ready to go at any time.

Unfortunately for Jake, when a trauma code was called and he was the chief resident on call, he would have to speed into the hospital in order to help out. This usually was not a bother for the OR crew unless Jake was having a beer or some other tasty beverage because he would need to spend a few minutes trying to sober up before heading into the hospital. This might translate in to the chief resident showing up late to the code or, worse yet, showing up drunk. Although Jake was irresponsible a great deal of the time, he rarely showed up to the hospital intoxicated.

Steve rushed to the ER, imagining several dramatic scenarios. He was sure to include a scenario that involved working by himself with no one else there to help run the code or the trauma. He was beginning to feel rather confident with what he could handle by himself, but he was not ready to handle a trauma by himself. The first thing he did when he made his way to the ER was to search for the chief resident.

Jake was nowhere to be found.

Steve saw the pre-trauma commotion. The nurses were trying to get the IV tubing situated and organizing the airway management equipment, including an endotracheal tube. Someone else was getting the paperwork together, including the orders and flow sheet for the trauma.

Steve continued to look for Jake. As the estimated time of arrival for the ambulance drew closer, the chief resident was nowhere to be found. Steve knew the ER doctor would be able to manage the trauma, but if a chest tube needed placement, he would be in a bind. Steve wondered if an ER doc would be able to help with a deep peritoneal lavage if that became necessary. The intern had seen all these procedures performed in the past but never had to tackle this alone.

A few short months ago, Steve would have panicked knowing he might be on this trauma alone, but he knew a third or fourth year surgery resident would be around soon. Even if no one showed up, Steve felt he could do any of the procedures necessary to stabilize the patient. Just then, everyone heard the ambulance rig pull up. Steve grabbed a face shield and gloves and then ran outside.

No sooner did Steve make it through the doors than Jake appeared out of nowhere. They almost collided as Steve was on his way out to meet the victim on the ambulance. "Glad you could join us, Dr. Douglas. I thought maybe you were going to skip town on us at this crucial moment."

Jake smiled as if he had cracked a joke to himself, "Now, now, Dr. Carmichael. I would never let you sink on your own, though I know without a doubt that you would be able to handle most anything that would come into the ER."

They continued out to the rig. On the gurney was a person lying limp on the backboard, moaning but not moving. The person's face, shirt, and pants were covered with blood. One shoe was missing, and the remaining one was covered with blood and glass.

Steve noticed the lack of IV tubing and fluid. "Hey, why don't you guys have any fluid running?"

"You gotta be kidding, rookie!" one of the paramedics said with a condescending tone. "We just scoop and run with these babies. You big doctors can fix them all up here." The two paramedics laughed as they took the gurney out of the ambulance. The condescending paramedic continued talking to Steve. "Alright, rookie. We have a very nice but unfortunate woman who was minding her own business driving some place when some asshole T-boned her. Probably some drunk shithead. He probably doesn't even know what happen. We just scooped her up and ran. She has just been moaning since we got her into the rig. She has a thready pulse, and her systolic was never more than the 90s. Her breathing is almost absent." He saluted. "Good luck, boys and girls."

Steve looked up. He hadn't realized that they were already in the trauma cell. Some people thought of it as the stabilizing room, but that's what the surgery interns referred to as the trauma room. Since the surgery interns got dumped on so much, especially during the traumas, they perceive the trauma experience as a life sentence without parole.

"One, two, three, and go," said a charge nurse.

Everyone took a hold of the backboard and lifted the unfortunate patient to a center table. The hustle of a trauma code started.

"Ok, Carmichael," said Jake. "What is the first thing we need to do in this situation?"

Steve didn't hesitate. "Primary survey," he shouted as the noise level continued to escalate.

"Go on, Dr. Carmichael."

"The first thing is airway, and then breathing."

"So what about it?" asked Jake.

"Well, her breaths are pretty shallow."

"Pretty shallow?" shouted Jake, "She is barely breathing, Carmichael! My cat snores louder than that. What should we do?"

"She needs to be intubated."

"Then let's rock, or you are going to lose her, not that she has much of a chance," Jake bellowed pessimistically.

"Get me a 71/2 tube and the rapid sequence intubation kit, and give ten of succnicoline and-"

"Steve!" shouted Jake. "She is about to arrest. I don't think she will give a flying shit if you stick that tube into her trachea. She may, in fact, appreciate that you are saving her life. Let's go!"

Steve grabbed the laryngoscope and began to slide the narrow plastic tube into the patient's airway. He stopped for a moment just before forcing the tube down into the lung. "Hey, ma'am, can you move your legs for me? Can you move your arms for me?" He could see her attempting to move. She did make a slight motion with both her arms, but her legs never moved. "Alright, let's be careful. She may have a cervical injury. Jake, stabilize her head!"

"Good going, Carmichael. Way to plan ahead. It's nice to know what kind of neuro status she may have prior to paralyzing her."

Steve continued to intubate her. "Suction!" he shouted.

Her face and hair were covered with blood. The scent of dried blood was like the smell of a drunk after puking a pint of liquor. Steve tried to ignore it the best he could. He and Jake were careful so as not to move the head around too much just in case there was a cervical neck fracture. However, blood was obstructing her vocal cords. The suction was used to help clear the blood in order to help provide a clearer view of the cords, thus enabling the tube to glide in the correct spot between the two vocal cords instead of sliding down into the esophagus.

After Steve placed the tube and felt he was in the correct place, the respiratory therapist gave a few breaths with the ambu bag. The CO2 monitor read about forty-two, which was normal and confirmed that indeed the breathing tube was in the airway.

"Nice going, Carmichael. What's next?"

Steve asked loudly, "Who has the pressure?"

A small voice was sounded from the corner where a nurse was documenting everything. "86 over 40, and her pulse is 125."

Steve continued, "Let's get two bags of LR hanging wide open. This lady is in shock! Let's get some trauma labs drawn including an ABG. Where is X-ray? We need a C Spine Chest and Pelvic X-ray." He glanced at Jake.

"Doing good, Carmichael. I think we should get four units typed and crossed and start giving universal donor blood. I agree that she is in shock, and she no doubt is bleeding aggressively somewhere, maybe her pelvis or chest. Let's start using blood as volume. Steve, what about the Primary Survey? Where are we?"

"We are getting ready to expose and look for any external injuries and neuro deficits."

"Good," said Jake, "but you missed something major."

Steve focused on his actions thus far. He could not think of what Jake had in mind. "I'm not sure what you are-"

Jake interrupted him. "You got this lady intubated with good CO2 levels, but we have not listened to her."

While Steve and Jake were carrying on their conversation, the x-ray tech was taking pictures. Neither doctor paid attention to the fact that they both were unprotected from the x-rays without lead aprons.

Steve acknowledged the breathing issue. He pulled a stethoscope off a nurse and listened to the patient's chest wall.

"Shit. I don't hear anything!" Steve shouted frantically.

"I gathered as much." Jake smiled. "The left side of her chest is not moving with inspiration. She may have a tension pneumo. That might even be why she has a low BP and is tachyardic. Let's get a chest tube in and see what that does to her vitals. How are you with chest tubes, Carmichael?

Have you done any yet?"

Steve thought about lying but knew that risked killing her. "I have assisted on a few, but I have not yet had the chance to do one solo."

"You assist in surgery, Carmichael, but you have either put a tube in or not."

Steve replied honestly, "Not."

"Alright, Steve. Let's get going. Someone get the chest tube tray and get the chest tube reservoir set up, NOW! Steve, get your gloves on and rock!"

Steve didn't wait. His gloves and gown were on in a few seconds, and Jake handed him the materials he needed. Steve knew the patient's injuries were serious and life threatening. He almost felt that Jake should put the tube in quickly and then they could continue to assess her, but he didn't have the chance to voice his thoughts. It was time to place the tube.

"What size tube do you want, Carmichael?"

Steve responded without hesitation. "A 40-French so we can evacuate both air and blood that maybe in the plerual space."

"Perfect, Steve. So here is your tube." Jake pulled a chest tube from the drawer and opened a 40-French tube.

Steve was motionless as the tube was opened for him. He realized that Jake was not gloving up. He was on his own for this one.

"Aren't you gloving for this?" he asked, just to be sure.

"I told you before, rookie, no assisting for chest tubes. Get a move on it, or this lady is going to code!"

Steve took the tube and turned toward the patient. He stared for a long moment before he began painting her left chest with betadine. His heart was racing, and he could feel every beat. As he reached for the sterile towels to drape the patient, he could see his hand shake uncontrollably. He knew that it was just the adrenaline running through his body. He grabbed a syringe in order to draw some Lidocaine to numb the skin before making the incision.

"What are you doing, Carmichael? She is about to code! Believe me, she won't feel the knife. She is somewhere between here and heaven, so let's move!" shouted Jake.

Steve took a 15-blade knife, and at the nipple level in the mid axillary line, he made a 2cm incision. He then dissected the tissue and muscle above the rib.

Jake was correct: she did not so much as flinch with these maneuvers.

As Steve continued with the chest tube, Jake managed the trauma code. He walked over to the x-ray view box and looked at the chest x-ray as the tech was putting it up. “Shit, Carmichael, you better hurry up. There is a total collapse of the left lung. Move, move, move!” Jake looked over his shoulder at Steve who was slowly dissecting the muscle off the top aspect of the rib. “Come on, Steve. Just pop the damn clamp through the muscle superior to the rib!”

Steve looked up at Jake and back at the clamp.

“Steve, let’s go! This should only take a second. She is about to crash and burn.”

Steve took the clamp, felt the rib, and pushed gently to the top of the rib. Then he pushed hard, but nothing happened. He leaned into it with his force of his body and felt finally a pop. He carefully spread the clamp. The entire room heard the loud rush of air as the tension was released.

Everyone shouted to congratulate Steve on his first chest tube.

“Good going, Carmichael,” said Jake. “Let’s see what her BP jumps up to. Who’s got the BP responsibilities tonight?”

One of the nurses alongside the patient was taking a manual BP. “100 over 50, doctor.”

“Okay, Steve, what else can we do for this lady? Her pressure is still sagging. I don’t think the tension pnemo is her only problem. What do you think, pal?”

Steve tried to provide the right answer. “She probably has some serious internal bleeding going on. Maybe we should do a DPL to see if there is free blood.”

“No doubt, Carmichael. While we get the DPL kit, what

next? Is there anything else we can do to get that pressure up?"

Steve had a thousand questions whirring through his mind. *What about the pressure? What about the peritoneal lavage they were about to set in motion? What kind of neuro trauma had she suffered that she is not responding to barely any stimuli?* The list of concerns continued. "Well, she needs volume, and if the blood is not here yet, then I would just pour in Lactated Ringers."

"Good," said Jake. "How are we doing for blood?"

"Dr. Douglas, blood is on the way from the blood bank, but we have a problem, sir."

"What now?" he demanded.

"We can't get another line in her. She must be so volume depleted that all her veins are flat."

Jake faced Steve again. "Alright, Carmichael. We only have one line. What the hell do you want to do next? Don't just think, Carmichael! She doesn't have the time. What is next?"

Steve took charge and shouted, "Someone grab me a central line kit pronto!" He stepped up to the patient's left side to start on that side for central line placement. With his bloody gloves, he tore the woman's blouse on the left side of her chest in order to do a sterile prep and drape of the shoulder and neck. Steve was so aggressive that he tore the entire sleeve off.

Jake gasped.

Steve was set on autopilot and took an extra moment with the other OR crewmembers to register disbelief. The room became quiet for what appeared to be an eternity but lasted only a few short seconds.

One of the nurses was busy calculating the chest tube suction when she realized the slight pause in the high-energy activity. As she glanced at the bare left arm, she cried, "Oh my God. It can't be! Oh shit, it just can't be!"

On the patient's upper arm was a tattoo of a pink and white dove. It was the most recent tattoo that Karla in the OR had painted on her left arm.

"Give me a wet towel, now!" yelled Jake.

As the doctor began to wash off the blood from the woman's face, the OR nurse began to scream. "Oh, shit, it just can't be. Not again, damn it!" She dropped the chest tube device and left the room sobbing.

"Alright people, let's keep it together. This looks like our patient is Karla, but let's keep it going. We have to. We have to for Karla. Steve, keep that idea of the central line going. Let's prep, and I'll give you a hand with this central line. On second thought, why don't you let me put this line in?

I'll promise you the next one."

Steve was relieved. "That sounds like an excellent idea." He quickly backed up.

Jake moved up to Karla's left side and started to place a central line in her subclavian vein.

A voice from the foot of the bed announced a dramatic change in the vital signs. "Oh shit, her pulse is beginning to drop. Oh shit, there she goes. Doctor, she is down to the thirties."

"Alright, alright," Jake replied. "Go ahead and give her-"

"Doctor, she just went into Vtach. Oh shit, make that Vfib!"

Jake shouted, "Steve, go ahead and start chest compressions." He looked at another nurse to rattle off more orders. "Let's give a hundred of Lido and charge at 200. Where the hell is the blood? Damn it!" He ordered a third nurse to go check on the blood. "CLEAR!" Jake shouted. He waited a second to allow people helping around the bed to drop what they were doing and step back from the table.

A small clicking sound was heard, and Karla's limp body

sprung up off the bed a few centimeters. Her arms flailed with the jolt of electricity that flowed through her body, but no solid pulse was noted on the screen. Just evidence of Vfib with a squiggly line for a pulse.

"Recharge up to 360 joules. Let's go! Let's go, people!" Jake shocked her again but nothing changed. The EKG on the monitor just showed a flat line. "Damn it!" shouted Jake. "Alright, let's get a chest tray NOW. We have to crack her chest. Someone put an NG down." Jake looked at Steve, "An NG will go into her esophagus and help us delineate the esophagus versus the aorta. Since there is no heartbeat now, the aorta will feel just like a hollow viscous. The NG will help determine which is esophagus and which is the aorta. Then we can clamp the aorta and stop the ongoing internal bleeding that is presumed to be causing her shocky state."

Steve listened and took mental notes.

"Let's give an amp of epi! Where the hell is the ches tray, people?" Jake was shouting orders as fast as people could get them done, but the fact of the matter was that Karla was quickly losing ground. Everyone knew it.

"Dr. Douglas, are you sure you want to crack her chest?" The voice was familiar to the surgery residents. Agusta, the ICU nurse, was there helping with the trauma code. "I mean, seriously Jake, she has been here for about thirty minutes with barely any perfusion to her organs. Are you really going to improve her life, or are you trying to make yourself feel better about this terrible accident?" Agusta put her hand gently on his shoulder.

"She is screwed either way, but her only chance for surviving this is to crack her chest and get that aorta clamped. Then I can get her to the OR and-"

One of the other nurses quickly interrupted Jake's attempts

at justifying his plans. “Dr. Douglas, she is flat line. She has had one amp of epi and a hundred of lido, not to mention several shocks.”

Jake looked up at the monitors and saw the flat line. “Try another amp of epi and a milligram of Atropine. Charge me up again to 360.” It was as if Jake was ignoring the pleas of the nurses to let this poor young lady go. “CLEAR!”

Yet another shock of electricity was delivered through the paddles on Karla’s chest. Her body sprung up as it had before, but the attempt was futile. She was still in asystole.

Jake looked up at the monitor and then down at Karla. He didn’t move for about a minute before glancing at the clock. “Unless someone objects, we’ll call the code at 12:34 A.M.”

The room was silent. Not one person made a vocal objection. One of the nurses disconnected the Ambu bag and the leads to the monitor. Another nurse took a wet cloth and began washing the blood off Karla’s limp body. Yet another person was finishing her charting. People were slowly picking up their tasks but not saying much.

Agusta approached one of the police officers who was standing near the trauma cell. “Hey, have any of you nice boys located kin nearby?”

“We have not made contact with anyone from her home. We will stop by in a few minutes. We are trying to get some information on the vehicle before we tell her family. As it stands, we probably have a drunken guy who seemed to have fled after the accident. His car just reeks of alcohol. And the real bizarre catch to this whole mess is that there are no plates or license for the car. Right now, I don’t even know where the car is from, not to mention who was driving it.”

Steve was leaning against the counter nearby, listening to the entire conversation and becoming just as confused as

Agusta.

"Well," Agusta blurted out, "if you don't have the plates or the driver, can't you get the serial number on the car and trace the records that way?"

One of the officers answered, "Why, yes, we can, ma'am. The only problem is that the serial number of the vehicle, the engine, and some of the car's insides are all missing. Very strange indeed. But before we go over to Karla's home and make contact with her family, we would like to have some more concrete information. Right now, I can't tell them jack shit."

Steve continued to listen to the conversation. *Why were the police unable to trace the car that took Karla's life?* He straightened up and headed back to the center of the trauma cell to help clean. As he worked, he played back most of that conversation, trying to piece together some of the missing links. Where was the driver? Was he hurt? How did he manage to leave the scene, and why was the car untraceable? These were some serious questions that needed to be answered. The more Steve thought about it, the happier he was about being a doctor instead of a detective.

Chapter 30

Steve kicked the door shut with his right foot and made his way to the couch. He collapsed onto it with his carryout dinner. Pudge realized his owner was home and rushed up to greet him. Steve quickly found a place for his dinner a safe distance from the jaws of Pudge. Then he took a moment to play with his dog. He appreciated the moment of unconditional affection.

After a brief welcoming from the dog, Steve heard his computer signal that it had a message for him. More than likely it was Sweetpea, and Steve couldn't ignore the need to talk with someone tonight. He had worked most of the day on the floor with the patients, but after lunch, Jake had decided to let the entire team head home except for Sally, who was on call. Steve spent the afternoon reading and sleeping. It was very difficult to study post call, especially after such an exhausting and mentally draining call night. Karla and A.J. invaded his thoughts throughout day. As hard as he tried, he couldn't get the vision of Karla and her dove out of his mind.

Steve didn't know many personal details about Karla, but he knew that she had family in the area and that she was well liked by all the staff. Without a doubt, many would miss her. Then there was A.J., who had just been buried a day earlier. Steve went back and forth, thinking about A.J. and his family and Karla and her loved ones. It was driving Steve crazy. He looked for Erica today at the hospital, but they hadn't crossed paths. He almost felt like paging her to talk but realized that it might mean taking her away from rounds. He really didn't know her well enough to pull her away from her duties at the hospital. Nonetheless, he was hurting and mourning for people he really didn't know that well and felt the need to get some thoughts off his chest. Chatting with Sweetpea tonight would be a relief.

He got up and let Pudge out as usual. Then he grabbed a beer and sat in front of the computer with his dinner. He logged on and answered his email, which was from Sweetpea. He told her to go to their chatroom so they could converse at a normal pace rather than slowly exchange emails. She showed up in their private chatroom immediately, as if she was waiting for him. It seemed like she has been there more and more, just waiting for him.

They said their hellos, and then Steve could not contain himself. He really needed to express his concerns about the recent week. "You wouldn't believe the last few days at the hospital. There has been so much going on, I can't believe it. It is like I am in this soap opera of dramatic events." Steve paused typing to let Pudge in and feed him.

When he returned to the computer screen, Sweetpea had responded with exclamation, "LIKE WHAT?"

"Sorry, I had to let my dog in and feed him," Steve typed. "A couple of days ago this anesthesiologist died in his sleep. He was really a great guy. Everyone just loved working with him and shooting the breeze with him. He was so laid back and mellow. I don't think there was a soul he would hurt, and most everyone that met him instantly liked him. It was so weird. I just can't believe he died." Steve paused for a bite of his sandwich.

Sweetpea responded quickly. "Well, people do die. What exactly happened? Do you know?"

Steve started typing with both hands, his sandwich balanced, hanging out of his mouth. He felt as if he couldn't waste a minute before responding. His fingers hit the keypad and started rattling off words. "That is the weird-ass thing about this. I mean this guy was pretty young, in his fifties I think, with a nice family. He was in great shape. I mean, the guy worked out every day, and sometimes on the weekends he would do triathlons and still have the energy for kayaking for several hours. No one ever expected a heart condition for this stellar guy in excellent condition." He took a break to tear off another chunk of his sandwich.

"Go on. This does sound strange. Did the guy do coke or any other drugs?"

"I really doubt it. I know he pushed gas during surgery, but never did anyone suspect any wrongdoing. I don't know if a drug tox screen was done, but I really doubt that he was a druggy. He just wasn't the type."

"No, he doesn't sound like the typical guy riding high all the time."

Steve added, "And that's not the entire story. A day after his funeral, last night, we got called for this trauma. My chief took his usual shit-ass slow time getting in for the code. And then he treated it like this major teaching case and was explaining everything to me and letting me basically run the code and do the procedures."

Sweetpea asked, "What is wrong with that? Isn't that what you have been begging for, to do a bunch of procedures?"

"Yeah, that would be the ideal situation, but unfortunately it wasn't until the lady was about to die that we realized she was one of the scrub nurses from the OR. It took us all by surprise, especially the people from the OR who responded to the trauma code. We were just in shock. And I think Jake felt like shit for letting me run the entire code. Of course, he couldn't know who she was because her face was all bloody. We didn't discover who it was until I pulled her sleeve down to get a central line, and then we all recognized her dove tattoo. We all just froze as we processed who she was and the shape she was in. It just freaked us all."

"SHIT!" Sweetpea responded. "I can't believe the terrible luck you all have had in the OR. Tell me, do you know if she was close with the anesthesiologist? I mean, did they have an affair?"

"I really don't think so. A.J. was a pretty dedicated husband and father from what people tell me. And besides that, it would be difficult to conceal a relationship like that in an operating room. Everyone knows everyone's business. It is really kind of sad but true. I mean, you know which nurse goes out with what resident, etc. I just don't think they were an item."

"Did they work a lot together?" Sweetpea continued her interrogation, which was a bit annoying. Steve wanted to vent his feelings, and she was grilling him on the details of the events of the last few days.

"Frankly we all work together. There are weeks they are in the same room constantly and then sometimes they might not be in on a case together for days. For example, just the other day before the anesthesiologist died, she scrubbed with us on that foreign guy who died during surgery. But I'm not done. There is more to this weird story."

Steve continued to type. "After Jake pronounced the scrub nurse Karla dead, I was cleaning up the trauma suite and took a break near the door. I leaned across a counter and overheard one of the nurses talking with the police officers. Apparently, they couldn't find the driver, who was presumed to be drunk. They said the car that had hit Karla just smelled like a kegger. And that the car had no license plates. Then the nurse asked about the serial number, and the officers said they couldn't find any on the car, the engine, or on any other part of the vehicle. That is really weird."

"Hey, I am so sorry, but I need to go now. That does all sound really freaky. And you're right. There are too many unanswered questions. I am so sorry to hear about your friends, but something just came up over here, and I need to go quickly. Please promise me to be careful. It sounds like working in surgery is a dangerous place these days. I will talk to you really soon, maybe even later tonight if you want. But I need to ask you a question and please do your best to remember a few nights ago. Who else was in the OR with you guys when you operated on the foreign kid that died?"

"I have to say that you sign off as quickly as you appear on my screen lately. But that night, it was late and just the OR crew that was on call scrubbed on the case. It was A.J. and Karla, of course, and me. Then I think Sue was the Scrub Tech, and Jake, my chief, was with us. Yeah, that was the crew. Why? What do you care?"

Sweetpea tried to rush off. "I can't explain now, but please be careful at the hospital and at home. It really sounds strange, but I hope there isn't a pattern to all this. It all may be coincidental, but don't take any chances…always watch your back. Talk to you soon."

Steve knew not to try to find her from his last experience. Once she signed off, she was gone. Steve had forgotten about his sandwich. He sat back and slowly finished his dinner with Pudge at his side.

Steve thought about the last few days, and he thought about recent conversations with Sweetpea. Everything was very screwed up, but he knew he was too tired tonight to come up with the all the answers. He finished his beer and closed his eyes. He started thinking of more relaxed moments when life was not so hectic and confusing, when he didn't have to take call and have all this responsibility. He remembered days when he and his family would go camping. They camped almost every summer up north, usually in the Boundary Waters of Minnesota. There they would canoe, kayak, fish, swim, and just enjoy the great outdoors. At night, they would relax with a campfire. If the weather cooperated, they would take their sleeping bags out of their tents and sleep under the stars. As Steve was about to fall asleep, he thought how wonderful those times were, especially without any responsibility. He had a sweet smile on his face as he drifted to sleep.

Chapter 31

Steve was afraid to go to work after talking with Sweetpea. She was making him paranoid. The first day after Karla died was terrible. He looked all around everywhere he went. He wasn't sure what he was looking for, but he felt as if there was something that needed to be noticed before something else bad happened.

He was wondering if anybody else saw him being so weird. He felt completely paranoid. He would get to his car and look around and then get into his car and look around and then park his car and look around. What did she mean by telling him twice to watch his back? He wasn't exactly sure, but he knew he didn't want to find out.

The surgery staff and crew were just beaten down. There were so many tears and sad faces. Jake felt bad about treating the code as if it were just some drunk in another MVA. He walked around in a trance most of the day after Karla's death. The next day he didn't speak to anyone except the staff doctors about their patients. Nobody seemed to pick at each other. Jake wasn't yelling at the interns or other residents, and the staff was much more cordial to Jake than Steve could ever recall.

The OR was very quiet, and few cases were added to the schedule. The elective cases that were already scheduled got done, but the surgeons tried to hold off on add-ons. Meanwhile, the medical students and residents enjoyed the lull in activity that provided extra time to read or study. Steve's team had just a few patients on the floor, and the floor work was completed in record time.

Steve was on his way to the library to study before evening rounds. He had checked with Sally and Tom, and they had no problem with it. As he made his way through the corridors of the hospital, he continued to think about the last week's trauma and bizarre conversations with Sweetpea. It was like a terrible dream from which he couldn't wake.

He heard the clunking of shoes get louder behind him. As was his new habit, he quickly looked back as if someone was going to attack him.

"Hey, Steve. How ya doing?" asked Erica.

"Shit! Don't do that!"

"Do what?"

Steve clarified, "Don't keep coming up like that from behind me. That's what!"

"Sorry, Steve. Maybe you have been watching too many scary movies. You should spend more of your time off studying than renting paranoia movies. Where are you heading?"

"I was just about to go in the creepy basement and sit in the dark for a while. Perhaps you'd like to join me?" he replied in a creepy tone.

"Funny. Very funny." She sobered. "I am really sorry to hear about the sad news in the OR department. They have had a bad week. The news is all over the hospital. What a strange coincidence to have such terrible news from one department! Are you okay?"

"Actually, now that you ask, I don't think so. I have been totally freaked out and can't stop thinking about everything. I mean, I try to, but the vision of Karla keeps haunting me, and then the fact that A.J. had an MI. It is all too weird! I tried to talk to a friend online last night, but all she did was ask a lot of questions and then freaks me out by telling me to watch my back." He made a face. "As you can tell, I am doing exactly what she told me to do. The only problem is that I think I am becoming paranoid."

Erica offered a comforting tone. "Well, I'm sure your friend had your best interest in mind. You know, I tried to say goodbye the other night when you left, but you were in such a daze that you didn't even notice."

"Sorry. It was not anything personal. I've just been a little preoccupied."

"That is certainly understandable. Maybe we should get together soon and hang out."

"Are you asking me out, Erica?"

She smiled. "I guess so, for sympathy's sake. I just feel bad for you and not for any other reason. Besides, I got tired of waiting for *you* to call *me* and make plans." They both laughed. "I'll give you a call sometime, but I need to run now. You know us fleas and our rounding on patients."

As Erica walked away, Steve thought about continuing toward the library. It was difficult for him to collect his thoughts in a civilized manner. Every time he thought about Karla and what Sweetpea had said, he would find himself down a scary road of bad possibilities. He knew with the way he was preoccupied, he would never concentrate on studying. He decided instead to walk back to the surgery ward and get some money from his locker for lunch.

As he walked through the automatic doors, Steve could sense the usual chaos and commotion of the OR. People in their blue scrubs were walking here and there. A staff surgeon was talking to one of the anesthetists, trying to plead his case to add on a difficult case, while three residents flirted with a few of the OR nurses. It was the usual hustle and bustle of the OR.

Seeing things slowly getting back to normal made Steve feel better. He walked past the nurse's desk on his way to the locker room and overheard two nurses talking to each other.

"I have never seen Sue this late before, Ruth. Don't you think we should call to see if she forgot about her shift? Maybe she has the wrong schedule and we should let her know what's up."

"I already tried to call her three times this morning, but she didn't answered. I left a voice message twice, so I think she will get the idea when she gets home."

Steve paused ever so slightly as he heard they were talking about Sue. They were right: it was strange for Sue to be late. He always thought of her as an early bird. She was usually at work by the time residents were making rounds. Steve had seen her several times in the cafeteria when his team stopped by for breakfast. Maybe Sue had, in fact, gotten her schedule mixed up. With all the commotion and stress over the last week, she might have simply read her schedule wrong.

Steve reached his locker, grabbed his wallet, and set off to the cafeteria.

"Carmichael, how the hell you doing today?"

The familiar voice of Jake Douglas made Steve want to cringe. "Not too bad, Dr. Douglas. How about you?" The man was still unusually pleasant, but Steve wanted to enjoy his break.

"Good. Nothing new since the last time I saw you a few hours ago. Where are you off to?"

Steve really didn't feel like company, and he knew which direction this conversation was going. Unfortunately, he knew he wasn't a good liar. "I thought I would get an early lunch. I don't feel like reading right now, so that was my best solution."

"That sounds like a terrific idea. Hey, you don't mind if I join you, do you?"

Steve tried not to pout. "Not really, if you want. I just thought-"

"Great, Steve. Give me a second to grab my money, and I will be right back."

"Super," Steve lied.

Steve knew that Jake was having a tough time with everything over the last few days, but the incident with Karla was the worst. Jake was usually not a very touchy-feely kind of guy. However, over the last few days he has been very talkative, understanding, and nice to be around. Steve actually felt sorry for the guy. He tried to remember if he had ever seen Jake with any friends in the cafeteria or around the hospital, but no such memories came to mind.

Jake came from around the corner and nearly plowed Steve into a locker. "Alright, Carmichael. Let's do it!"

"You must be pretty hungry," Steve joked as he dashed out of the other man's way. They headed out of the locker room and toward the automatic doors in the front of the OR near the nurses' station.

The mood of the operating wing had already shifted. The three residents were no longer flirting with the nurses, and the staff surgeon was no longer pleading his case for getting his surgery on the schedule. Instead, all attention was on the two nurses behind the desk at the front of the OR. Police officers stood on the opposite side of the desk talking to the nurses.

One of the officers was leaning across the counter that separated them with a small notepad open. He looked up occasionally to ask questions. Then he would look back at his notepad and scribble something down before repeating the process. This continued for several minutes.

Meanwhile, people in the hallway, including Steve and Jake, lingered to eaves drop. All of a sudden, one of the nurses put her hands to her mouth in horror and screamed, "I don't believe it. I just don't believe it! It just can't be. I just talked to her a day ago. She is just late, damn it! Now leave me alone and get out of here, now!"

As she started to cry, the other nurse put her arm around her shoulder and tried to console her. Soon they were both crying as the officers continued to ask them questions.

Steve and Jake didn't move. Their appetites were gone. One

of the nurses walked closer to them and started to cry. Jake put his arm around her and asked what had happened.

"I just can't believe it," the young woman cried softly. "Apparently Sue was attacked last night in her home. They think she was raped and then killed. It is so not right. I just can't believe all that has happened to the OR staff in the last few days."

"You got that right," Steve agreed sympathetically.

Jake gave the nurse a big hug. "Don't worry about a thing. This is all just coincidental, and hopefully this will be the last incident for a long time." Jake said a few other things to the nurse, but Steve could tell he was more interested in the conversation between the cops and the nurses at the desk. After Jake stopped talking, he leaned closer to the nurses' station to absorb as much from the conversation as possible.

Suddenly, as if he had heard enough, Jake looked up at the clock and then stared out the automatic doors. He didn't move and looked mesmerized as he continued to stare out the doors.

Steve asked several times if he was okay, but Jake never responded.

Finally, something clicked, and Jake looked straight at Steve. "I need to go out for a while. Steve, I need to take off. Listen, tell Sally that I had to go talk to a friend and will be back after lunch, maybe about an hour or so. Okay? Great. Thanks." He turned away. "We'll make rounds early this afternoon."

Dr. Douglas shot through the doors as if he were late for a meeting. Steve never had a chance to say anything. Jake just took off. Steve could sense there was something wrong. Besides the news about Sue, something else had triggered Jake to fly out of the OR in a flash.

Steve didn't know what came over him, but he felt that he should follow Jake to see what he was up to. Maybe that way he could get some answers to all the bizarre happenings around the OR lately. Steve reached in his pocket for his keys and took off after the chief.

Before he exited the OR, he picked up the phone near the door and called Sally's call room. "Sally? Hi, this is Steve. Jake and I are going out for a bite to eat and will be back early this afternoon. See ya." He quickly hung up without giving Sally a chance to ask questions or otherwise delay him.

He scrambled down the stairs in order to keep up with Jake. He headed out toward the resident parking lot, staying about a hundred yards back from the other man. He wasn't sure what he was getting himself into, but he was determined to find some answers to this mess.

Chapter 32

Steve watched Jake get in his car and make a phone call on his cell phone. Steve's own car was nearby, but he didn't want to look away in case Jake only made one call before returning to the hospital. Steve pulled a paper from his lab coat to hide his face.

Steve watched Jake shut his phone and throw it against the front passenger seat with what appeared to be great frustration. Although Steve was a short distance from the other man's car, he could see Jake banging his hands against the steering wheel. Jake finally stopped to rest his head on the steering wheel. He stayed in that position for about a minute. Then, like a bolt of lightning, he sat upright and started his car.

Steve didn't waste a moment of time. He shoved the paper back into his pocket and jogged to his car. By the time Steve closed the driver door, Jake was on his way out the parking lot. Steve started his car and followed.

Steve kept his distance safely behind Jake's car to avoid being seen. Jake seemed to be in a rush, speeding down narrow roads. Steve could hear the tires of Jake's car squeal as his car would take a turn. Nonetheless, Steve kept up.

Steve tried to figure out where they were going and why the phone call had made Jake so angry. As they continued through another neighborhood, Steve noticed that Jake would look occasionally down at the passenger seat and frantically back out the window, as though reading directions to a certain address.

While Steve was trying to put some pieces of the puzzle together, he realized that they were driving into a shady part of town. This alone made things interesting. Who would Dr. Douglas want to see down here? Was Jake involved with drugs or hookers? As Steve's imagination filled with possibilities, he nearly missed Jake's last minute turn.

Jake's car was moving slowly now, so Steve thought they must have been getting closer to his destination. Jake took another quick right, went down a half block, and stopped in front of what appeared to be a vacant building. Since there was minimal traffic, Steve continued on the previous street without turning. He drove to the next block, shoved his car into park, and ran back to the intersection. As he made his way to the corner, he stopped just shy of the road to carefully spy on Jake around the building.

Steve was so interested in what Jake was doing that he didn't notice the kids approaching him. He felt eyes looking at him and glanced away from Jake for a moment to find five faces staring at him.

They had gathered around Steve as if he were some character at a freak show. He noticed that four of the five had tattoos on their arms and two of them were smoking cigarettes. He felt a little uncomfortable but pulled his head away from the little hoodlums in order to see what Jake was doing.

He could see Jake trying repeatedly to open the door but failing against a solid lock. After several useless attempts on the door, Jake walked over to a window and leaned closer to peer inside. He raised his hands up to each side of his face to try to get a better look. He slammed his hands against the windows two times and then just laid his forehead against the glass. After half a minute, he straightened himself and then kicked the building's brick wall. He slowly turned around and walked toward his car. Steve couldn't make out what Jake was saying to himself, but he was obviously cussing. He got in his car and nearly burned rubber as he sped off.

Steve waited a few minutes to make sure Jake wasn't going

to return, and then he started to walk toward the brick building. He had hoped the kids would get bored and disappear, but one of the kids stepped in front of him now. Then two others moved behind him and a couple alongside of him. They didn't say anything but just stood there. They seemed so little that Steve thought he could handle them, but he figured where they came from were probably more and bigger. Their pants were huge and baggy, able to conceal a small tank, so he did not want to mess with them too much. He thought a little small talk might make it better.

"Do any of you guys know what that building is over there?" He pointed to the brick structure.

"What's it to you, punk?" said one of the kids.

Steve couldn't believe his ears – punk? "As a matter of fact, it is kind of important, so I just need to know."

Another kid answered, "Yeah, sure looked important to that guy you were following too. He seemed a little pissed off, huh? What's it worth to you?"

Steve reached in his pocket to see if he had any money. He pulled out a twenty.

The kids all laughed.

"Hey, that's all I've got," said Steve. He pulled his pocket inside out to show the testy little hoodlums.

One of the kids finally caught his breath after laughing, "Alright, punk, so you's got no money. How about that twenty and your watch?"

"What? No way! That watch was a gift from my- never mind. Fine. Here you go. Now tell me about that place."

The older kid who seemed to be the leader started talking as he led Steve and the other kids across the street.

Steve initially wasn't listening. He was more interested in what was inside the building than its history. Steve peeked through the windows just as Jake had done a few minutes ago. "Nothing! There is nothing in there," said Steve quietly.

"Yeah, duh. There hasn't been anything in the joint for about three years," answered one of the kids.

Steve turned around and tried to understand what Jake was looking for or what he needed from there. He gazed up at the sky, at one of the kids, and then down at the pavement. There he saw a matchbox. He reached to pick it up about the same time another kid noticed it. Steve got there first. "Huh, nice try. Besides, I don't have any more money."

"Yeah right, punk," said a little voice.

Steve looked at the box and saw 'Joe's Pub.' It had the address 402 East Third. Steve looked up at the address of the building, and on the door, it read 402 East Third St. The address was correct, but no bar was inside. There wasn't even any evidence of a bar – counters, tables, chairs, liquor, or anything suggesting that a bar once existed there. What was Jake trying to find at this Joe's Pub anyway? Steve had a lot of questions.

He turned to the little gangbangers. "Was this place ever a bar?"

Once again, the little leader took charge and answered, "There hasn't been notin' in that building for like a real long time. But comes to think 'bout it, there was this like, uh, like a party or something about two or three weeks ago. They had all these people and stuff for the night, but there were like these security guys that wouldn't let you get too close to the building, if you know what I mean."

"So you never could get close enough to see what was happening inside?"

"Yep, you got that one right, punk. And that pissed me off 'cause this here is our territory, and we have the right to see all that goes on. You know what I mean, punk?"

Steve looked at him and then at the building again. “Thanks for your time.” Steve slapped his hand on the kids shoulder. “You have been a great help.” He turned around, slowly made his way to his car, and then drove off as quickly as possible.

Chapter 33

The next day at the hospital, Steve made an effort to watch Jake for more clues. After rounds, Steve followed Jake through the cafeteria and up to the OR where it was business as usual. Jake had two surgeries scheduled, and he was discussing the anesthesia plan for one of the patients when he noticed Steve close by.

"Carmichael? What is your problem today? You are following me like a little puppy. Oh, I bet I know what the deal is. You need some time in the operating room today, don't you? I'll talk to Sally to see if she can manage the floor work today. Let me finish up here, and I will let her know about the changes for the day. But when we are done, I need you to get back on the floor and help…"

Just as Jake was finishing up, they heard Jake getting paged to the floor stat over the intercom. "Dr. Douglas, please come to Med Surg immediately. Dr. Douglas, please come to the Surgery floor immediately."

Jake and Steve stared at each other, "I never got a page like that before." Jake said. "I wonder who could be coding. And more important, where the hell is Sally? I better get down there." As Jake headed out of the OR, he added, "Steve, make sure the patient gets in on time and prep her. I'll get Sally to manage the problem down there, and I'll be back in a few minutes."

Jake left the OR, and Steve wondered if indeed there was a code, then why the "Code Blue" wasn't used instead of specifically asking for a certain doctor. He walked over to the preop area and gathered the needed information for the first patient. He recognized her from clinic as he introduced himself.

She had problems with varicose veins, and the plan today was to strip the veins in her legs. Steve certainly was not following Dr. Douglas to get into surgery, but he was sure happy that it turned out that way.

Just as Dr. Douglas dictated, Steve got the patient into the OR and anesthesia was putting her to sleep. Steve looked up at the clock and noticed that nearly fifteen minutes had transpired, but Jake was nowhere to be found. Steve called down to the floor and asked for Dr. Douglas.

"Dr. Douglas never came down here," answered one of the nurses. "I heard that strange page for him, but we never actually needed him. All of his patients are fine."

Steve heard the words and began to put the bizarre intercom page into context. He looked at the patient on the table already asleep. *Where did Jake go? Who paged him to the surgery floor and why? And most importantly, where the hell was he now?*

Steve looked at the operating room door, hoping to see Jake walk through and start bitching about this and that. But the doctor was nowhere in sight. Steve glanced at the clock and realized almost twenty minutes had passed since the time he disappeared. Steve looked at the OR team and then the door again, but still no Jake.

"Dr. Carmichael, let's get on with it. Where did your beloved leader go to this time?" asked Charlene, the circulating nurse.

"I'm not sure, Char, but I'll call Dr. Jenson. She'll be up in a second." Steve picked up the phone and dialed the cafeteria. He explained the bizarre situation to Sally. "She'll be here in a few minutes," he announced as he hung up the phone. "I need to go and check the floor work, but Sally will be here soon." He walked toward the door.

"Dr. Carmichael, you can't leave until Sally or another one

of the doctors from your team arrives. We can't have this patient unattended from your service," said Char. "Dr. Carmichael? Dr. Carmichael, do you hear me? You can't leave yet!" she shouted.

Steve had a different agenda. He needed to find out where Jake was and why he had been paged over the intercom. Steve was out the door and down the hallway as Char continued to scream at him.

He rushed to the elevators first and pushed down. He hoped Jake would realize there was a mistake once he was on the surgery floor and head to the cafeteria to get a bagel or something.

Steve waited impatiently for the elevator. Finally, he glanced up and realized that it was stopped on the top floor. The cafeteria was only two floors down, so he decided to take the stairs.

He opened the door and started taking two stairs at a time. He was racing down the stairwell when he thought he heard something. He paused his pace to listen for a second but heard nothing, so he continued down the stairs. Half a flight later, he heard another moan. He looked over the railing of the stairs and saw a body against the railing another floor down. The person had a white lab coat with a dark red stain. Steve's first guess was that one of the hospital employees or a resident missed a step and fell down a few stairs.

He quickly ran down another flight of stairs, but as he approached the body, he began to get nauseous. The odor in the stairwell was horrific. As he approached the body, Steve confirmed that the stain was definitely blood, but there was also blood near the person's head. The body was faced down. Steve reached down to carefully roll the patient over. The airway needed to be open, and the intern wanted to make sure the person was still breathing. He thought about getting some help to properly brace the body, but getting the airway open and protected was a time sensitive issue. Someone else was likely to take the stairs anyway, and he could call for help then.

Steve put one arm around the person's shoulders and used the other to stabilize the head as best as possible in order to protect the neck and prevent further injury in the neck. As his hand traveled under the body, he felt something wet and knew it was most likely blood. He slowly rolled the person over.

When the face came into view, Steve gasped in disbelief. There in the middle of the stairway was Dr. Douglas, blood oozing from several large tears along his scalp.

Steve cradled Jake with his mouth wide open, but no audible words came out.

Jake's breathing was labored and shallow. Steve released one of his hands in order to check Jake's pulse. He could barely palpate the pulse, but it was there. It was very thready and shocky but not completely gone. Steve quickly looked up and down the stairs but saw no other passersby. Jake was going down the tubes, and no one was around to help. Steve had to get help, and his only option was to let Jake rest on his own on the stairs.

As Steve was adjusting the chief's head to rest on its own, he noticed Jake opening his eyes. "JAKE! What the hell happened? What's going on?"

Unfortunately, the man had no energy to answer questions.

Steve then started to get up but felt a hand grab his coat. He quickly moved his eyes to Jake's face.

"Carmichael?" whispered Jake, "Is that you? Carmichael, is that you, damn it?"

"Yes, Jake. It's me. What the hell happened here?"

Jake tried to get up, but he barely had enough strength to breathe.

"Jake, just chill. You are in major shock. Let me go and get help."

Jake tried to talk again. "Steve, there is no time for that." He took a long but shallow breath. "You need to get out of here now. They are after you too!"

"Who? Who the hell are they?" Steve asked.

"There is no time for answers. Just don't trust the CIA. There is some sort of scam going on, and they are all after us. I mean it…" Jake's voice sounded increasingly fatigued. It was getting difficult for Steve to make out what was being said. "Steve…I mean it…get to Milo-Kerr and leave. They…are all over and will get you too."

Steve heard a door in the stairwell open, followed by several footsteps, as if several people were in a rush. He glanced up the center of the stairwell and saw two or three men in black suits. Steve thought to himself, *CIA suits*.

"Jake, they're back!" Steve rasped. "They are upstairs and…" He looked down as he felt Jake's head fall. Jake wasn't breathing any more. Steve glanced up the stairs and quickly back at Jake. Finally, he lowered Jake's body to the ground.

The footsteps and voices were getting louder, so Steve popped up and looked for the nearest set of doors. Just adjacent to him was a set of doors leading to the cafeteria. He glanced down at his coat and saw blood. In one fierce motion, he ripped his coat off and dropped it next to Jake's body. He then flew through the doors in a terrific panic.

As he dashed into the cafeteria, Steve nearly decked Erica, who was making her way to a table with a tray of food.

"Shit, Steve. Slow it down!"

Steve didn't say a word.

She noticed his face was white as a ghost and filled with fear. "Dr. Carmichael! Dr. Carmichael, wait for a second-"

Steve disappeared as quickly as he had entered the cafeteria. Erica realized something was seriously wrong, but Steve was gone in a flash.

Steve sprinted through the main corridor of the first floor in attempt to reach his car before the CIA could figure out where he was. As he cut through the ground floor, he saw Mike, one of the medical students on his service. "Mike! Tell Sally I am sick and going home!"

Dr. Carmichael dashed through the front doors without another word.

Chapter 34

Steve hurried to his car without looking back. He pulled out his keys from his pocket and started the engine. Just before peeling out of the parking lot like a mad man, he decided to look in his rearview mirror to see if they were hot on his tail.

Nothing.

Without active pursuers, Steve figured it would be best not to make a scene. He pulled back from his parking spot. He looked again – still nothing – so he placed the gear into drive and took off at a normal speed.

He turned on to a frontage road and veered to the left to get on the highway. He glanced in the mirror again and saw no cars or police lights. As he fell into the driving routine, he replayed all of the events from the morning, including his last conversation with Jake.

The bogus intercom page for Jake was an obvious attempt to get him to take the stairs. Steve wondered how the enemies were able to get to the intercom system, but if they were with the CIA, then they had sophisticated gadgets to connect to the system. *Probably not a big chore for those guys,* Steve thought. Once they had Jake in the stairwell, they beat him up thoroughly but still made it look like he was in so much of a hurry for this code that he missed a stair or two and fell. *But why?*

Steve glanced out the windows, through the mirrors, and even over his shoulder to make sure the coast was still clear. He watched a few cars behind his to check for unusual people following him. After a few minutes of vigilant watching in all directions, he felt confident that he was not being followed.

He went back to thinking about why those people were after Jake. Maybe Jake owed someone money, but then why would the CIA want to kill him? Why would they give him money in the first place? There were so many questions to be answered, but the one with all the answers was dead.

As Steve considered Jake's death, he started to think about the other people who had mysteriously died in the preceding week. *Very strange.* He remembered Jake's last few words: "They are all after us." What did Jake mean by *us*?

The more Steve thought, the more pieces he put together. First A.J., who was in excellent shape, died from a heart attack. Then Karla and Sue were each attacked. Then Jake was dead. Steve felt his heart flutter with panic. A.J., Karla, Sue and Jake. They were all together the night that foreign kid had come in with the abscess. Maybe Jake wasn't the final one. That was what he meant by *us* – they were after Steve as well. Steve was the final link to that OR crew. They, whoever they were, were trying to kill the entire OR crew. *But why?*

Suddenly Steve heard tires screeching. He noticed a black suburban turning onto the ramp behind him. He saw the vehicle fishtail as it pulled onto the highway. He knew it was no coincidence.

Just as Steve felt another panic attack rising in his chest, he noticed an off ramp. Rather than reduce his speed, he accelerated down the ramp. The black suburban was right behind him. A line of cars was waiting at a stoplight, but he quickly swerved around them to turn right on the street. People honked, but no police cars were in sight. The one time that Steve would love to be pulled over, there was not a single cop around.

Suddenly Steve realized the reason why no cops were appearing. There was one chasing him. The suburban had its own flashing lights. Of course: it was the CIA.

Steve floored his car down a little road, swerving away from cars in order not to hit any of them. He noticed an opportunity to get away from the chase as a semi was delivering some goods to a little store. Steve floored the car as the truck was backed up toward the other side of the street. His car barely made it through, scraping the passenger mirror off.

He heard the suburban slam on its brakes. He could just barely see the tires of the suburban from under the truck. He took a deep breath of relief.

Just as he was thinking it was over, Steve noticed another suburban pull on to his street with flashing lights behind him. This vehicle was also black. Steve slammed the accelerator down to the floor again. *This is crazy!* Steve thought. He half expected to find helicopters flying overhead.

Steve had been on this street several times – but never flying at the present speed. He turned the steering wheel from side to side to avoid cars and people. He once glanced down at the speedometer and saw 95mph, the fastest he had ever driven.

He saw a small side street with a 'one way' arrow. He took a quick turn, trying to lose his pursuers but to no avail. That new suburban was glued to his backside. The faster he went, the faster they went.

They finally came to a stretch of road that was straight and more country than city. Steve watched his speed reach 110mph, but that suburban was behind him by just a few feet. He noticed a small lake alongside a turn in the road up ahead. Steve wasn't sure he could control the car at this speed and make the turn, but there wasn't enough time to reduce his speed.

Steve tried to ease the car into the turn, but before he knew it, the momentum started to roll the car toward the lake. He felt the car roll at least twice but lost count as he saw the water quickly approaching. With a quick jolt, his car landed upside down on the water.

Steve quickly looked back and saw the suburban slow down behind him on the shore. He could feel water seeping inside his car. He noticed that the front end was facing the opposite shore. Without even thinking about the risks, he took a huge breath of air, kicked through his window, and pulled himself out against the pressure of the water coming in from the window. He rose to the surface in front of the car and took a couple of breaths. The car had not yet sunk completely, so the tires and underside provided Steve temporary visual protection from the men in the other vehicle.

He took another huge breath, turned toward the opposite shore, and pushed himself under the surface to swim for safety. He lasted over a minute before his body demanded a fresh breath. He rolled onto his back so his face was pointing toward the sky. He brought only his mouth up to the surface, exhaled, and quickly sucked in as much air as his lungs could hold. Then he flipped back over to swim again. This time he lasted longer before needing to exhale and inhale. He never took a chance to bring his head out of the water to see what the men were up to, but he was confident that would protect his escape.

At last, he felt his arms hit a tree branch. He carefully navigated through the debris until he was hidden in the middle of the growth. He refilled his lungs again without showing the rest of his face but then rotated his face so that only his eyes were exposed.

Steve determined that he was on the other side of the lake. Fortunately, the tree gave him some camouflage to see what those men were doing by his overturned car. They appeared to be waiting for Steve to pop up at the surface nearby. Steve watched them get something from inside their coats. He couldn't tell what they drew, but soon he could hear them shooting pistols toward the submerged car as if to ensure that Steve was dead.

Steve shuddered with each gunshot.

Chapter 35

Steve didn't move for what seemed like an eternity. He was paralyzed in the water. His body started to shiver, but he didn't move even after the men left. He couldn't be sure if they had seen him alive. Even if they hadn't noticed him at a distance, they might return, in search of his lifeless body. Regardless, trauma from the day's events had caught up with Steve, and he just could not move from the shock of it all.

Once he lost sensation in his legs from the temperature of the lake, he figured that was nature's cue that he better get out. He looked toward the shore behind him and saw that he was only a few yards from land. As he waded over, he considered his next move. He had no doubt that they would eventually realize that he was still alive and begin their pursuit all over again.

Before they caught on, he had to get home to get dry clothes, more money, food, and a few extra items in case he couldn't make it home for a while. He took a few minutes to realize where he was and the direction he needed to go in order to make it home. Then he started his walk home. He knew he would be conspicuous since he was soaking wet, so he took back roads to stay out of people's view.

The crazy car chase had taken him closer to home, so he had only a few miles to cover on foot. Dazed by recent events, Steve didn't notice as his clothes became a little stiff from the cool weather. They weren't frozen but getting close with the temperature outside dropping toward the forties.

As he walked, Steve's mind tried to figure out what the men were after and why Jake had been in such trouble. Steve could not believe that they were real agents, so he could understand why Jake told him not to trust the CIA, but why would they do such a thing? Were they also responsible for the deaths of A.J., Karla, and Sue?

Steve was contemplating the answers to those questions as he subconsciously approached his duplex. He could see several marked and unmarked sedans and SUVs parked outside his house. Several agents were walking around the yard. He stopped one house away and jumped behind some bushes to watch the activity. He could just make out figures in the house moving about as if they were looking for something. He noticed two men near the door who were discussing something with the energy of an argument. As Steve roamed the area with his eyes, one thing was certain: he wasn't going to make it in to his house for dry clothes, so there was no need to stay there and get discovered.

He checked his surroundings and then slowly backed away from the bushes. Just as he started toward the back alley, voices startled him. He sought shelter at the nearest house. He quickly placed his trembling hand on the handle of a sliding glass door. The door miraculously slid open, and Steve slipped into the house. His heart was pounding as two men in suits walked by that side of the house just moments later. He was relieved that they failed to notice the door was slowly closing as they walked by.

Steve held his breath for a minute. After deciding that the agents were not coming back, he sat down on a chair in his neighbor's kitchen. It took a few moments for him to acknowledge that he had just broken into this house. He needed to determine if anybody was home. He didn't want to attract attention from the men outside by yelling, so he walked through the house calling out quietly instead. No one was home.

Steve developed a few ideas, none of which was legal. The first thing that he needed to find was some dry clothes. He found a bedroom and started to go through the closet. The clothes were a little big for him, but it was nothing a belt couldn't fix.

Steve was not in a position to be too fussy, though. As long as he was breaking and entering, he figured he might as well take extra clothes. It would be a while before he could get back into his house. With all the activity next door, Steve was not sure when it would be safe to come back to the neighborhood. He scrounged around the house until he found a backpack. Then he rummaged through the wardrobe to find jeans, shirts, and a sweatshirt.

Steve took a final glance around the room for anything else that he might need. For a split second, he thought about underwear, but that was too much to tolerate. However, he remembered that he was standing in soaking cold clothes, so he gave in to just one oversized pair of briefs.

After he changed and packed the extra clothes, he took a moment to check the scenery outside. He quietly made his way to the dining room, which had two large windows that overlooked his house. He gently pulled the drapes open from one side and studied the landscape.

A fair amount of commotion continued around his house. Three or four agents were standing in front talking, and a few others were walking around the perimeter. The action inside appeared to continue as well.

Steve peered through the living room windows too. There he saw more activity than he expected. Several cars were still in place along the street. He could not figure out why there was so much activity at his house. What were they looking for? It was not like he was involved in some sort of scandal or robbery.

Maybe that was it. Maybe Jake was involved in a robbery or a drug trafficking deal, and the guy in the overcoat all those times at the hospital was really a drug lord or a runner or something like that. Steve knew his imagination was running wild, but he just didn't have enough answers to separate fantasy and reality.

Steve sat down in the living room and continued to analyze the situation. If this was indeed a robbery, Steve could not believe that A.J. and the nurses were involved. Steve was definitely not involved. *Why were they in his house?* If they thought they had just killed him, then what did they want in his house? Were they interrogating Pudge?

He thought for a few more minutes, and then a light bulb clicked on in his head. Actually, it was a vision. A vision of the OR on the night with the young foreign man who had a belly full of pus after an apparent appendectomy.

Steve remembered Jake's possessive attitude regarding the abscess mass. Jake had been adamant about taking the specimen to Pathology himself instead of allowing the nurse as usual. Steve recalled Jake's anxiety over the entire process once the specimen was found and removed.

Steve wondered if it would still be appropriate to view the Path report to get a better idea as to what was going on. He knew it wouldn't be safe to call into the Path Department and ask for the report himself. The CIA was all over, and then Steve's location would be identified. They would probably stall the call unnecessarily while they tracked him. It was better if they still assumed he was dead. His snooping around needed to be covert.

Steve thought for a while longer, comfortably seated on his neighbor's couch, and then came up with a terrific idea. He needed to get to the public library, sign online, and go through the hospital computer system to get the results. If the CIA was indeed trying to track outsiders, they would just get the public library's identification, and Steve would remain under the radar. He still needed to wait until all the activity from next door quieted down before he could escape from his neighbor's house, but then he would hurry to the library.

Steve looked at the window and then at a clock on the mantel. He figured he had another hour or two before he would have to vacate to avoid being caught by the house's real owners. He closed his eyes for a while to pass the time waiting. Just as he was about to doze off, he heard the car doors slamming and engines being revved up. Steve slowly made his way to the window and saw the cars leaving in a major exodus. After all the commotion, two vehicles remained in the street, which meant people were still in the house. *What were they searching for?*

He decided this would be a safe time to sneak out. His only remaining problem was transportation. He thought for a moment and then just shook his head, no way. Yet he couldn't resist walking to the kitchen door and peeking into the garage. Parked there was a hot red Corvette. It wasn't a very subtle car, but it would certainly be able to outrun most CIA SUVs.

Steve looked around near the door, found a key rack, and identified the key for the car. It had a tiny Corvette on the chain. He grabbed a winter cap on his way toward the car. He lipped inside the car as he pushed the button for the automatic garage door opener.

In full view of the lingering CIA agents, he backed his new Corvette down the driveway and on to the street. He nodded his head as two agents waved a polite hello and got on his way.

As Steve calmly turned on the next road, he considered what just transpired. In front of a clan of CIA agents, Doctor Steve Carmichael broke into a house, stole several articles of clothing, and drove off with a stolen vehicle. What an extraordinary day for a surgery intern!

Chapter 36

Steve enjoyed his sweet new ride on the way to the library. He tried not to think about the fact that he had stolen the car. As he pulled up in front of the library, he realized that he didn't see any CIA agents or dark SUVs. He also felt like a free person again.

He parked the car and looked around but saw no conspicuous people. He was grateful for a break to collect his thoughts and make plans without having to worry about being killed by the CIA or whoever they were. How fortunate that they all thought he was already dead.

Steve walked into the library and looked the place over. He had never been in this particular library before, so he wasn't sure where the computers were. As he gazed from left to right, he heard a calm voice.

"Can I help you out, young man?" a sweet older woman asked.

Despite the quiet tone, Steve was in such deep thought that he nearly jumped to the moon.

"I'm so sorry," the old woman giggled. "I didn't mean to startle you!"

Steve forced a smile. "Oh, that's okay. I was just trying to remember where the computers were."

The lady returned his smile and said, "They are on the second floor."

As he followed her directions, Steve thought about what he needed to do. He had to check the pathology on the specimen from the night they were all in the case. He wanted to make contact with Sweetpea since he didn't know the next time he would be online. He needed to ask why she said he should watch his back.

He decided to email Sweetpea first. He told her about the bizarre course of events and the rotten day he was having. As he started to address what she had said, she appeared on instant messaging.

"Steve, you need to be very careful. These people you are dealing with are really bad, and they are trying to kill you like the others!! Where are you? Let me help!"

Steve did need help but now hc was skeptical as to who this person was and how she knew so much. He debated ditching the computer so they couldn't track him, but probably it was too late. "Who are you? And why should I trust you? Why didn't you tell me before that you knew about this and that I was in danger?"

"I needed to protect you and still bring these guys down. I work for the CIA, and you need to trust me because you are in a lot of trouble, but if I don't know where you are I can't help you or protect you."

Steve stared at the screen. *CIA!* Jake told him not to trust anyone from the CIA.

He wrote back, "I am sorry Sweetpea or agent whoever, but I need to go."

"STEVE!" she wrote back immediately. "Here is my home number 544-9130 and my cell 870-2244 just in case you need it. We already tracked you to the public library, and they can too. If you'll just stay where you are, I will have agents over there in just a moment. Steve, don't move!"

Steve quickly copied the numbers and signed out of his email account. He needed to get the heck out of there, but first he needed to see the Path report. He logged into the hospital system and entered his code and password. He didn't want to analyze whether CIA queen Sweetpea was on his side or not.

He typed in Ziamuddin's name and found nothing. Steve gritted his teeth with frustration. He quickly looked up the date of the surgery but found no path for that entire night or the next day with that kid's name. Whatever that mass was never made it to pathology.

Steve knew he didn't have time to contemplate this problem here. He signed off and rushed downstairs to the main lobby of the library. He cautiously checked the lobby but found it clear of dark trench coats, so he bolted to his car. At the door, he nearly bumped into two teenage girls talking. Steve overheard one saying, "Don't worry about that homework. I already did it, and it is in my locker at school. I can get it before class tomorrow."

Steve stopped in his tracks for a second but then remembered he had to get out of there. He ran to his car, and as he shut the door, he saw several SUVs pull up to the front door of the library. As he watched from the safety of his new stolen car, he saw two more black SUVs pull into the back parking lot. They were a different shade from the ones at the front door, and they slowly pulled through the parking lot but left without talking to the agents in the front.

This was all too weird for Steve. Why would the cars bother coming at all if they weren't going to check inside? Why didn't they talk to each other? They may have been communicating via cell phones or radio transmission, but it just didn't make sense. Why were the vehicles different?

Steve started the car and realized that he might want to get a new car soon. His neighbor would probably be home soon and notice the missing Corvette. However, now was not the time to get out and walk.

As he drove off, his mind drifted to the conversation between the two girls. It seemed to trigger something in the back of his mind. He tried to recall why he would have heard about homework or lockers.

He drove about fifteen miles out of town before parking the car to think. He decided to just call his neighbor. The poor guy would never believe the whole story. Steve dialed information for the number.

"Hello?"

Steve recognized the guy's voice but started to sweat.

"Hello, hello?"

"Dan? Hi. This is Steve Carmichael."

"Hey, how's it going, Steve? You know, we haven't seen you too much. I think you are working a little too hard."

Steve replied, "You're probably right, Dan. Hey, listen. I have a huge favor to ask. Can I borrow your Corvette tonight?"

"Sorry, ol' buddy, but I have some bad news. I just pulled in, and I think I was robbed. They must have been hungry 'cause they raided my fridge and took off with my Corvette."

"I am sorry to hear about that. Did you call the police yet?"

"No. I just walked in. That was going to be my next step."

Steve's voice started to crack. "Dan, let me help you out with that. I really don't have time to explain all the details, but I can tell you for a fact that your car is safe. *I* took it. But I can explain! I just can't explain it right now. It really is important that you not report it. Otherwise, frankly, I think I might get killed."

Dan interrupted abruptly, "What kind of trouble are you in, son? Maybe I can help."

"Dan, I appreciate the offer, but I think that would put you in a lot of danger. Remember all those people who have died at the University Hospital in the last week or so? I am next on the list. I needed some wheels to escape, and my car ended up in the lake. I can't explain much more, but please trust me that I will bring back your Corvette!"

"Alright, Carmichael, but you be careful! You hear?"

"Thanks, Dan. I really appreciate it. If any one comes snooping around, don't mention this conversation. Whatever you do, don't say you talked to me. That would put you and your family in grave danger. Talk to you soon. Thanks again."

Steve hung up thinking that the conversation had gone surprisingly well. Next, he had to figure out why those girls' conversation was bugging him. He turned the motor off, leaned back, and closed his eyes.

After about a minute, his eyes snapped open, and he felt his heart in his throat. He said to himself, "Milo-Kerr, Milo-Kerr." Then he drew it out, "Mi-lo-Kerr." He said that a few more times and realized what he was thinking had to be true. The last few words from Jake were Mi-locker. Steve had thought it was a name of somebody, but it was Jake trying to say my locker…his locker. Steve started the car and turned around. He had to see what was in Jake's locker.

Chapter 37

Steve knew that going back to the hospital was outrageously dangerous, but he had to see what was in the locker. It had to be important or else Jake wouldn't have wasted his last few breaths on those words. As he drove, Steve tried to put together why Jake was involved with the CIA and why he didn't trust them.

Steve pulled into the parking lot of the hospital, and all seemed normal. No SUVs were parked around the entrance or the emergency room entrance, suggesting that all agents had made their way to another part of town. Nonetheless, Steve chose a parking space up close to the building in case he needed to take off quickly.

He hoped not to bump into anyone he knew, like Sally or Erica. However, he needed to go through the OR to reach the locker, and he would surely run into a few staff members who would want to know what the hell was going on. Steve made a promise to himself just to say hi and continue with his business.

He took the stairs to avoid any elevator conversations, but it was hard to ignore the memory of that last time he had used that shortcut. He went straight to the OR. As he walked through the doors, he tried to look too busy for anyone to bother.

To Steve's astonishment, the OR was relatively quiet. No nurses or staff were in the vicinity. Steve quickly glanced at the clock and realized it was way after hours for the regular staff. He had been so busy most of the day that he hadn't realized it was coming to an end.

Steve made his way to the locker room to find Jake's locker. In his eagerness to find out what was inside, Steve forgotten that he had no way to get past the lock. He took a chance and tried to open it, but no such luck.

Steve looked around for a paper clip to pick the lock without a key. He absentmindedly thought, *You already burglarized a house and stole a car – why not continue this delinquent behavior and pick a lock?* He looked around and pulled on the locker handle again. As he did so, a voice nearly sent him to the moon.

This time it wasn't a calm gentle voice of a librarian. "Dr. Douglass always kept his key on top of his locker. I think that way he always knew where it was."

It was Joe, the nighttime janitor.

As startled as he was, Steve offered gratuity. "Thanks, Joe. I just needed to get some books that Dr. Douglas left for me." Steve didn't want the janitor to think that he was breaking into a dead man's locker.

"No problem, Dr. Carmichael. His locker has been very popular today."

Steve frowned. "What do you mean?"

"The day janitors said some creepy looking guys were asking where Dr. Douglas's locker was. Of course they didn't tell them, just pointed them in the direction of Human Resources."

"Did they ever get in to his locker?" asked Steve.

"Not as far as I know." Joe turned back to his work. "I'll see ya later. Have a good night, Dr. Carmichael."

"Good night, Joe." Steve reached for the key. Whoever was after him must want whatever was in Jake's locker. Maybe if he gave it to them, they would back off.

That was how a normal person would think, but he was dealing with some bad people. They probably would do what they did to A.J. and the others to him anyway.

Sweat was building up on Steve's forehead as he placed the key into the lock and turned it. His hands were shaking, and his heart was racing as he opened the door.

Nothing stood out as different from any other locker. A backpack, some clothes, and a few books.

Steve was confused. What was the big deal about this locker? Whatever those agents sought, they would surely be disappointed.

He brushed through the items on the top shelf, which were just goggles and masks for surgery. He checked the pockets of a pair of pants and found a wallet with a few bucks. He looked down at the bottom of the locker and noticed Jake's shoes and the backpack. He knew that the shoes couldn't be too exciting, so he turned his attention to the backpack. He bent down and nervously opened it.

Steve gasped. He quickly looked up to see if anyone else was around. He turned back to the contents of the backpack. He reached in and pulled out several hundred-dollar bills. He reached again and pulled out another handful of bills. The entire backpack was filled with them. Steve guessed there were several hundred thousand dollars, if not more.

No wonder those guys were after Jake. Maybe Jake stole this cash or was in bad with gambling. There were a number of possibilities, but Steve didn't want to waste time in a smelly locker room trying to figure it out. He quickly went through the pockets of the backpack just to see if there was anything else that was important. In the second pocket, he pulled out a piece of paper with an account number to a bank in Argentina. He quickly placed it in his own pocket, closed the backpack, and stepped toward the door.

"I am glad you did all the foot work for us, Dr. Carmichael," said a deep voice as four men in black trench coats entered through the door to the locker room. "My men and I have been trying to hunt down my backpack all day. Thank you for finding it for me." He smiled. "I am sorry, Steve. Let me introduce myself. I am Agent Thomas with the CIA." He reached out his hand.

Steve hesitantly offered his own hand, but his heart nearly stopped when he saw the starphire ring on Agent Thomas's hand. It was the same ring that Steve saw on the man in the hallway with Jake. He remembered the sparkle. Sally had thought he was a lawyer, but Steve didn't think he had the look of an attorney. Steve was right.

He was in a tough spot with no place to run. Agent Thomas and his friends didn't appear to be so friendly. Whether they really worked for the CIA or not, there were definitely more of them, and they were much bigger than Steve. He tried to remain practical for a moment while the apparent leader was making bogus introductions. He realized he needed to use this unpleasant encounter to his advantage and gain as much information as possible.

"Steve, if you would be so kind as to hand over the backpack, that would be greatly appreciated. Then my associates and I will be on our way," Agent Thomas concluded.

Steve stalled by asking, "Sir, could you please show me your ID? I am sure Jake and you had some agreement, but I really don't know you at all. The contents in this backpack were very special to Jake. He made a special request when he was dying in the stairwell, and I don't want to dishonor his memory."

"What a good friend you are to be so careful! Jake spoke very highly of you, and now I know why." While the man spoke, he reached inside his coat pocket.

Uncertain what the guy was reaching for, Steve took a few steps back.

"Here it is, my friend." Agent Thomas showed Steve his

CIA badge.

It appeared to be kosher. Thomas then pulled his coat back under the disguise of replacing his ID, but the motion provided a glimpse of the revolver that was stowed in his shoulder harness.

Steve took a deep breath, trying to control the panicky feeling in his chest. He could feel his heart pounding wildly and wondered if the other men could sense it. "So what do you think Jake had in here that makes it yours?" Steve asked with more confidence than he felt.

Thomas stared at him. "Dr. Carmichael, while I appreciate your concern for the contents, I don't think you should play games with me. Frankly, we have had a terrible week. You really don't want us to take out our frustration out on you, but if you keep this up, you will leave me with no choice. Do I make myself clear, doctor?"

"Sir, I understand perfectly," Steve replied. "But I promised Dr. Douglas that I would take care of the contents in his backpack."

Thomas sighed. "Now I know why Jake spoke so highly of you. You are a devoted friend. That is a noble quality, but in this instance, your devotion to your dead friend is a mistake! Let me rephrase my request here." He tried to make the atmosphere a little less threatening by sitting down.

Steve watched him move, and he moved as though in a lot of pain. Steve also noticed the other men appeared to be Middle Eastern, not American agents. Steve wondered if the CIA often outsourced their missions.

Once sitting comfortably, Thomas began to speak again. "Sorry, Steve. I'm moving kind of slow these days. I have been a little sore since that prostate came out. They found cancer and had to yank that little thing out. Too bad 'cause things don't work the way they used to, if you know what I mean. Now let's get back to business. Steve, you are holding a backpack with a shit load of money that belongs to me, and I want it. Please don't try my patience anymore."

Steve could see that his plan was coming to an abrupt end. He needed to come up with another plan and fast. Just as he was about to try stalling a second time, the locker room doors swung open. The four agents looked over their shoulders to see who was walking in. Without a moment's hesitation, Steve ran with the backpack toward the door to the OR. He had only a split-second advantage, but Thomas motioned for his colleagues to stay calm and walk out of the locker room calmly to avoid attracting unneeded attention.

"Good evening, gentlemen," said Thomas as they crossed paths with the entering staff. "Just looking for a friend, but I think he took off into the operating rooms. We will just wait for him out in the lobby." The four men made their way to the front of the OR to catch Steve on his way out.

Little did they know, Steve had taken the back stairs and was already running through the cafeteria toward the parking lot. Once through the doors outside, he slowed to a brisk walk. He saw black SUVs all over. He took one glance at his borrowed car and knew he was in trouble. Several people were standing in front of his car. One guy was nodding his head as he talked on his cell phone. "Yes, sir. We have the perimeter secured. I will make sure he doesn't escape, sir."

The man talking on the phone glanced up and noticed Steve. "There he is! Apprehend him now! *Freeze!*"

Steve dashed frantically toward the city bus that had just pulled away from the hospital shelter. He jumped onto the first step of the bus and pulled himself through the open door. He looked back and saw his pursuers stop in their tracks. They were putting their guns back into their holsters, giving up the chase to avoid public casualties.

As Steve continued to watch, he noticed that several of them were jumping into cars and falling in line behind the bus. He heard tires screech even over the bus's engine and realized that they would trail the bus until he got out. He had to make a move before they caught up.

The bus made its first turn, and the cars still were not directly behind the bus. Steve needed to get out without waiting for a regular stop. He tried desperately to make a plea to the bus driver. "I am so sorry, sir, but I made a bad mistake. I meant to jump on the 175 not the 54. Could you please let me out here?"

"Are you joking?" laughed the bus driver. "I can't stop the bus for every mistake people make. I can let you off at Elliot Street and 36th, and you should be able to pick up the 175 there, okay?"

"No, it is not okay!" Steve screamed frantically. "I need to get out NOW!"

"Settle down, kid. We'll be there in just a few minutes," responded the driver.

Steve looked back and still didn't see the cars. He needed to make a move immediately. He thought quickly and then shouted, "Let me out now or I will blow this bus up! Yeah, I've got a bomb in this backpack. Don't make me do it!" He made a motion with the pack.

The bus driver took one look at Steve and slammed on the brakes. Purses and bags went flying. An elderly lady fell forward and hit her head on the seat in front of her. People started to scream, but Steve didn't notice. His eyes were watching out the back of the bus: still no SUVs.

Before the bus came to a complete stop, Steve jumped off the bottom step and ran into the nearest store. He watched through the windows the bus started rolling again. Not more than twenty seconds went by before a train of black SUVs went speeding by. After what seemed to be the caboose, Steve took a deep breath.

He turned around and realized that he was in a clothing retail store. He looked at the store clerk who was staring at him with panic in her eyes.

“Don’t worry. It’s not what you think,” said Steve. “Do you have a back door to this store?”

The young lady was so scared that she didn’t say a thing. She nodded her head and pointed to the door that led to the alley.

After a quick thank you, Steve disappeared through the back as fast as he had burst into the front.

Chapter 38

The phone rang just as expected. Though reluctant to pick it up, he knew he didn't have a choice. He reached for the phone and picked up the receiver with shaky hands. His nervous trembling caused his ring to clank against the phone. "Hello?"

"How are we doing?" answered a familiar Middle Eastern voice. "It has been a few days, and I am getting anxious, my friend. I was hoping to talk to you by now. Are all the birds in the coop?"

Agent Thomas thought quickly. He couldn't disappoint his caller. "Things are going well, but we have one more bird on the loose. I think we are very close to capturing it, perhaps even by tonight. Yeah, I think tonight we should be all set, and then all the birds will be in the coop."

"My friend, please don't lie to me. Dishonesty portrays a very bad character. Where I come from, people who are dishonest lose their life. I have been watching you and your associates very carefully. Although you have most of the birds, there is one that seems to have escaped your capture. I will give you a short while longer. If all the birds are not found, our deal is off, and the payment for birds and the package will be nullified. I will be in contact."

Agent Thomas kept the phone to his ear long after the disconnection. He studied the situation in his head, trying to devise a plan that would help capture Steve. He also considered whether there was a way he could just take his money and run. It wasn't all they promised, but maybe he could find a way to get into the foreign account they had guaranteed as well.

Thomas knew better than that, though. They probably had those accounts frozen until everything was completed. He finally hung up the phone. He glared at it for a moment and then picked it up again to dial one of his associates. "Well, how are we doing? Did you locate that kid? He has to be around somewhere!"

A voice on the other side of the phone answered, "No! It is like he just vanished into thin air. We have searched the streets up and down the entire bus route. I have no idea where he went. He just disappeared."

Thomas tensed. "We all will be in a lot of trouble if you don't find him. Go back to the house, and make sure he doesn't go back there to hide."

"Already done. I sent two guys there right at the get go, and then I sent two more back to the hospital. I have his home line tapped as well as all the lines at the hospital in case he tries to make connection with anyone who might help him out," responded the man on the phone.

"Fine. Good work. We will just have to see if, or rather *when*, that little doc makes a mistake, and then we will be all over him."

Chapter 39

Steve slowly opened the back door of the store and looked in both directions of the alley. No SUVs and no men in black suits. It appeared to be clear. Steve walked out, trying to act calm, but his pounding heart was beginning to give him a headache.

He thought maybe now his house would be a safe haven since nothing was there that would interest them. He was holding a backpack filled with a lot of money, so perhaps the house would be clear.

Steve saw a dirty hat on the ground and picked it up, dusted it off, and slipped it on. It had a terrible odor, but he needed to hide his face. Buying something at that store might have been a good idea, but the clerk seemed too scared to tolerate a normal transaction.

Steve's mind returned to the backpack full of money and why Jake was involved. He remembered the bag of powder in the OR: probably the drugs that showed on the tox report. Steve didn't think of Jake as a drug dealer type of guy, but residency sure didn't pay well. Even if Jake was dealing drugs, why was the CIA involved? It should have fallen under the jurisdiction of the DEA.

Whatever it was that they were after, it must have been important. They had killed some wonderful people, another unlikely CIA habit. If they were truly CIA agents, they would interrogate through the legal system before killing people. Maybe they were only disguised as agents to get in and out of places without question. Then why were foreign players so involved?

As he continued to ponder this whole thing, Steve realized he was nearing his house. He snuck around the block to avoid being seen if any agents were already waiting outside his house. He crept up along a neighbor's fence until he could get a good view of the front of his house. Sure enough, his house had unwanted visitors. He didn't waste any time staring at them. He quietly backtracked.

So now plan B was in effect. Steve had no idea what plan B was yet, but he did know that returning to his house with those slugs outside was sure to end poorly. He knew it couldn't just be about the money. Agent Thomas saw Steve with Jake's money at the hospital, yet they had thoroughly searched his house.

Steve had pondered this issue for the last few days without resolve. Now was not the time to sit twenty yards from the enemy to wonder what was happening. He tried to concentrate on the immediate situation at hand and come up with a plan. The town appeared to be filled with these agents or whoever they were. Steve felt it would be best to get out of town. Then maybe he could contact Sweetpea, or whoever she was, to find out why she was so worried. Maybe, just maybe, she could shed some light on the situation. He didn't know if she was good or bad, or if one of Thomas's thugs was pretending to be a woman online, but his gut demanded that he give her a chance to tell her side of the story.

His biggest problem was transportation. Both his personal car and his borrowed car were useless, not to mention that taking public transportation was out of the question. They knew he had no wheels and had to rely on the bus for mobility. That only left Steve a few possibilities, one of which was getting himself another vehicle. He knew that adding to his list of crimes by stealing again wouldn't impress any judge, so his next option was to buy a car. He thought for a few minutes and then looked at the backpack as a wide grin slowly spread across his face.

It wasn't his money, but under the circumstances, Steve thought Jake would understand. He probably had enough to buy a few Mercedes and then some, but he just wanted wheels to get him around to and fro. Why not make it a fast car to get him to and from without the help of those agents? He couldn't get something that would attract too much attention, but a car with a 'hemi' would probably do the trick. The guys on the TV commercials sure got where they needed to get to without any problems.

He started on foot toward the nearest Dodge dealership to pick himself up a 'hemi.' He remembered a dealership about a mile down the street. As he walked, he realized that paying cash for a brand new car would also attract a lot of attention. He decided to only shop for a used car and not to look for the most expensive car while he was at it.

By the time he arrived at the lot, the sun was going down. Steve hoped that the dealership was still open. He walked up to the door just as the salesman was closing up.

"You're not closed yet, are you?" asked Steve.

"As a matter of fact I am, and you know I am actually late." The man looked at his watch. "Can you believe I stayed here for an extra twenty minutes showing this old lady a freaking car, and then after all that, she said she wasn't interested? What a waste of my time!"

Steve smiled to himself. *Just twenty minutes late...* He thought about all the hours he put in each week – or for that matter, each day. He thought about the times post-call that he still had to work the whole next day in order to get all of his work done. There were times he would put almost forty hours in just over a two-day period.

Never mind all that. He had to stay on task and find a way to get this guy to let Steve shop for a car. "If you give me just a few minutes, I am sure I can make it worth your while."

"Right!" responded the salesman. "It is not like I haven't heard that one yet today."

Steve turned around so as not to let the guy see what he was doing. He put his hand into his grab bag and pulled out a hundred-dollar bill. He then quickly turned around and dangled the bill in front of the man as he was turning the key to the lock the dealership. "Would this make you believe?" asked Steve.

The man straightened. "I think I have a few more minutes. I mean, what the heck! I am already late, right?" he said. "Now, I have a few new cars inside that I think would suit you perfectly. I get the feeling that you might want the kind of car that can take you-"

Steve had no time for sales bullshit, so he quickly interrupted the guy. "Sorry, I hate to be rude, but I am also in kind of a hurry, so let me tell you exactly what I need. Then you won't have to guess what kind of guy I am and the right car for me." He continued, "I need a truck with a hemi, like the ones they have in those commercials with those two guys who can never win the car race. Do you know what I'm talking about? If you do, then I think you have figured me out, and that would be the car I want. Okay?"

"No problem," said the guy. "You want a Durango. I have a few brand-new beauties right here in the showroom."

Steve chimed in again to save time. "How about a used one with a few miles on it?"

The man turned to face Steve and smiled in a hesitant manner. After a few seconds, he smiled in a manner depicting greater confidence. "Alright then, I think I know just the car for you. Just got in last week with a trade in, and it has your hemi with about 50,000 miles on it. Sound good so far?"

"Perfect," answered Steve.

"Great!" said the man. "Just follow me over here to our used car lot. The guys just finished going over the vehicle yesterday and gave it a good report card."

Steve wasn't really listening. He was glad that there was only one person to deal with instead of a full store of people. Heading out of town would be the best next step. There was a small town about one hour north of Minneapolis where he used to hang out near the St. Croix River. It would be a great place to sit and collect his thoughts.

"How about this one, sir? This was the one I thought would go well with you. What do you think?" asked the salesman.

Steve drew himself back to the present. With a quick glance at the Durango, he asked, "Does it have a full tank of gas?"

The man chuckled and gripped Steve's hand. "Don't you want to take it for a test drive?"

Steve shook his head and said, "No, this is perfect. You deserve a raise because this is exactly what I had in mind. Let's get the paper work done, and then I will take this baby out for a quick drive."

The sales person couldn't believe his ears but didn't argue. The paperwork was done in a flash. Fifteen minutes later, Steve was driving away in a beautiful black Durango. He smiled to himself, thinking he needed to purchase a nice black suit to go along with his black car. Then all he would need was the dark sunglasses to blend perfectly with his pursuers.

Steve turned on to the interstate and glanced at the clock on the dashboard. He could get up to Taylors Falls without much trouble, and there he could sort things out. He glanced at his mirror just to make sure he had no followers. Only a few cars were on the road, and they didn't seem to be the SUV type. He felt he was in the clear, so he sat back and pondered the entire situation as he drove northward.

Chapter 40

While Steve was taking a leisurely drive along the picturesque St. Croix River, a different brand of CIA agents was interviewing people at the hospital. They had a list of people to interview about recent events. Most people didn't have much to contribute, but Sally, Tom, and the medical students Mike and Roger were interrogated endlessly.

Sally just looked at the man with a blank stare as he tried to explain the situation to her. Other CIA agents were questioning people and running about. She couldn't believe what was happening. It seemed like a televised drama, not something in her real life.

However, those people had really died in her hospital. They were her friends and staff. There was nothing fictional about that. She would never be able to hear another A.J. story or listen to Jake complain about annoying details. The nurses who had died were way too young with too much to look forward to, not to mention their poor families. These people were really dead, not ever to return.

Sally wondered if Tom was getting the same story. Was his mind filled with the same thoughts and concerns as hers?

"Ma'am? Ma'am? Did you hear everything I said? Ma'am?"

Sally was indeed in her little world, but unfortunately, she had heard it all.

"Yes, yes, yes, I heard it all! It is just kind of hard to believe and digest everything you have just told me. I mean, this shit happens on a movie screen with actors, not in my hospital with my friends!"

"I appreciate your disbelief, doctor, but my staff and I are trying to protect the last person out there. We don't know where he is or what he is going to do. But if he makes one mistake, they will be all over him in a flash."

Sally stared at the agent. "How do I know you and your thugs here are the real thing? They could be just like the first group. *Then* how will this end? And really, who are the bad guys and who are the good guys? No offense here, but there seems to be a lot of agents running about, and we are supposed to trust you guys? I mean, who killed four of our colleagues? Really, what the hell…Help me out here!"

"I understand your concerns, ma'am, but all I can offer is this ID badge and a phone number direct to headquarters. Otherwise, you just have to trust me and the men who are here now. And the quicker you do that, the sooner we can put the pieces together to protect Dr. Carmichael."

Sally thought for a minute. Steve was still out there, running from some thugs who were out for his life. But if she trusted the wrong people, she might lead the enemy directly to Steve.

Never did Sally imagine that this could ever happen where she worked. She remembered during med school on the last day when all the senior students found out where they were going to complete their residency. Some were going to do surgery at Duke and others at Stanford. She was just excited to stay in Minnesota where life would be nice and quiet. Little did she know that she would be in the middle of an international mess that would leave several of her friends dead.

"Sally, have you thought about this enough? We need to ask you some questions."

Sally sighed. "Fine. Let's get on with it."

The agent balanced his pen over a pad of paper. "We know through our undercover agents that Jake was making direct contact with several foreign men. These men are terrorists from

Afghanistan. They may have ties to other larger terrorists groups like Al Qaeda, but they may be working independently. Nonetheless, they have possibly obtained some very classified information concerning our country. We will leave it at that for right now. The more information you can give us, the better we may be able protect the country. Do you have any questions? If not, I would like to know if you have ever seen any unusual men talking with Jake or Steve."

Sally looked away to think. She glanced up and said, "I don't recall any major encounters, but there were times that Jake was late for rounds, and he would be seen talking to a man in a black suit. I wasn't ever close enough to listen to their voices. I would never have guessed that he was foreign. I remember one time that Jake was seen talking to a guy near the ICU during rounds. He looked very American."

"That's a start," replied the agent. "It sounds as if you never heard any of their conversations, but what about gestures or exchanges? Did you ever see anything transferred back and forth, like a briefcase?"

"Sorry, but I never got that close to their encounters. Jake was acting a little more concerned the last few days before his death, but he never said why." She paused. "Jake seemed a little uneasy right after the night they operated on that foreign guy, too."

"What foreign guy?" exclaimed the agent. "What foreign guy did they operate on, and why? Do you know any of the details? Is that guy still in the hospital? Can I see him?"

Sally glared at the agent with the barrage of questions. "I am afraid you are out of luck with the hospital visit. That poor young man died post-op from sepsis. They said he came in with a presumed appendicitis, but they found a large mass and a lot of pus when they operated. They took out the mass and irrigated his belly, but he developed sepsis and died."

The man in the black suit repositioned himself on his chair. "Can we look at the mass? Who else was in the OR for that surgery? Do you have a record of what transpired?"

"Yes, we have a record of everything. Everyone who has died so far was in that room, and so was Steve Carmichael. As far as the pathology goes, we can look that up right now." Sally grabbed one of the computer keypads and entered the date of the surgery. She gave the screen a funny look. "That's weird," she said. "There is no pathology recorded for that surgery." She typed in a few more things but found nothing.

Sally was perplexed. She grabbed the phone nearby and punched in the extension to the Path Department. She waited for someone to answer and then asked a few questions. She listened to the response and slowly hung up the phone. She had a blank stare in her eyes. She turned to the agent. "They said there was never any path delivered from the OR that night and that I was the second person in a day or two to ask that same question. They said Dr. Carmichael called just a little while ago and asked for the report."

Without a moment's hesitation, the agent grabbed his phone and walked away from Sally. "John, they took the package! I repeat: they have the package. You need to notify Washington immediately! I don't know where they are, but I do know they are trying desperately to destroy the last link. We need to find Carmichael pronto! They won't want to use any of that info until all their witnesses are destroyed." He looked back at Sally and asked, "Do you have any idea where Carmichael is? This is for national security, damn it. I don't need any bullshit now!"

Sally looked perplexed and scared at the same time. She didn't know what to say. She had no idea where Carmichael would be. Outside of work, she didn't know Steve that well.

She didn't know his likes or dislikes, and she didn't have a clue how he spent his time outside of work. He was just a coworker, so why would she know where he was now?

Sally replied nervously, "I have no clue where Steve would be or where he would go. I don't hang out with him very much, and conversation here at the hospital is limited to hospital stuff. I understand the importance of the matter here, but I just can't help you or your staff anymore."

"How about acquaintances, people he would meet or hang out with after work?"

Sally shook her head. "I have no idea. I never talked about those things with him. He interned with Dennis Burrows, so he might know something, but I don't know how close they were. I just knew they went through orientation together and sat together at the surgery conferences."

"Alright, Dr. Jenson. We are making progress. Where is this kid? Is he here at the hospital?"

"Last I heard, he was on the Vascular Surgery service, but the surgery office would have information as to what rotation he is on now. You could find him a lot quicker that way instead of my just guessing where he is."

"I appreciate your time today, Dr. Jenson. I will contact the surgery office and go from there. We request that you stay near the hospital today until my staff and I are done questioning everyone. You may be needed if there are any further questions or leads to follow up. Thank you again."

The man walked away toward his colleagues, and Sally tried to find Tom Formin. She was walking down the corridor when she saw Erica Miller, the Internal Medicine resident who Steve had talked with as if he had a crush on her. Sally turned around to see where the agent went. She saw him talking with another agent near the cafeteria, so she walked back.

"Hello again, Dr. Jenson. Are you alright?" asked the man.

"There was just one more person that Steve talked with quite a bit here at the hospital. I think he had a crush on her."

"Who was that?"

"That lady over there." She pointed. "Her name is Erica Miller, and she is-"

The man cut her off nonchalantly. "We already talked with her, but she didn't offer us much. Thanks for your time and information." He turned around and smiled at the other man as they walked away.

Sally looked confused. Why he didn't care about Erica? Maybe she had told them about a romantic side to Dr. Carmichael. Still Sally thought it was strange response. As she walked down the hall again in search of Tom, she thought about their questioning. She wondered where Steve was hiding out and what he was doing. He seemed to be the last link to this international mystery.

Chapter 41

The commotion at the hospital was winding down, and the CIA agents were packing up and leaving the hospital just as Steve was signing into a motel near Taylors Falls. He was unaware of the day's events at the hospital, and he hadn't a clue there was a 'bad' and a 'good' CIA. He only knew that thugs were chasing him and that somebody wanted him dead.

Steve finished writing his name and address for the check-in book at the motel. He figured that he was remote enough to feel safe using his real name and address. No sooner did he think that and hand his credit card over to the clerk than he realized that they might have bugs on the credit card.

He snatched the card from the clerk's hand. "Sorry, I forgot that one is getting a little full. Can I pay with cash instead?"

The clerk looked a little surprised, but money was money.

Steve prepaid with cash from his grab bag and got his key to his room without any questions. He didn't have much with him, so he grabbed what he needed from the car and headed to his room. He looked a few times over his shoulder but realized that – at least for the moment – he was invisible to the people looking for him. They would have no idea where he was or what his next move would be.

Once the door was locked, Steve threw his stuff on an old recliner. It was a typical motel room but with a twist of small town leisure to make it feel like a bed and breakfast more than a motel. The beds were made up with a soft country flower comforter. The furniture was an antique collection. It would be fine for a few days while Steve got his thoughts together.

It was too weird to be true. The events over the last few weeks were filled with more drama than he thought imaginable.

He thought of the people who had died. Correction: the people who were *murdered.* This was supposed to happen in a movie but not in his real life. He began to long for his family and friends, and in a most bizarre way, he was really missing Erica. He knew if he attempted any contact, they would be able to track his access to her.

But who were *they*? That was the million-dollar question. It seemed to come back to the drugs. *What a waste of life for a bunch of drugs and money*, Steve thought. A.J. and the nurses who lost their lives wouldn't have thought it was worth it, neither would their families.

Steve realized he was staring at the TV even though it was off. Several days had passed since he'd even had a TV on, so he decided to sit, watch, listen, and try to relax for a bit while considering his next move. He thought it would be much easier to just use a remote and continue to vegetate on the chair that he was in, but it was nowhere in sight. Begrudgingly, he made his way to the TV to turn it on.

As the screen lit up, he went to the bathroom to do his thing. He was barely listening when the voice on the tube caught his attention.

"This is Drake Johnson, reporting live from Sydney, Australia. The people here are in dismay. They just can't believe their eyes. This has been a country mostly immune from terrorist threats and actions until now. Just a few hours ago, the US embassy was bombed. Several people are reported dead and many more injured, but the exact numbers are not in.

We do not want to speculate on the depths of this tragedy."

"Drake, this is Kathy from the New York office. Do we have any idea who did this or why? Is there any connection to the bombing just yesterday in London? This all appears to be directed toward the US."

Steve quickly and attentively returned to his spot on the bed directly in front of the television. He was stunned by this news report. He couldn't help but wonder if there were any connections. He continued to watch.

"Well, Kathy, we are trying to get all of our information straight and make sure all the details go hand in hand before we report to the public. What we do know is that both bombings happened internally. That is, they were detonated from within the buildings themselves. This is very important because it means there was some inside connection. No car or truck was run into the building. A person actually got inside and then set off the bombs from within the buildings. It is much too early to determine if this was international sabotage or if it was a plot constructed by one of our own. It could be a terrorist group or just an employee who went off the deep end."

"But Drake," Kathy interrupted. "If this was someone from within the embassy, an employee of the US government, how could they get to both countries less than twelve hours apart to plant and detonate these bombs?"

"Exactly, Kathy. The concern is that we might be dealing with an organization rather than an individual or small group. An organization is a bigger problem because, if they have access to our embassies, then who knows how much more information they could have? Depending on what they do know, does that mean they will be coming to our country, within our own borders in the United States, to create threats and bombings locally? The authorities are sorting out many questions before they feed the media information. There are reports that the State Department is going to give a formal press conference in the next hour to explain the situation to the public and what it means both nationally and globally. I think it is safe to think that this might be the work of Al Qaeda or a smaller faction of that group. Al Qaeda might take some time to announce their role in these bombings. The talk out here is that this is too big of a mastermind to be just a small group. In fact, just to get into these buildings and dodge all the security is a great concern not only for the government here but also back home."

Steve started to tune out the announcer as he analyzed the entire situation. Sad as it was, what if the whole thing at the hospital was related to these bombings? He thought it would bc a long shot. Yet, the patient who had started this entire escapade was probably from somewhere in the Middle East. Maybe he could have been part of this terror group. If that was the case, perhaps the money was still important, but then why would Jake have been involved? Was the money just too good to turn his back on when he was so in debt? Many more questions, but still no answers.

Steve wondered who he could talk to in order to get more answers. That could very well help him find a way to save himself from getting murdered. He didn't know anyone who could give him all the answers, given that Jake was dead. Perhaps it didn't have to be a person to provide all his answers.

He turned around and looked at the backpack with all the money. He crossed the room to peer at the treasure. There was a lot of money in that little pack. Mixed with the cash was a piece of paper with a bunch of numbers. Steve suspected that they represented some account that could point to a few answers. He carefully reached for the paper, his heart pounding.

The number of digits listed first on the paper convinced Steve that it was an account, but there was also a phone number. No bank name was listed, nor a person or anything else. Where would this lead Steve, and was it a safe direction to go? It might be a trap to find and destroy Steve.

He sat with the backpack on his lap for nearly an hour. As the clock eased toward 10:30, he picked up the phone. Cautiously he started to dial the number, but before he put in all the numbers, he hung up the phone. He just felt that it wasn't safe and that something would happen. He thought about it for a few minutes more. He turned the paper nervously in his hands and finally noticed that more digits were written on the back of this piece of paper. He studied the numbers for a long time and wondered if this was some Internet address. He knew that if he went to this site there was a distinct possibility that his location might get discovered, but he might also get some answers. He figured the CIA would hack into his computer or his account while online, but that was a chance he was going to take.

He took out a laptop computer that he stole from the hospital to stay in contact with Sweetpea. He hooked everything up quickly but turned it on with some hesitation. Fortunately, the motel had Internet access. He paused for one more moment and then decided to go for it. It took a few minutes to get online before he could carefully type the address that was on the piece of paper. He slowly pushed down on enter as if relinquishing his last chance to back down.

The computer started its search. It seemed to be a strange password to a complex site that made no sense to Steve. Then the screen started to spew a random series of letters and numbers. As this weird configuration continued to flow, he saw different languages appear intermittently on the screen. First, it was Chinese, and then some Arabic characters popped up.

Steve panicked and thought what he most feared from doing this was happening. There were hackers trying to identify his location, thus causing the different languages.

Well, he wasn't going to sit and ponder the possibilities. He quickly closed the site and screen. He could feel his heart pounding again.

It was obvious to Steve that his assumption was correct. Getting into that site would give him answers to some of his questions, such as who the people involved were. However, it was too risky to go back there and get himself busted. He pushed the laptop away from himself in disgust and frustration. Now what?

Sweetpea was not an answer, but as long as his computer was out, he figured he should check in with her. He pulled the computer back toward him and began typing away. He found her quickly and wrote that he was on a little vacation.

Her reply was baffling. "Steve, can't tell you everything right now, but you just exposed your whereabouts to the world. They know where you are, and you need to move quickly. I can tell you that they want to kill you, and it has nothing to do with a drug deal. Now, be safe and move immediately! Take care."

Steve looked at the screen as if this was another joke, but he knew better. No more jokes, this was all serious stuff. He looked out his window immediately as if they were already at his door, which was more or less impossible. All was quiet outside his door.

As he stared out the window, he noticed a huge bluff overlooking the town. He was about to take the advice of someone he didn't even know. He was going to ditch the comfort of the motel and just sit on the bluff for the night. He needed to see if she was telling the truth.

He quickly grabbed the blankets from the bed for warmth during the night. He stuffed them with the rest of his belongings into the car. He figured the motel would be a little ticked about the blankets, but he could always return them later.

He checked himself out as quickly as he checked in. He drove up to the bluff and found a comfortable place to settle in for the night. It was a starry night, and he had a great view of the town. What a shame that he wasn't just enjoying a casual camping trip!

Chapter 42

By the time Steve was settled on the bluff overlooking the town, the clock was close to midnight. He had found a perfect place to oversee the quaint town without being visible. A few lights on the road showed Main Street. Steve could see the motel where he had been for a very short stay. He could make out the grocery store and the old-time movie theatre. He remembered going to the theater when he was younger. He had never envisioned that he would someday be living a real-life movie with murder, intrigue, and mystery.

Most importantly, he could view the roads leading in and out of town. He could even see the interstate nearby.

Steve was happy with his location. He could see everything yet felt invisible with the brush and trees around him. With that comfort zone, he snuggled up under the motel blankets. As he drifted asleep, his mind wandered over how comfortable he was a criminal, stealing this and that, bucking the rules, and causing mayhem wherever he went. This was a new Steve Carmichael.

He slept very lightly. At about 2:00 in the morning, something startled him awake. He jumped up from his sleep, thinking that someone was nearby. He jerked upright. He looked around and found a deer. It quickly became scared and scurried away.

In a few minutes, he was dozing off again. Before long, the sun was making its way into the sky. As darkness was replaced by sunlight, the clock read 6:57AM.

Steve stretched and looked out at the town. No activity down below at first glance, nothing out of the ordinary for this little town. A few people were up and about, probably opening shops and getting to work. The interstate had its usual flow of traffic. As he watched the people down below get started with their day, he realized that he would be spending a good portion of his day on the bluff. Unfortunately, he had failed to stock up on food before leaving town, and now his stomach was making all sorts of funny noises. He would probably have time for a visit later, but he wished that he had planned better in case the morning on the bluff proved long and slow.

No sooner had he realized his mistake than he saw two black suburbans drive into town from the interstate. Steve looked toward the highway to see if other cars were making their way into town but saw none. He focused on the vehicles as they rolled to a halt directly in front of his former motel. *Sweetpea was right!* he thought.

Two men got out of each vehicle and looked around. The men from the first car walked to the entrance of the motel. Steve was much too far away to recognize their faces, but clearly, the first two men were in charge. The two others waited outside while the first two talked to the clerk. They both looked unremarkable. One pulled out a package of cigarettes, and they started to smoke. They rested against the car but barely had a few puffs when the first two came storming out of the motel office, clearly upset. Steve just smiled to himself.

One of the men kicked his car a few times and then began throwing his fist against the hood of his car. Although Steve could not hear a word of the conversation, he did recognize that they were after him.

The four of them talked for a few minutes, then jumped into their respective vehicles and made their exit from Taylors Falls. Steve was not sorry in the least to disappoint the men. He wanted to talk to Sweetpea to tell her she was right, but that would just lead those men back to him. Since they were already on their way out of town, Steve thought he would take the opportunity for a nap. He closed his eyes and snuggled back into the blankets.

He couldn't have been sleeping long when the humming of sirens woke him. Steve rolled over to examine the latest situation down in that little town. "What could be going on down there that was worth calling the troops?" Steve asked himself. When he saw black suburbans again, he quickly sat upright. Instead of a pair, a dozen vehicles paraded into town this time. Steve tried to figure out why they came back and in greater force, especially since they knew that he was gone. Did they discover something else? Did they get a tip of his whereabouts up here in the bluff? The cars were intent on staying down in Taylors Falls, so he scratched that idea. They quickly surrounded the motel, much more aggressively than the first time. It was very strange, but why should that bother Steve? The whole thing was strange.

This time, each vehicle held several men, and each stepped out with a mission. Some went into the motel, some started to set up equipment they pulled from the cars, some were on cell phones, and more. No one leaned against a car to smoke.

These agents held Steve's attention more carefully than the group of four. He continued to observe their behavior and activity. This was obviously a more intense search for Steve. He hardly knew if that was good or bad. He noticed that the men who went into the motel were still there. Their questioning must have been in more detail because they didn't immediately come out of the building kicking and hitting cars. In fact, it was nearly an hour before those men exited the motel and began discussions with the other men and on cell phones.

Steve finally realized that the two groups of agents weren't collaborating. *What was going on?* Too many new questions bubbled in Steve's mind. He had wanted to focus on saving his own life, but this morning just opened a new can of worms.

He wondered if Sweetpea knew this when she warned him. He wondered if she knew that two different groups of agents were chasing him down. *But why? Why so many men, and why didn't they all arrive together?* As he watched this second group, he considered if there was a good group and a bad group, perhaps imposters. If so, why would both groups want Steve? Did they all want him dead? Were both looking for the same thing?

Steve continued to watch their each and every move. It was obvious that they knew he wasn't there, but they weren't leaving. They continued to talk to strangers in the streets and went from house to house and shop to shop, presumably asking questions.

Never did any of them ever look toward the bluffs, so Steve remained comfortable as he watched all the action and tried to piece it together. What he really wanted to do was talk to Sweetpea to see if she had any answers, but he knew that was just too risky. Instead, he had to start planning his next move because he couldn't make the bluffs his home forever. His hungry stomach was a dominant reminder.

At this point, he knew both groups were looking for him, but he was not sure if they all wanted him dead. He wondered if one of the groups were good guys and trying to protect him.

Still, it was certain that somebody wanted him dead. He didn't have anything except a lot of money, but they had killed A.J. and the nurses without anything – but did they know? Maybe they wanted him dead like the others because of what he saw or knew from that surgery on that foreign guy. If Sweetpea said it wasn't just about drugs, then maybe there was something else that came out with that mass. *What???*

It really didn't matter what was in that mass because whoever wanted A.J., the nurses, and Jake dead would also want Steve dead. This was the fact that Steve knew for sure. So the next step was to protect himself. In order to do this, he had to kill them before they killed him. *Oh, shit,* he thought. *Now I am going to be a murderer too.*

He didn't have to kill anyone. He just had to capture them or detain them until the right authorities came to incarcerate them. Steve started to think about how to do this. It would have to be perfect and go without any hitches, or they would kill him first. This would have to be a very well thought out plot.

Steve's stomach gurgles fell silent to his ears as his mind worked. He had to come up with the perfect plan to save his life. He lay back on the grass and stared into the sky, trying to come up with a strategy.

An hour later, he sat up and smiled. He had gone through several scenarios and plots, but many were too Hollywood. If there were any mistakes, he wouldn't get a second take with a director shouting, "Cut!"

He smiled. *I need to use my brains with something I am comfortable and know inside and out,* he thought. *So why not head up to the Boundary Waters in the wilderness and use my skills up there to capture my enemies?*

Steve had loved nature since he was a little kid. His dad would take him up north several times a year to backpack, canoe, and camp. He knew how to protect himself from nature's wildlife, and now he could protect himself from the city's wildlife. He found some paper in the car and made a list of everything he was going to need. After all, money was not going to be an issue.

Chapter 43

Steve spent the better part of an hour plotting and organizing his thoughts. After writing a list of all he was going to need, he decided it was definitely time for a bite to eat. The only problem was that the present town was not a safe option. He packed up the car and left town.

He needed to head up north toward the Boundary Waters and Canada. He stopped at the first gas station he saw to go the bathroom and fill his stomach with food. He grabbed several bags of junk food and hit the interstate.

While driving, he realized that with all the things he was going to get, including a kayak, he was going to need a larger vehicle like a pickup truck or a big SUV. He still didn't want to attract too much attention by buying a car or truck with cash. It would be nice to use the car he had for a trade-in, but since it was only a day old, that would also attract attention. He decided to look for another used vehicle.

He exited at the first town he came to along the interstate. He drove until he saw a car dealership and then parked on the street to buy yet another car.

Thirty minutes later, he drove off the lot with a nice used Yukon, perfect for all that needed to get done. He stopped by his day old car to pick up most of his supplies. He left the blankets and the car keys behind for some other lucky thief.

The next step was to eat a real meal and to get supplies to shave. Everything on his head and most of his facial hair had to go. He planned to leave only enough to grow a goatee.

He visited a local diner for a real meal and then stopped at the Super America, which was conveniently busy. No one noticed him around the bathroom: in with a full head of hair and out with nearly nothing.

Next was Ely, Minnesota. This was a town right on the edge of the Boundary Waters. He could shop there safely. He needed supplies to survive outside in the wilderness for a week or so, not to mention a few extra things to protect himself from the urban wilderness and agents.

It had been a while since he was in these parts of the woods. Driving up north brought back many memories about his childhood and camping in the great woods. He remembered a time when he, his father, and his brothers were hunted for nearly a day by a mother bear trying to protect her cubs. His brother got too close one day to those cute little bears, and mama bear was not happy. She chased Steve and his family hours, but they got smart and left that part of the woods.

Steve forced himself to focus on the animals that were chasing him now. He was going to have to cut down his hunters one by one. Was it going to be just four hunters or a group of several men? What a difference that could make in how he approached his own chase.

Finally, he decided that the large group of men that showed up in Taylors Falls seemed much more professional. They went about their business systematically. The first four men just wanted Steve. They didn't wait around to discover any leads to direct them toward their target. They just showed up and left. If he had to put his money on one or the other, he would have to guess that the four guys were the imposters or bad guys, and they would be the ones hunting him down. Both groups might be after him, but the four men were more likely to have killed the others and to want Steve dead now.

If his hunch was correct, Steve needed to lure four men in and detain them in some way until real authorities could apprehend them. Then, and only then, could Steve move on with his life. He had to devise a way to attract only the four men instead of the whole cavalry. Both sides had showed up at Taylors Falls. He needed to figure out a way to entice only those four men and not the others.

His brain was working overtime trying to sort things out and plan during the drive. Consequently, he failed to realize how close to Ely he was getting. Signs on both sides of the interstate advertised local businesses. The sign that caught Steve's attention was a wilderness store. Steve remembered going there in the past. It had most everything a Boundary Waters camper could ever dream of. The sign said it would be another twenty miles, so Steve returned to plotting what he would need.

Suddenly, his answer clicked: the bank account. The enemies probably had the account closely monitored so that they could trace Steve's computer if he entered the numbers online. The other men or FBI agents probably didn't even know that account existed. That was the perfect solution to attract one team without the other.

As far as capturing them after that, Steve had a good idea of what he wanted to do. He had already spent a great deal of time thinking about it. He was going to show these men some quality time up in the great north. The important point of this unique camping experience was that everything had to be perfect, without any loose ends, or those friendly city slickers would be after Steve with a vengeance.

Steve pulled up at the wilderness store for a shopping spree. The first thing that caught his attention was the kayak collection. He was going to need a whitewater kayak to get him around quickly in the Boundary Waters. If he needed to get away from his hunters in a hurry, this would allow him to escape safely on the water through tough river currents. Setting up traps for them near the river access would be wise so that

Steve could make a clean get away and leave them on shore. He was certain they would not come comparably prepared to deal with the elements.

He knew exactly what he wanted from years of paddling experience. There were many options, but the Mamba would be perfect. This little boat would get him in and out of trouble quickly, have enough room for storage, and have the ability to handle any whitewater and rapids that he would encounter.

To play it safe, Steve planned to buy all the essentials and then set up camp himself before summoning the bad boys. There was no need to be in a rush. He was in control now.

After selecting the kayak and supplies necessary for a good whitewater experience, he was off to purchase camping equipment. Steve just wanted the essentials. He had spent enough time in the wilderness growing up that he had the knowledge to make it through up there with the bare minimum. This was important with such limited storage space in the kayak.

Steve enjoyed that money was not an issue but rather space on the kayak was. He acknowledged he would have to make at least two trips into the Boundary Waters even with the bare essentials. He could set up camp somewhere within the Boundary Waters and paddle back to his car to make a second trip.

He spent about two hours at the store stocking up for a wonderful camping and paddling experience. They had great-prepackaged food specially made for camping. It didn't take up too much space, it was easy to prepare, and it wasn't too bad for the palate. All in all, the shopping spree was wonderful. It was some of the most fun Steve had in a long time.

As he was checking out at the register, he grabbed a small newspaper for this little town of Ely. After packing everything up in his car and finding a safe place for his kayak, he searched through the wanted ads. It took a little while, but he found some of the extra things he needed, like a bear trap – but not in case he encountered another overprotective mama bear.

He started to reach for his phone to call the number listed for the trap, but he realized he wasn't ready to attract the troops up. He went back into the store and asked to use the company phone. The man he called said he would be there for another fifteen minutes, so Steve got directions and hurried on his way.

The man was pleasant and eagerly showed Steve the traps that he had for sale. Steve inspected them carefully and decided to buy two. As he was waiting for the guy to get everything ready to go, Steve noticed the news on TV. There was a story about the mess Steve was in. It discussed the weird situation and informed that authorities were looking for one more person involved with the murders: "Steve Carmichael. If you see him, please use caution as he is armed and dangerous. Please call the authorities if you spot this man."

Dangerous! thought Steve. There was no way in the world he was dangerous, armed, or a murderer. It was a good thing that he had shaved his head and grown out his goatee, quite different from the picture they were showing on the national news.

Sweetpea was right. They were really looking hard for him!

The man with the traps asked if there was anything else he could do to help. Steve looked around the room as if it were a store, but his mind was caught up in the news story about him as a wanted criminal. He had a glazed look in his eyes and responded with a slow drawn out no.

Steve left with his traps and a criminal record. He figured that he would need a few days in the Boundary Waters to set everything before he would alert the authorities of his whereabouts. His car was packed with his gear, food, and kayak, so he drove to the entrance of the Boundary Waters. There were a few places people could enter this huge park that covered territory in both the United States and Canada, but Steve was most familiar with the Ely entrance.

Steve got the air bags blown up, his wetsuit on, and took as much gear as would fit on the first kayak run out to his campsite. He would come back in a week to tell people in town what islands, lakes, and rivers he was planning to camp on so that his hunters would have an easier time finding him. First, however, he needed to get his traps set. He stuffed rope, the traps, a foldable shovel, and the tent into the storage compartment of his Mamba kayak. Then off he went.

Steve paddled to the first lake and found a nice camping ground on the opposite side. He had never camped so close to the entrance, but he knew he had to make at least one more trip out. The trip out took about ninety minutes, but he was in no hurry. No one knew where he was, so he enjoyed himself. If any of this failed, he would be a dead man anyway.

Steve fit everything else in his second trip with the kayak, so he took off into the great Boundary Waters. It was a great day with the sun shining and cool air beating down on his face. He had all the things he needed to set these guys up for the chase. He set up at camp with a small fire and his tent. As the fire blazed, Steve took out the map of the area and started to plot and plan. There could be no mistakes: any error in the details could mean his life.

Chapter 44

Steve was hoping it would take only a few days to set everything in order, but there was so much more to do than he had planned. For one, the ground was cold, so it took longer to dig the pit. Nonetheless, six days later, Steve paddled back to the Ely entrance to the Boundary Waters.

He had put everything in place just how he planned it. Once everything felt perfect, he would go through it over again from a different viewpoint, second-guessing himself and playing the devil's advocate from each angle. He had to make absolutely certain that everything was in place now and would still be when he returned with the CIA hunters.

Steve brought his sleeping bag back with him to camp near the entrance to the waters but still close enough to the town of Ely so that he could track the CIA agents coming to town. He was sure they were going to come without equipment, so he wanted to see what they bought to town for the waters. The spot he was going to set up camp was a place he had known for years. He and his brothers would sit atop a hill about five minutes from the entrance. With the aid of binoculars, he could see all activities in and around the town.

First, he needed to leave a trail toward his whereabouts. He was going to spend a day in town asking questions about the Boundary Waters, certain lakes and rivers, and where the best whitewater was located this time of year. He would only ask about the areas in which he wanted to be chased.

He paddled the kayak up to the entrance and placed it in his car. After taking off the wetsuit, he hurried up the hill. As he found the perfect spying spot, he reminisced about how he and his brother would sit there for hours, watching the town. Now it was the offseason, and Ely was quiet. The advantage was that his pursuers would stick out like a sore thumb as some of the only 'tourists' around town.

Steve sat for a long time, reflecting on his childhood, medical school, this horrific experience, and much more. Eventually he decided it was time to mingle with the locals and yak his head off. The locals needed to be able to rattle it off perfectly to the CIA agents when they arrived in town asking about Steve's movements.

He gathered his thoughts and made his way to the Ely coffee shop for a bite to eat. A number of people were there as he ordered something to drink and some food. While waiting, an older gentleman greeted Steve. "I haven't seen you in town before. What's your business?"

That didn't take long. Steve smiled. "I thought I would catch one more trip before winter sets in and ice covers these gorgeous lakes. Besides, it's so nice to head up here when no else is around. It is so peaceful and quiet without all those tourists."

The older man nodded his head in agreement. "You sure got that right. It's great to get rid of all those pseudo campers and have our town back. So where are you planning to go?"

Steve could not have planned this any better. He told the man every detail of his alleged trip. He explained where he planned to be and how long he was going to be in each spot. It was a perfect conversation.

After a short two hours, Steve managed to tell a varied group of locals about his plans of camping and river running and where he planned to hike and set up camp. He even shared thoughts about where to store food during the nights. Several locals had gathered and listened to his conversation with the older man and then added their own opinions. This could not have worked out any better.

Steve had been thinking of visiting town again tonight and having a beer at the bar down Main Street, but that would no longer be necessary. He had a perfect crowd, so he had no reason to repeat the same conversation with another group of strangers. He finished his meal and sat around with the group for a short while longer before asking where to find a public library. He paid his bill and shook hands with everyone in the group. It was a sweet goodbye.

Steve grinned as he walked out the door. Not only did he share everything he wanted with the group, but also over two hours, not one person asked for his name. Phase one had been completed without any difficulty.

Now on to phase two. He walked outside and paused for a moment. He stretched his arms and looked toward the sky. He wondered if he was ready for the fireworks. Everything was set up in the Boundary Waters. He was ready to be done with this terrifying nightmare and move on with his life.

He followed the easy directions that the man had given him to the library. Steve was daydreaming about the possible outcomes of his plan and almost walked right past his destination. He knew once he logged on to the foreign account he would have about twenty-four hours before the crowd would arrive.

Suddenly it occurred to him that he should make contact with Sweetpea. If something did go wrong, she should know to get into contact with the right authorities. It would be fun to contact her anyway to just regroup his mind and thoughts. He really just wanted to take a few minutes to get away from this bad dream and talk to an old friend. He wanted to remember what normal life was like and learn if anything new had happened during the past few weeks.

The library was a cute, older building. The walls were brick, and it looked like an old, one room school from years ago, with the smell of mildew in the woodwork.

Steve searched for computers. He wondered if he'd made a mistake. What happened if there was no computer in this public building?

No sooner did he start panicking than he glimpsed two computers in the corner. He dragged his feet as he proceeded in that direction, knowing that once he got into that account, he would initiate mayhem for this small town and himself. The aisles were quite narrow in order to fit everything into this small building, but after about thirty seconds of shuffling, he could delay no longer.

Steve was ready to get to work. He logged on and then looked around as if someone were already monitoring him. It took only a few seconds for the computer to warm up and get him to the Internet. He pulled the folded piece of white paper from his back pocket and hesitated only for a second before typing information regarding the foreign account. Once he clicked enter, he decided to stay in the account and look around. If it was going to be the connection that sent them after him, he might as well pretend the account was actually his.

Steve poked around for about five minutes to make sure that the computer was tracked without difficulty. They probably had it tracked within a few seconds, but he needed to be sure they'd come after him. After he felt there was sufficient time to get busted, he logged out of the account.

He quickly typed Sweetpea's account info into the chat search engine.

She was waiting for him again. "Where the hell are you? I have been so worried about you! Are you okay? Is there anything I can get for you? Do you have enough food?"

Steve thought she was being a little over protective but knew that she was only concerned about his welfare. Unlike the general public, she didn't recognize him as an outlaw but as a guy in a lot of trouble with the wrong kind of people.

"Hey, I am doing great," he typed back. "Just hanging out in Ely. Thought I would do some off-season camping since I really didn't get a chance to go this summer. How about you?"

"Steve, that is not funny! I have been terribly worried. You drop concerning messages and then have to leave so quickly. Are you okay?"

Steve debated just how much to tell her about his intentions, but he *did* want her to get some information in case something unplanned was to happen to him. He quickly told her his camp and kayak plans and which rivers he was going to be on, and then it was time to get off.

They said their goodbyes. She told him to be careful, and he laughed to himself. "Thanks, Mom!" he jokingly typed. "I promise to be good, and safe!"

Steve waited at the computer for a few minutes, just staring into the empty screen. Everything was in place, and now his plan was in motion. He wondered how long it would take those men to make it to Ely and how many people there would be. Maybe the real CIA agents would blend with the bad ones and arrive at the same time. Maybe they were all involved with this situational drama together after all.

Steve shook his head. He couldn't really believe that everyone was on this same side of this mess.

He knew he had at least a few hours before trouble would arrive. It was early evening, and he figured that, by morning, there would be a few new people in town. His plan was to head to the grocery store for a few more things. He spent about twenty minutes in town getting what he needed, including a fantastic pair of binoculars. After his shopping spree, he made his way to the top of his hill and set up camp. Tonight he wouldn't allow himself a fire. He didn't want to attract attention to himself prematurely. He ate a lukewarm dinner and some snacks. He wrapped himself up with his sleeping bag but stayed sitting up. He was not going to miss anything.

Chapter 45

As Steve was tucking himself in for the night, a foreign delegate from the Middle East with a strong accent was busy on the phone lines. “We need to pass it on that Carmichael is located in a town in Minnesota called Ely. He tried to access the account! He is trying to make a run for it, and we need to locate him before he takes all the money. You need to pass this on, and we need them to find and kill him once and for all.”

The return voice on the other end of the phone also had a Middle Eastern accent. “Relax, relax, my friend. We will capture this Mr. Carmichael, and then we will be able to complete our plans with no other worries. We need to contact our friend in Minnesota to get his team to take care of this Carmichael.”

Click.

Another phone call was placed. “Good evening, my friend. I am calling with the whereabouts of a Mr. Steve Carmichael. Once I give you this information, I trust you will complete our mission as previously discussed. I don’t want any more loose ends. My friend, he is in Ely, Minnesota. I don’t know where that is, but I trust you will greet Mr. Carmichael with open arms. There is no room for any more errors. I hope you understand that if there are any more problems, the deal will be off.”

A voice with an American accent responded, “Yes, I understand completely. Dr. Carmichael has been evading us, but my team will finish him now. You should have no worries.” Agent Thomas hung up the phone, and the phone lines went quiet.

Chapter 46

The information had been passed to the appropriate parties. Although Steve did not know the specific content of those conversations, he knew that they were taking place. He knew they were making plans to hunt him down and do away with him. Steve knew that if he were to make any mistakes, then they would win and he would die.

Several hours later, Steve was sleeping on his perch when he heard the echo of car doors slamming shut. He quickly opened his eyes and focused down on the town. Just as he had hoped, two black SUVs were parked outside the library. He glanced at his watch and saw it was already 8:30. He had no idea what time the library opened, but it was obviously closed now. The men looked like small ants from where Steve was sitting, but he could see that the doors wouldn't open for them even without the binoculars.

The men must have started with the library because they were tracking the computer, not the man. Steve was confident that the men would eventually make their way to the coffee shop and find the info they wanted from fellow diners. Steve used the binoculars for a while to see with whom the agents came in contact. He noticed that they had a picture of him to show people. It would only be a matter of time before the men showed it to someone that Steve had talked to at the coffee shop.

Steve figured he had a while before the men would have all the information and supplies that they needed. He broke the tedium of watching the town to open a bottle of juice. While having a bite to eat for breakfast, he jotted notes and kept track of every detail he could grasp about the men. It was a team of four men driving only two vehicles. Steve scanned the vehicles with his binoculars multiple times but never saw anything to suggest other men. He was able to recognize the man he had encountered in the locker room, Agent Thomas, but he wasn't sure if the men were the same as before.

It didn't matter who was there, just how many people he had to deal with. The numbers were important; the thugs themselves didn't matter as much. The men finally made their way to the coffee shop and spent a great deal of time in there. Steve hoped they were talking with a few people from his visit yesterday. Nearly an hour passed before they came out of the coffee shop and headed toward their cars. *Good,* thought Steve. *They found the bait and took it.*

The SUVs headed to an outfitter where they could buy the essentials to get them through an unknown camping experience. Steve imagined the humor of seeing four men in business suits shopping for gear that would ordinarily be used with rugged attire. Nevertheless, they spent nearly two hours inside, presumably shopping and plotting their adventure route. They were probably using clues from the conversation at the coffee shop to plot on a map. Steve hoped they wouldn't hire a guide. That would mean another innocent bystander who did not need to get hurt.

Eventually they filed out. They had several bags of supplies. Steve had binoculars but not x-ray vision. He really wanted to see what was in the bags to get a better idea of how well they were prepared to weather the great outdoors. He was pleased to see their two canoes. Those guys would never be able to keep up with Steve in the rapids or anywhere else on the water given the maneuverability of his kayak. *Two points for Steve,* he thought.

Steve could see backpacks and paddles, but he could not see what or how much food they had. With good advice, they would have meals enough for seven days. No fishing poles protruded from the shopping bag. Steve jotted a few more notes and then felt he should get going so they wouldn't catch up with him paddling in the middle of the lake. They wouldn't need a close proximity to shoot Steve on open water, but he didn't want to give them that opportunity.

He gathered his belongings, mostly garbage at this point, and then hiked down to an isolated lake access. He found his kayak where he had left it near the secluded shore. He knew the place from camping as a kid. He got his kayaking skirt on now and hurried out on the water. He paddled in the direction to his first campsite, the one he had mentioned to the townspeople. There he would begin his adventure.

Steve figured he had at least four hours before they would reach the first site, but he had a few traps to set up for them. His kayak cut through the water without much difficulty, providing him a safe advantage over the CIA thugs.

As he paddled, he contemplated whether to start the action that day or let them set up camp and orient themselves on the island first. Meanwhile, Steve noticed that water was choppier than it had been the day before, which would give him even more time to get organized ahead of the canoes.

Once Steve was close to his site, he looked back but didn't notice any canoes. Once on shore, he climbed a tree to spy on Ely with his binoculars. He couldn't find any canoes near shore, which meant plenty of time to check his traps. The first stop was a deep pit. He had shoveled that while attached to a rope to be able to get out after the pit was completely dug. He tried to make it close to twenty feet deep to ensure that whoever was to fall in would not be able to get out. If two men fell in at the same time, they still wouldn't be able to stand on each other's shoulders to get out.

Steve walked another two hundred yards to where he had marked off the next trap. The bear traps were set up just as he had left them. Steve knew this would be fatal unless the men were to leave and get medical help immediately. The traps were designed with the strength to sever the leg of whatever bear – or man – stepped on it. If a poor human victim were by himself for any period of time, he would probably bleed to death. Steve felt a touch of guilt at the prospect, but he reminded himself that his intended victims had already killed more than one innocent soul. The traps were in perfect position. He would just have to remember the exact location so as not to land on it himself as he dashed by.

Before examining the last snare, which was meant for two, he took a break with food and water. He had left two rope traps adjacent to a hornet's nest. As if it wouldn't be bad enough to hang upside down, he anticipated a nice greeting from the hornets.

He was thinking about this last trap when he thought he heard voices off in the distance. He froze. There was no way those thugs could have made it out this far in such a short time. He jumped up and started to run to the shore. No sooner did he get to his kayak than he saw the canoes. The weather and winds had calmed down, and the waves were almost non-existent. Steve's pursuers were only about a hundred yards away from the shore. With a panic-stricken face, Steve heard them scream out, "Hey, there he is! Let's get going!"

Steve had not planned to start the chase on this shore just standing around. He had wanted them to be much further into the island and closer to the traps.

He frantically jumped into his kayak, quickly remembering that he wasn't wearing his kayak skirt. He jumped out, put the skirt on, and leapt back into the kayak. He paddled his kayak as he had never paddled before. He took off along the shore, unsure where to go. If he were to take off into the middle of the lake, he would be nowhere close to the traps, foiling his every plan. He didn't know where to go along the shore either. The island was quite large, and to just paddle around the lake would serve no purpose.

As Steve wasted time contemplating his next move, the agents were moving into gunshot range. Just then, Steve noticed an entrance to a small river. He was not sure exactly which river it was, but he had no choice as a loud gunshot sounded.

The entrance was narrow, but once through, Steve smiled to himself: sharp turns filled the path ahead. He glanced over his shoulder and shouted, "Oh, shit!" They were catching up with him much quicker than he thought they could paddle. He paddled faster as he heard another gunshot. He was moving as fast as he could, dodging overturned trees and boulders in the river. The current was not moving very quickly, so he had to make that speed up with his own strength.

Steve was a little unsure of where he was in the island, and he definitely was not familiar with the river, but he didn't have time to care. They had twice the horsepower per canoe, and they were more comfortable with the canoe than Steve had predicted.

Steve wondered if the river would get the best of him, but then he caught a sound that was music to his ears. It sounded like a loud washing machine. As he paddled forward, the churning of water got louder and louder. "Rapids!" he shouted with relief. He realized where he was and exactly which rapids he was fast approaching. He had been on them before, but it had been a while. He didn't have time to look them over now. He figured it would take at least class three rapids to knock over the canoes.

As he turned the next bend in the river, great delight filled his face. They were easily class four or five rapids. The water was already moving quite fast but only accelerated as Steve continued forward. He knew that those canoes wouldn't stand a chance against these rapids. The holes were huge and strong, the eddies few in number. Even with the most experienced hands, canoes were no match against those rapids. Within seconds, Steve started to bounce from one current to the next.

After about two hundred yards, Steve found a small eddy to pull his kayak and watch the enemies. By this time, the four men had started down the rapids. They actually were doing all right as they hit the first few rapids, so Steve turned himself around and continued downstream. Unexpectedly, a current caught an edge of his kayak and nearly rolled him over. He gave the river a quick and sharp slap with his paddle and bounced upright in no time. He moved on without a moment to breathe.

The next two hundred yards were incredibly difficult. Steve barely made it through. He found another small eddy and turned his kayak around in order to observe the canoes as they chased him.

The first canoe held Agent Thomas, and it was doing okay. The second canoe was having more problems getting down the rapids. Suddenly it flipped over a large rock and into a huge strong hole. One of the men popped out of the hole right away, as did the canoe, but the second paddler in the canoe did not come up.

Steve glanced at his watch and noted the time, 3:52. He continued to watch in disbelief. Nothing has gone accordingly to plan, but this situation was still working to his advantage. Steve knew that, after seven minutes, the missing guy would be a dead man, and the only thing that would pop out of the water then would be a lifeless body. Holes were notorious for taking people's lives. They acted as a suction device, pulling water back deep into the river as the current flowed over rocks. The bigger the rock, the faster the water current and the more dangerous the hole. As time went on, the likelihood that this man would survive was decreasing.

3:58 was the time when Steve checked his watch again. He

turned his kayak to pull out of the eddy, but he wanted to watch a few more minutes. This was not how he planned any of his victims to perish, but he didn't care much as long as he was one person closer to living a normal life.

After ten minutes, Steve felt comfortable moving on. He knew the three other men saw him take off. Steve took one peek back and saw them fussing over the canoe and trying to grab the supplies that had fallen out when it overturned. Steve decided to catch the next eddy just to see what they would do.

He saw all three men get into one canoe and paddle toward shore. Steve figured they had decided to bag the rapids and just get to dry land. He noted where they were, assuming they would set up camp nearby. He was certain they were done for the day, as they still need to pitch a tent and gather wood for a fire to dry their clothes and other supplies. Steve eddied out and went down stream to a safe place for portage and to find his camp. There he could keep an eye on where the other three set up their camp.

Chapter 47

Steve shot the rapids for about a mile more before he decided that he should get to shore and locate his camp. The monstrous rapids were a lot of fun, but they seemed to go on for a long stretch.

He looked up stream and unsurprisingly saw no one. He knew they wouldn't waste time trying to fool him by pretending to get out and then jumping in their canoes once Steve was out of sight. They would never have survived those rapids anyway.

Steve pulled his kayak up on to shore and covered it with brush, ready in case he needed a quick getaway. He looked around to see if he recognized where he was on the island. He noticed a thinning out of trees to his left and figured it would be close to the lakeshore. He made his way through the trees toward that break but soon realized that he was wrong and completely lost.

He returned to where he got out of the river. He was trying to determine how he could find his campsite when he came up with a completely different plan. The three remaining CIA agents knew that he was downstream, but they had no idea what or where his plans were. Why not set up a mock camp to make them think that this was his actual campsite? Then they might not spend as much time or energy seeking his real campsite.

He walked up about fifty yards and started setting up a campsite. He didn't have a spare tent but arranged a fire pit and lit it. As he was putting together brush for a bed, he thought he heard voices but told himself there was no way those men could have made it through either the water or woods that fast. He stopped to listen to the forest for a few minutes but then continued to work.

Only a few more minutes went by before he heard another noise. This time it wasn't voices but rather some brush moving about. It sounded as if it was coming from just beyond the campsite he was creating. He stood paralyzed for a minute with a million thoughts running through his head. *What if it's the men and they're getting ready for the kill and I'm not even putting up a fight? What if it's some other weird stalker just hanging out on the island, taking humans as prey??*

Steve shook his head. He couldn't let his mind create drama when none was really there. He figured he was hearing things and that his mind was playing games with him. Nighttime was fast approaching and twilight was setting in. Steve needed to get back to his real campsite and settle in for the night. He looked all about the site to be sure that everything was in proper position. As he did, he heard another bunch of leaves move about just a short ways a way. He glanced in that direction and found himself looking straight into another pair of eyes.

Alarmed, he couldn't make out if they were from the men or not. The creature slowly came forward, and Steve released a quiet shriek. It was an automatic response to the huge black bear standing directly in front of him.

Never in all of his experiences camping had Steve ever encountered a black bear. He turned toward the river and ran, jumping over tree branches and rocks along the way. He could see his kayak but could also hear the bear chasing him and grunting. He didn't want to know just how close this monstrous creature was behind him, but before he hopped into the kayak, he turned his head to see.

The bear was only ten feet away, so Steve grabbed his paddle, jumped into his kayak, and pushed himself out onto the river. He didn't even consider taking time to put his skirt on. As soon as he felt the rush of the current, he realized just how important those skirts were. Brisk water splashed against his legs in the kayak immediately. The fast approaching darkness worsened the effect of the cold water. He wanted to take a moment to put the skirt on but had to check for his latest pursuer first.

The bear wasn't as brave as Steve, or maybe it was a bit smarter. The creature didn't dare step into the aggressive rapids. It remained near shore and watched Steve bounce along the rapids, one wave to the next. Steve turned around in disgust. That big bear had scared the pants off him, and now he was in the river without a skirt while the bear comfortably watched from shore.

He wanted to take a few minutes to put the skirt on, but the water was moving terribly fast. It would be better to wait for a break in the rapids before he could position himself properly to get the skirt on without tipping the kayak over.

Just like that, he hit a rock in dark water. The kayak leaned upstream as it bounced off the rock. Once Steve leaned upstream, he could feel a rush of cold water start to fill his kayak. He had to use all his energy to bounce the kayak back up and downstream before the boat filled completely with water. Leaving off the skirt was becoming increasingly regrettable: it would have covered the kayak cockpit to keep water out and would have helped roll the kayak back up in case it flipped. Now Steve just needed to get to shore safely so he could empty the water in his kayak.

Despite a full moon and cloudless night, he was unable to see clearly on the river. As soon as he recovered from one near catastrophe, he hit another rock. He leaned back to get himself off this rock, but the massive pressure from upstream took his kayak sideways again. Before he could blink an eye, the kayak was pulled down from the pressure of the current. He tried desperately to flip his kayak back upright, but it was to no avail. The boat already had too much water. It finished filling in a quick second and then flipped over. Steve was dumped into the water with little chance of rolling the capsized kayak, so he bailed.

The water froze even his soul for a moment. He quickly realized that he was still in a tumble position. He assumed the proper position as he surfaced. He was on his back with his legs bent up so he looked like he was driving a go-cart. His legs would hit rock after rock, but he would be able to bounce off each one as he made his way to the shore.

He leaned backward and used his arms for a strong backstroke. He was gaining ground toward the shore when he hit a particularly big rock. He bounced off with ease, but right away he could feel the sucking pressure of a hole start to drag him to the downside of the rock. He frantically backstroked with his arms, but the current of the hole was too much for him. He could feel himself being dragged underwater.

At this point, he knew it was hopeless. Only by mercy of God was he only going to be able to survive this ordeal. He took in a huge breath of air just before the current pulled him into the depths of the river.

As he was pulled into the hole, he tried desperately to keep his wits about himself. He hoped he could push off the rock down below as the current kept turning around like a drying cycle. Then he could use the force of the hole itself with his own strength to break free from the gravity holding him in the current. He prepared to touch the bottom with his feet, but he got to the bottom without any warning. He felt himself hit bottom and start to ascend back upwards. He had no time to push off, so he was at the mercy of the hole again.

He gasped for another huge breath of air when he reached

the surface. He tried frantically to swim free from the grasp of the current but had to go with the pull of the current from the hole. He could feel his body being suctioned like a piece of dirt in a vacuum cleaner, but he tried to stay more focused as he went down this time.

He bent his legs like a baby in order to offer as much spring and force as possible to break the suction of the current. *Boom!* He felt himself hit the lower edge of the rock. With every bit of energy and strength could muster, he kicked off the rock with his hands straight above his head. Just like a slingshot, he could feel himself being flung with the upward current to the surface of the water. As his head reached the surfaced, he forced his arms down to his sides to pull himself free from the strong grip of the current.

He shot up through the air and free from this hole. He knew he was going to land back in the river, so he gasped for more air. Once in the river again, he resumed the position of being on his back and using his arms to direct himself to shore. He hit a few more rocks but gradually felt the peace of an eddy swirling around in circles at the river's surface.

Steve sighed with relief. He knew how lucky he was and that most people – like the agents upstream – would never survive encounters such as this one. He pulled his weary body up to the shore and lay on his back as he regained his senses. He stared at the sky and watched the nearly full moon and hundreds of stars in the night sky. That horrific experience had drained his energy. His eyes began to fall shut, but he knew he was still being hunted with no idea where he was on the island. He wanted to get up and get back to his camp, but just as he'd had no option in the river hole, his body fell asleep right there on the rocky shore of the river.

Chapter 48

Steve woke abruptly as his body shivered from the cold. He never had a chance last night to change into dry clothes, and now his body was terribly cold. He was glad he was wearing body thermoware that prevented his body from getting too cold from the water and night temperatures. He could still feel his fingers and toes, so he knew he would be okay. He thought of ways to warm the rest of himself. A fire would be nice, but that would just attract attention. He thought about trying to find his original campsite, but the sky was still dark. He tried to keep his eyes open and to get up, but his body was still exhausted. He tried to lift his head, but it felt as though it weighed a hundred pounds. He gave up trying for a moment and stared at the sky.

The moon lit the sky like a Hollywood movie opening. The stars added their own cast characters. He decided from their stage position that it must be getting close to dawn. He only had limited time before the agents were on his tail, so he rolled his tired body to one side and slowly picked himself up. He stood on the rocky shore, listening to the river moving down stream, reliving the nightmare from just a few hours ago. The moon shined brightly on the rapids.

He began walking along the shore. He found what looked like a break in the brush and woods, and he veered off with high hopes for a hiking trail. Despite the tall trees, the moon's brightness lit the way for Steve. He tried diligently to recall where he was or where his campsite was. He thought he knew the island well, but not so much in the middle of the night and soaking wet. He recognized some trees from setting his bear trap. He suddenly thought how miserable it would be to fall into one of his own traps.

He moved about slowly so as not to set off one of the traps. He saw where his rope trap was set and then knew exactly where he was. Now that he was reoriented, he took a moment to process what had happened just a few hours ago. He had rolled his kayak, hit a few bumps, almost died in a river hole, and lost his kayak. He'd had a fair amount of equipment still stored in the compartments of the kayak, but worse was that the kayak was his transportation back to Ely. He no longer had any means to get back to the mainland. He knew the agents had already dumped one of their canoes, so that left only one possible canoe to get back.

He needed to concentrate on capturing the agent with the ring and putting a stop to the manhunt. Steve's stomach grumbled, and he realized just how much he had lost on the kayak. He had his backpack on with a few essentials like water and snacks, but the rest of the food was gone. He stopped for a break and pulled a bag of trail mix out of the backpack. He was devouring the treat but then realized he should eat in moderation in case he was out in the wilderness longer than expected. He drank a little water and then put everything away. Eating would have to be a rare luxury until he was safely out of the Boundary Waters.

The sun started to make its rise along the eastern sky. Steve needed to get close to his campsite and start the manhunt. He took a step in the direction but froze when a sound in the background startled him. This time he knew they were human voices. He heard males speaking to each other but was unable to pick up what they were saying. They were coming from the direction of Steve's campsite. They must have gotten an earlier start, just one more thing to backfire for Steve. He climbed a nearby tree to get a better view of the situation. Sure enough, his campsite was about twenty-five yards away, and three men were going through his tent.

That didn't matter much. Steve was more concerned as to which way they were going to go. The plan had been for them to be chasing him so he could direct them into each trap. Now they were in position to have Steve chase them instead, which is exactly what he didn't want. He needed to have the upper hand to stand any chance of surviving this mess.

He was trying to think of a way out of this dilemma when the three agents started to walk in the opposite direction of the snares. Time was running out quickly for Steve's strategy. He hurried down from the tree and ran toward the campsite. He had to dodge the pit that he dug and the bear trap. He got close to the camp and started shaking a tree violently to get their attention.

As soon as Steve started to rattle the trees, he heard one of the men shout, "Hey, over there! I think I heard him that way. Let's go!"

The chase was on. Steve was not exactly where he wanted to be, but he was just going to have to do some maneuvering to get himself closer to his intended route along the traps. Steve ran as fast as he could through the brushy forest, reminding himself that he just had to trap each man and then summon the correct authorities.

As he was running away, Steve almost passed his first trap, the bear trap. It was a large metal ring with huge teeth that would snap shut and lacerate, if not amputate, whatever leg stumbled into it.

Steve slowed down enough for the agents to catch up and spot him. They needed to follow his exact trail. Steve was almost at a walking pace when he saw the men behind him. He passed the trap, slowly walked over it and beyond.

"Alright, Dr. Carmichael," called one of the men. "This is enough! We have chased you long enough, and this is ridiculous. We just want to have a few words with you."

"How come you didn't just call?" Steve remarked quickly. He felt comfortable sassing them because he knew they were after his life.

"Very funny, Dr. Carmichael. This topic is very important and sensitive to me, and I would rather we discuss it in person. That is why I made the trek out here to find you."

Steve recognized the voice of the ringmaster, Agent Thomas. "If that is the case," he replied, "I am right here in front of you. Let's talk."

Steve stood still and watched the men slowly make their way through the brush. He was glad that at least one thing was going right as they walked directly along the path of the bear trap. He was disappointed to see that Thomas was second in line with some bulky man in front. He wondered where the guns were hidden.

They were only about ten feet from the trap when Steve said, "Okay, close enough. I can hear everything that you want to say to me." He didn't want it to be too obvious that he was prepared for them to walk up to him without any hesitation or concern. He hoped that they would ignore his request.

They continued to slowly walk toward him. "Dr. Carmichael, we have made a long voyage out here, not to mention that a very dear friend of mine died yesterday, so I'd prefer to see you up close."

Steve replied with a somber voice, "I understand. I lost some very good friends as well recently. They were wonderful, innocent people. Funny how we both must be suffering from their losses." He wanted to continue but realized that they were only inches from the trap. He needed to be ready to bolt once that trap snapped shut because he would be well within gunshot range.

The ringmaster started to reply, "Yes, Dr. Carmichael. Those losses were very unfortunate, but they lost their lives honoring their country as-"

A loud snap sounded.

"Ahh! Oh, my world! *Ahhhhh!*" screamed the front man.

Steve didn't need to continue this conversation any longer. With a quick turn, he was gone. He was well oriented and ready to continue the chase. Although he was only yards in front of them a second ago, he was out of sight in a few seconds. He could tell the other two were attending to their front man because no shots sounded for at least fifteen seconds. By then, he was hidden deep in brush. He took off at a different angle too, so shooting in the direction of his previous position would be useless.

He ran nearly a hundred yards and found the tree from which he knew he could see them at the trap. He climbed the tree as easily as a ladder. The branches were in perfect position.

The poor soul, Steve thought when he saw the wounded man. His moment of sympathy passed quickly as he remembered that their sole mission was to kill him. Still, the victim had blood gushing from his leg. The trap had evidently locked onto his lower leg. The power of the jaws of the trap must have nearly amputated his leg, but it was dangling in the air. The other two men were trying frantically to release the jaws of the trap, but it wouldn't budge.

Steve was far enough away that the agents wouldn't be able to see him, but he could see them and hear almost everything they said. Agent Thomas looked up every few minutes as though hoping to see Steve. Steve could hear him swearing at the trap and at Steve.

"Damn that Carmichael! When I see him, I will rip every organ out of his body with my bare hands!"

Steve could feel the anger building up in Thomas. It was obvious that they didn't come prepared for all of this. Although Steve felt bad, he realized it was him or them. Another thing he realized is that this must be their whole team because they never attempted to call for backup. He was confident it was just the three of them, soon to be just two, left for him to handle.

Twenty minutes passed before they finally unhooked the trap, and the victim had nearly bled to death. Another few minutes passed before they started a tourniquet to help stop the blood loss. Steve figured they were so focused on getting that trap off they had forgotten about the leg itself. Now the man appeared pretty limp as they tried to stand him up.

Steve could sense that the man was in hypovolemic shock since he had lost a fair amount of his blood. Unfortunately, there was no way to get any volume back in him, no IVs and no saline. The two others tried to carry him for about twenty-five yards, leaving a trail of blood, but Agent Thomas was growing increasingly frustrated at being slowed. The two healthy men finally stopped for an earnest discussion. It appeared to be more of a disagreement as the other man was throwing his arms up and shouting at Thomas. The man finally kneeled beside his friend and started to wrap his injured leg with an extra shirt. As he was working on the man, a gunshot echoed.

Steve couldn't believe it. Thomas had just shot the injured man in the head. He heard the kneeling man scream, "What the hell did you do that for, you idiot? You didn't even let me try to wrap him up or anything!"

Steve could just barely hear Thomas' calm reply. "He was a goner. He lost too much blood, and he wasn't even complaining or hurting anymore. He was only going to slow us down, and we need to move quickly to catch Carmichael. Let's just dig a shallow grave to protect his body from any animals, and we'll get him on the way out."

He pulled out a fold up shovel from one of the backpacks and started to dig. Steve knew this was going to be a long process, so he climbed down from the tree and made his way closer to the pit. He was hoping both pursuers would fall into it, and then he'd be done with the ordeal.

Chapter 49

As Steve was walking thoughtfully, Agent Thomas was digging thoughtfully. He was frustrated with this entire ordeal. When he was initially approached on this matter, he couldn't imagine the endless problems that would result. He thought it would be easy money. He hadn't even bothered to consider what the foreigners would do with whatever they were transporting. Thomas just wanted some money to pay off his bills and to finish his life in paradise.

As one partner lay dead next to him and another was lost in the river, Thomas began to see that this was not the best decision he had ever made. Perhaps these were not the right people with whom to have made a quick buck.

After digging a shallow grave, Thomas sat next to it and thought for a few minutes. He quickly reviewed his life. As a kid, he had always liked espionage and mystery shows. He would daydream often about life as a secret agent. He would imagine running through the forest, driving fast cars in chases, and jumping out of high-speed trains in order to catch the bad guys. As he sat now by this makeshift gravesite, it seemed he was the bad guy. *How did this happen?*

His dream of being a spy had continued through the college years. Some dreams fizzled, but this never once faded from his thoughts. He would be in the library to study but would catch himself daydreaming about capturing some double agent after a long chase through international territory. His alias would encounter battles, fistfights, gun battles, and close encounters with death, but he would always end up as the victor.

Reality seemed so far from his ideals of yesteryear. He had become a CIA agent, but it was a distant second to the heroic spy of his dreams. The work was exciting at times, but he never got to visit the world or chase international thugs. His life had proven rather dull, especially outside the realm of work. His professional life never became what he had hoped, and his social life was even worse. Relationship after relationship, but he never could find the right one. Later in life, he met a woman who seemed nearly perfect for his lifestyle, but soon after they were married, they realized they were unable to have children. They tried to work on the marriage despite this major shortcoming, but she had asked him for a divorce just a few years ago.

That seemed to be the beginning of the end. One thing lead to another, and his okay life started to fall apart at the seams. His social life began to fade again, and his professional life headed down a dark path. He was unable to get the cases that had any promise of upward mobility. He was constantly getting reprimanded at the office and slowly being ostracized by coworkers and friends alike. He was at work constantly, and his partners were switching with unusual frequency. It was just not where he wanted to be at this point in his life.

If the downfall at work was not enough to break him, he began to have issues with his sexual wellbeing. As time went on, he dared to get an opinion from a doctor. He soon discovered he had prostate cancer. There was talk about various treatments, but ultimately the surgeons recommended removing his entire prostate at his relatively young age to aggressively treat the cancer. Thomas had spent hours on the computer and talking with others to get different opinions, but the consensus was to have surgery and just move on with his life.

His life continued to sink downward until he received a most unusual call from a man with a strange Middle Eastern accent. It was strange indeed. He always dreamed of international activity but never as the bad guy. The talks with his new contact were short but seemed to provide everything he needed at the moment: money, freedom, and a chance to move away from this awful place. Every time he talked to this guy, the possibilities seemed endless. What they needed from him and what they offered didn't seem so bad at first, but as he sat next to his dead partner, perhaps it was not such a lucrative payoff.

The money his ex-wife was able to pull from him with the help of an exceptional lawyer had taken him to the bottom. His bills too were quickly adding up. The call from this man came at a most opportune time, but then the man had done his homework and knew he found an ally in need of financial help in the worst way. They knew what they offered to him was too good to pass up.

Now Agent Thomas was in a much different place than he expected. He had no money, no wife, no prostate, and no morals. He was on the run from the very same people he had worked alongside for years. If that wasn't bad enough, he was sitting next to a makeshift grave that he himself had dug for a partner who never even knew exactly what was going on. Thomas's team only knew they were going to get an undisclosed amount of money. Thomas had done his homework too and found a few men with a situation similar to his.

Agent Bill Thomas was just another miserable person who was moving to the dark side with the consequences that resulted from his poor decisions. He quickly looked at the only other living person on his team as the man dragged the dead body to its temporary resting place. Thomas wondered for a moment if he should disclose the full truth. Should he tell him about the chip? Should he just shoot him now and keep the money for himself? That would be one less person to worry about. Thomas studied him and even reached to his holster to grab his gun. The other man, unaware of Thomas' reflections, looked up for help. Thomas stared at him for a brief moment longer before dropping his arm. He stood up to assist his partner in burying their fallen comrade.

Chapter 50

Steve walked through the forest without a particularly quick pace, certain that the two agents would be busy for at least a few hours burying their partner. *Agent Thomas doesn't really seem to have much patience for the people he worked with,* thought Steve. He knew that the agent was on a mission, but he was still uncertain as to what it was. This entire experience seemed surreal, especially for a young surgery intern just minding his own business.

Steve wished he had more knowledge as to what sparked the entire ordeal. So many people were involved, but for what? So many questions remained unanswered. He acknowledged that one certainty still stood out: they wanted him dead. If they did capture him, they would have plenty of ways to disguise his death, including his own traps.

He pushed the prospect out of his mind. He was close to his pit, so he picked a tree to use for spying. As he was climbing, he tried to listen for voices but heard none. He continued to climb until the point after which he expected the branches to break under his weight. He looked in the direction from which he had come but saw no sign of his enemies. He glanced in every direction but still nothing. Steve was surprised not to find them still digging. He scanned the area again in case they were setting him up with discussions of burials while really planning to take off after Steve. He climbed out of the tree somewhat anxiously, thinking they could be anywhere. He looked from side to side as he made his way down the tree. He couldn't see anybody anywhere.

Suddenly he thought he heard voices, so he stopped quickly and turned his head slowly in the direction of the voices. They were just ten yards away. Steve tried to quietly come down the rest of the tree, but Thomas' partner shouted, "Hey, there he goes!"

So started another fast pace chase through the brush. Steve didn't have the upper hand this time with a good head start. He dodged tree after tree as he heard one, two, and then three gunshots. Fortunately, he knew exactly where he was and where the pit was. He ran as fast as he could with a few quick turns here and there to avoid the bullets rocketing from the guns.

Before long, he recognized his pit, covered with camouflage just as he had left it. He zigzagged around the pit with an extra turn to confuse his trail. He ran about twenty yards past the pit before turning around. They were already near the edge of the pit. Steve stopped and stared as they moved toward the pit.

Agent Thomas saw him and stopped running himself. His face revealed concern as to why Steve would have stopped.

Steve noticed and realized that he had stopped too early. He was mistakenly giving the agents another advantage with time to consider the situation.

Thomas returned his gun to the holster. He picked up a log and asked, "Was this what you were hoping for?" He threw the log dead center into the camouflage of the pit. The log and the brush over the opening fell quickly to the bottom.

Steve turned and started running as fast as he could in a crooked path. He could hear Agent Thomas laughing as he started in after him again.

"Not so smart after all, huh, Carmichael?"

Steve refused to consider how poorly that had worked out as he ran for his life. He continued redirecting himself in varying directions as he heard the intermittent gunshots. He was trying desperately to get further away from the two men when he tripped on a fallen tree branch. Quickly he darted up and continued to run, worried that the few seconds on the ground slowed him too much. He didn't want to take the time to look back.

He was so concerned about getting away to safety he wasn't even sure how close he was to the next trap. He realized he had only one more chance to take care of at least one of the men. He would have to find some other way to deal with the last man, but he couldn't skip the rope trap near the hornets' nest.

As he rushed past several large trees, he identified where he was in proximity to the rope. He wasn't taking any chances this time: he was going to keep running after he passed the rope. If they missed it the first time, Steve would loop them around again. The extra distance would be better than having them discover the trap.

Fortunately, Steve heard a loud scream. He knew not to get too excited because it could be a few possibilities. One thought was that the men discovered the rope trap without getting caught, and the scream was to lure Steve back. The trap may indeed have captured one or both of the men, but Steve would have to be cautious if he wanted to backtrack to check.

He didn't want to make his return obvious, so he started to walk back toward the hornets' nest in a big half circle rather than back track the exact route he came from. A few steps later, he decided to climb a tree to get a view of the rope trap and watch the men from afar instead. As he was climbing, he could hear outrageous cries of pain. The more he heard the screams, the more sure he was that they were real screams of pain.

Nonetheless, he made his way up the tree and saw the horrific view of a man dangling by a rope lassoed around his left leg. He was trying desperately to reach up to his leg as if to get the rope off. Meanwhile, hornets were attacking him left and right. His arms were swinging back and forth trying to swat at the hornets, which was only making matters worse. With each swat came a few more stings from the hornets.

It was disturbing for Steve to watch the helpless man unable to release himself. His colleague was unable to help him because he was too high off the ground, and the hornets were sucking the life out of him. Unfortunately for Steve, the man dangling was not the ringmaster. Agent Thomas was jumping up trying to help free his friend, but he was well above reach for anyone on the ground.

The man's screams quieted after a few minutes, and his movements were slower with less effort to free himself. The hornets were swarming all about him and appeared to be covering most of his body. Soon there was no movement at all. The hornets buzzed around their victim as if to acknowledge victory.

"Carmichael!" screamed Thomas. "I am going to kill you! I am going to inflict so much pain on you like you have never envisioned. You are going to wish you never had become a surgery resident. You are going to wish that you never worked with anyone from the hospital. You are going to wish that you never knew me because when I get a hold of you, I am going to torture you to the point of no return! You are going to wish that you never even considered any of those torture traps! I am going to kill you!"

Steve felt terrible about those traps. He hadn't wanted to make anyone suffer or die, but he didn't want to die himself either. He wanted to shout out his apologies and hope the man would keep them in mind before torturing him, but he knew better. Thomas was not only out to keep Steve quiet; he wanted painful revenge for his partners. Once he had Steve in his custody, he would destroy him. There was no alternative: Steve still had to get the job done. He had to finish off this man, or he was going to be killed.

Steve noticed Thomas' voice growing louder, and then he remembered he was being chased. He flew down from the tree and started running away from the hunter. He darted through the woods and didn't look back. From the amplitude of his voice, Steve could tell that Thomas was much closer than was safe and that he was gaining the proximity. He knew where he was when he first took off from the hornet's nest, but now, as he was running for his life, he realized he was lost again.

With his heart pounding from exertion and panic, Steve made his way quickly through the trees. He nearly fell when he glanced up and saw the end of the forest. No more trees, no more brush, no more ground, and no more hope. He had reached a cliff at the edge of the forest and could run no further. He glanced over his shoulder. He could not see Thomas, but he could hear the rustling of brush as he follow.

Steve looked down and saw a river flowing about fifty feet below him. He thought it might be the same river he had been on earlier but had no recollection of where he was now in relation to the big lake. He knew he was losing valuable time just standing there, but he needed to clear his head to plan a quick escape.

He looked down again. He studied the surroundings all the way down to the river. He noticed for a quick second how beautiful it was but then recognized what he could hit on the way down if he jumped. Trees and brush extended from the side of the cliff all the way down. If he got a good thrust off the ground, he might be able to miss most of the branches. However, he had to hit the water just right in order not to break every bone in his body. He couldn't enter headfirst with the rocks and underwater tree branches. So many possibilities could contribute to a rather dim outcome, but the torture Thomas had promised was not a comforting alternative.

Just as he heard Thomas coming through the clearing in the forest, Steve noticed a kayak making its way down the river. He quickly glanced over his shoulder at the man with his gun in hand and then back to the kayak riding the current downstream. As he focused on the kayak, trying to understand why anyone else would be kayaking this time of year in the Boundary Waters, he realized he recognized the person paddling.

He heard Erica Miller scream, “Jump! Jump, you moron!”

Steve couldn’t believe it. What was Erica doing out here in the middle of the Boundary Waters?

It didn’t really matter. He glanced at the man whose only interest was in torturing Steve to death. He knew Thomas couldn’t see Erica. Steve had an outlet, dangerous, potentially fatal, but at least one outlet that would remove him from a slow death by an angry enemy. Worst case, dying from a dive into the river would give Steve a very quick, painless death.

He decided to take this situation as far as he could before getting shot or plunging to his death. He wanted some answers. He looked at the kayak below and then turned to Thomas. “What was this all about? Since you are going to kill me regardless, just tell me why. *Why the hell do you want to kill me?*”

Thomas slowed his pace. “You have seen too much, and you know too much. You are the last problematic link to this entire mission. To have you around flapping your lips and telling the proper authorities on me, what you had seen and who you had seen me with, would jeopardize my future. So I have to destroy you and all the knowledge you’ve stored up in your head.” He suddenly pointed the gun at Steve and fired a shot.

Steve jumped back a step as if there was more than a foot of safe ground behind him. He felt the bullet pass with a hissing sound. His heart was pounding right out of his chest. The man deliberately missed him.

"Kind of scared now, Carmichael? Nowhere to run now, huh?"

Steve looked at the man and then down to Erica who was still shouting, "Steve, just jump! It's almost twenty-five feet deep here! I have a depth finder for God's sake. Just please jump before he kills you!"

Steve faced Thomas one more time. "But why the others? Why did you have to kill the others? Why the innocent nurses and A.J.? Why them?"

"Because you all were loose ends," shouted the man. "I didn't know who saw what, and I couldn't take any chances. Once you are gone, I will become a very rich man!"

Steve had heard enough. As Thomas raised his gun again, Steve turned around and jumped as hard as he could away from the cliff. He heard another gunshot, but he was already past the edge and on his way down to the river.

Chapter 51

The dive down was more fun than being shot at, but Steve had just enough time to wonder what the water would feel like before he splashed through the surface. He was engulfed by freezing water in a split second. All other thoughts vanished as he focused on the abrupt change in temperature. The wet cold gripped his veins quickly. He became motionless as the water penetrated his clothes. He never felt the bottom of the river, but his body reached a plateau downward, then began its assent toward the surface. His body was so cold that he barely could move his arms upwards to help swim to the surface.

Breathing was not even a question for those few seconds under water. The cold shock numbed Steve's mind. His head bobbed up out of the water, and he was in a daze. Erica was shouting his name, but he couldn't comprehend her words. He was unable to focus on her at all.

She was waving her hands wildly, trying to get Steve to swim to her as quickly as possible. She was afraid the man was going to lean over the edge and start shooting.

Steve finally noticed her and wanted to make his way to her, but he was paralyzed by the cold water. Multiple gunshots fell from the cliff, and his daze dissipated. His brain recognized the situation he was in and forced him to swim toward Erica as she paddled desperately closer.

"Get in for damn sake, Carmichael, before he kills both of us!" shouted Erica.

He leaned over the front cockpit of the double kayak and tried to pull himself inside. With as much energy as he could muster, he pulled himself over the front end of the kayak.

Erica started paddling downstream as the gunshots continued. "Hang in there, Steve," she offered. "Let me get past this curve up here, and we'll get you inside. I brought some clothes for you, thinking you might need a few warm items, but first we need to get back to my camp and away from Mr. Gun-Happy."

"What the hell are you doing here?" asked Steve with a confused look.

"There will be ample time to explain everything to you, Steve. First, let's get safe, and then we will get you warm. On our way back to Minneapolis, we will talk," explained Erica.

As she paddled, the gunshots grew more distant and less frequent. Steve slowly maneuvered his body into the cockpit of the kayak. He had no paddle or skirt for the kayak, but he was glad to be out of the river. He wrapped his soaked sleeves around his very cold and wet body. The shivering was continuous, and his teeth would not stop chattering.

Erica could see his body shake but ignored it as she paddled as hard as she could to get to her campsite. She had dry clothes and a blanket for him there.

There was no more conversation, no shared words, no explanations, and no answers. They both were silent as they traveled the river waterways to her safe haven. Although it felt like eternity, they were there in about ten minutes. Steve was colder than he could imagine, but he was grateful to be alive.

They pulled up to the shore off a rather large eddy in the river. Steve sensed that he was finally safe. Still in shock from the cold temperatures and still confused as to why an Internal Medicine resident was in the middle of the Boundary Waters saving his life. Erica got out of the kayak first and pulled it up to land. She stood behind Steve and lifted his freezing body up and out of the kayak. She laid him next to the boat and quickly ran over to her tent. She pulled out an emergency blanket and ran back to him. She laid the blanket open next to him and began taking off his clothes. “Don’t mind me, Carmichael,” she teased. “I have been wanting to do this for a while but maybe under less duress.”

She wrapped his naked body in the blanket, and she began patting his body down to dry off the water. She ran back to the tent for warm clothes for him to wear. She dropped them on the ground next to him, then looked away.

“What?” Steve laughed. “You don’t want to dress me too?”

“Don’t get me started, Carmichael! Be careful what you wish for,” Erica said with a smile. She turned around and began packing up her campsite.

While Steve was getting dressed, he noticed what she had for camping gear. She was prepared. She had at least enough supplies for a week. She obviously knew what she was doing, and Steve grew more confused about her role in this mess. Nevertheless, he had an awkward feeling of comfort and security with her there, as if he knew she was supposed to be there to protect him.

Erica was ready to go. She kneeled over Steve and asked, “So, hotshot, are you all warmed up and ready to do a little paddling? Or will I have to do all the work again?”

“Hey, I kind of like being taken care of by such a nice, warm internal resident or whatever you are,” he responded.

“Such a typical male response, and the egotism of a surgeon!”

As she was bending over him, Steve saw a gun stashed in her chest holster. Their eyes met, and a thousand new questions filled his mind.

Erica looked down at the gun and then back to Steve. “I guess you are wondering about this latest medical technology.”

“Either you get into some very serious kinky sex, or there is more to you than I know about!” said Steve, knowing it had nothing to do with the hospital.

"I will tell you everything once we're back on the main land," said Erica. "But I can assure you that I am the good guy. Or gal." She flashed a grin but then continued softly. "It is very complex and may even sound a bit bizarre, but you are in the middle of an international nightmare. You've been amazing! You protected yourself and used resources appropriately to get to the truth and protect the innocent. You are safe now, and you'll be home soon. All I need you to do is paddle like the wind!"

No more questions were asked, but the two worked together as if they had been partners for years. They finished loading gear into the kayak and pulled back onto the water. This time Steve had a skirt to keep him and the boat dry. Steve sat in front, and they paddled like never before.

Every so often, Erica paused to look in all directions for a follower, one with a gun and a mission to kill. The ride back to shore would only take an hour or so, but Thomas could very well follow them on the remaining canoe. She thought they had at least a half hour head start with two paddlers. The other man would probably try to remove any traces back to make himself invisible to the real world before pursuing them. However, a lot had happened that Erica hadn't anticipated, so she paddled harder.

The trip back proved to be a very simple, mundane kayak ride. Erica had hidden her car and other supplies along a rocky shore about two hundred yards south of the public access. They unpacked and gathered what needed to be placed in the car with few words. Erica was in a hurry to get Steve home safely, and Steve wanted to hear Erica's story. They worked expeditiously and efficiently. The dark suburban was packed in a few short minutes. Steve felt as though they were working the Indianapolis 500 as a cockpit crew. They were driving toward Minneapolis in no time.

After nearly twenty minutes of silence, Steve could not take it anymore. "How much longer do I have to wait?" he asked impatiently. "I would like to know everything. No, actually, I *deserve* to know everything! My friends and coworkers have been killed. Innocent people are dead. Families have been torn apart and changed forever. I need to know why this guy wanted all of us dead!"

"Bill Thomas," responded Erica. "Bill Thomas is a very dangerous man. You are right: he wanted you dead in the worst way. Of all the people he held responsible, you are the one he wanted dead most of all."

"Why?" Steve interrupted.

"Because you knew too much, you saw too much, even though you had no idea what was going on. You were just there at the wrong time in the wrong place. Although several people died, they helped prevent the death of thousands more people. We will make absolutely certain those people who died will have done so as heroes who protected innocent children, mothers, fathers, families and so many more. Their families will be honored as such, and the country will know of their patriotism."

Erica continued. "Agent Thomas was a CIA agent who was approached by foreign terrorists. They recognized his vulnerable state, recently diagnosed with prostate cancer and broke from his divorce. Broke financially, physically, and emotionally. These terrorists did their homework when they discovered Thomas. They offered him a deal too good to be true, a deal that would create a foreign threat to the United States. Although Agent Thomas was a good man and a good agent devoted to his work and country, he had hit rock bottom, no money and no one to lean on."

"So why me, Jake, and the OR crew?" demanded Steve.

"Honestly it wasn't you, Steve, or the OR crew. It was Jake. Thomas did his homework too. He found a poor, vulnerable soul in Jake. Jake was a surgical resident in a similar flight pattern, cycling out of control toward the bottom of the pit. Money was scarce with bills to pay, not unlike many surgical residents. Otherwise we are not totally sure why Jake. Thomas probably had several possibilities that could have been substituted for Jake, but he agreed. He probably didn't even know the details of what he was involved with. He just was supposed to deliver a package – that surgical specimen. I suspect he had no idea that it contained a computer chip that provided immense intelligence. That small chip contained a wealth of information from international and federal agents, their locations and real names, the locations of defense satellites, vital intelligence, and counter terrorism. It was primarily a new way for them to communicate to each other across borders without the use of the web, computers, or cell phones. They have been concerned for some time that our intelligence was picking up on their communications and needed a way to communicate with each other, especially from one continent to another, without being discovered. The chip also had the whereabouts of several terrorists in the United States, addresses, phone numbers, ongoing and planned plots and attacks on targets in this country and others, and so on. Honestly, there may be more, but that is all we were briefed on. I don't think even Agent Thomas knew exactly what was on that chip. They just needed a discrete way to transport information about their organization to members in the United States, and Thomas was a perfect guinea pig with resources to make something like this work but without any moral conscience. The point is that, if the chip would fall into the wrong hands, many lives would be at risk. Not just the agents involved or their families, but certain cities and countries would be at significant risk for terrorist threats. The list could go on and on. So those people from the operating room who lost their lives did it for the sake of thousands of others."

Steve felt confused and overwhelmed. He had wanted to know what all this was about for so long, but now that he was beginning to know, he was numb all over again. "So what does this have to do with you? Why are you involved?"

"Agent Erica Miller." She reached out her hand as to shake his in a formal introduction. "Also known to you as Sweetpea."

Steve gasped. "You mean…You mean you have been Sweetpea online as well as Erica my friend in the hospital? *Why?*"

"Because we had to protect you! But also we had to protect all of those agents. We knew Thomas would be inquiring about a few chief residents, and we knew you were going to be on Jake's service early on so we had to befriend you and gain your trust. That paid off since you were one of the few who were in the OR the night that the package came and then the only one still alive. We had to keep you protected and keep in contact because you were our only source connected to these men. Without you, so much more would have been at risk. It was truly a foreign threat in every sense of the term. You were our last hope at capturing Thomas and the chip."

Steve was doing his best to process all of this drama, none of which he would ever have imagined for himself. He had wanted to be a surgeon in the worst way but never an international spy or agent or whatever he was turning out to be. He was still perplexed as to how he ended up being involved. It was all just surreal to him.

As he pondered more, Erica pulled into the streets of Minneapolis.

He had more questions. "So what about you? Are you really a doctor? Are you just an agent? Is there anyone else I need to worry about? Any more bad guys lurking about? And most importantly, where is the chip?"

"Wow, I can see how you have taken such good care of yourself out there in the real world!" answered Erica. "I am not actually a doctor. I just play one on TV! Just kidding, sorry. I am not a doctor, but I went through intense training before arriving at your hospital, and I had a real doctor inside my ear the entire time I was in the hospital. So every decision I made was from real doctors based in our department out east, and the patients were always safe. As far as Agent Thomas, we have intense tabs on him. All of his team were real agents originally, but Bill coaxed those over to his side who he knew he could trust to work on his behalf for a lump sum of money. We think… Actually, we *know* they were all on the island with you, so it is just Thomas we are after now. The intelligence we have is that if Thomas could not destroy and take care of all the loose ends, the deal was off and the terrorists he was working with would not want the chip. They didn't want to take any chances at getting caught and blowing their cover. We would very much like to find out who they are to prevent other situations like this in the future, but we are more concerned about the issue at hand and the lives we can save by obtaining that chip. We need to find that chip before Thomas sells it to another source and threatens the lives of thousands."

As they pulled into the hospital parking lot, Erica said one more thing. "We still need to find Thomas, and we need to find the chip before it lands in the wrong hands. But Dr. Carmichael, you are now a free man."

"Just like that, I am done?" Steve questioned. "I have been involved with an international espionage ring, my life threatened multiple times, my friends killed, and now you'll just leave me be?"

"Actually, Steve, you'll have to be debriefed. Another agent will want to ask you many questions and obtain as much information as he can get before we let you go."

"What about you? Will I get to see you again?"

Erica paused. "I don't think you want to get involved with my kind of life, Steve. It gets very complex, and there is no organized schedule to my life and work. One day I could be in Washington D.C., and then I could be in Tehran a few hours later."

"Perfect!" Steve laughed. "That will match my schedule, too. Do you know many surgeons? We don't have a set agenda either. Perfect! So when can we have our second date?"

They both laughed. Then she grabbed his hand with a serious expression. Looking into his eyes, she asked, "Are you serious?"

He grinned. "Absolutely!"

Erica leaned over and gave him a warm and genuine embrace. "Soon…"

Chapter 52

Steve was a free man again. Nobody was chasing him. No one was trying to find his whereabouts, and no one was trying to kill him. Although he was free to go, he felt the need to stay. The experience had been an addicting process, more than Steve had realized. He wasn't ready to just get out of the car and walk away from the drama. He wanted to see it through at least until the case was closed with Bill Thomas and the chip in custody and Erica's real phone number in his hand.

Steve fumbled with the seat belt as he tried to unlatch it and then looked at Erica. He wanted to say something unique and wonderful, but as he stared at her beautiful eyes, the words that were in his head dissipated. There was nothing there to come out of his mouth. The sweet words he wanted to share with her vanished. He tried to think of something to say as filler while he tried desperately to recall the words he wanted to share with her.

"What about if I could hang out with you until this case is closed? After all, I did act as an agent and help apprehend the suspect!" Steve suggested. "I would stay out of the way and just offer medical advice as it deemed itself important. I could help locate the chip and I…"

Erica cut him off. "Steve, we so appreciate your help and that you risked your life as we attempted to apprehend Bill Thomas, but legally we can't take a person off the streets as a pseudo CIA agent without any training. There are so many risks involved. You proved yourself to be very cautious and wise as you protected yourself while trying to get Agent Thomas, but there is a lot more training before you could become one of us."

Steve replied, "But you quickly became one of me – I mean

a doctor. You jumped into the world of medicine and took great care of patients."

"But Steve, I had an earpiece in my ear the entire time! I was connected to several physicians in our office. They were the ones who took care of the patients, not me. Let me try to explain it in terms that may be closer to home for you. What if I wanted to be a surgeon? I couldn't just walk into the operating room and start doing surgery. I couldn't just ask for a scalpel and then complete a Sigmoid Colectomy. I wouldn't even be able to do that with an earpiece in my ear! That is the same situation we have here."

"I am not ready to be done with this!" Steve insisted. "It is kind of addicting. I mean the adrenaline rush, the thrill of fighting the bad guys, the adventure, all of that stuff. And besides, I don't want you to run off just yet."

Erica blushed and didn't know what to say. She wasn't ready to leave Steve either. She had enjoyed many wonderful moments shared on the computer as Sweetpea and Steve. She had learned about his life. She felt connected to him as if they were actually dating. She had shared intimate moments about her life online as well as in person at the hospital. She was just as attracted to him but didn't know what to do about that. It was totally unprofessional to fall in love with clients or colleagues, even pseudo colleagues. Still, she had thought many times about Steve when she probably shouldn't have. She couldn't remember feeling this way before toward another man. She really did want him to stay and help, but it would be all wrong.

They gazed into each other's eyes across the car, each trying to find the strength to part but trying more desperately to find excuses to stay together. A long moment of silence passed before Erica slowly and somewhat reluctantly reached for Steve's hand. She gently placed her soft fingers over his and was about to say something when they were interrupted by a loud knock on Erica's car door window. Disappointed in the timing, she reluctantly rolled down her window.

"Miller!" It was one of her colleagues. "We got some info on the whereabouts of Thomas. Looks as if he was quicker than you in driving back from up north. He already spent a quick fifteen minutes at his apartment and now is parking at the airport. Let's move! Miller, we can't lose that chip!"

Erica had no choice now but to include Steve, at least for the time being. She put up the siren that was stowed by her ankles and threw the car in reverse. The siren went on, and the car bolted forward with thrust that Steve hadn't experienced since the rides at the amusement park. Erica glanced over at Steve and then down at his waist. "I guess you…I mean, *we* both get our wish. But buckle up, Carmichael, because I don't plan to use any brakes, only the accelerator!"

They sped along parkways and side streets that Steve never knew existed in his hometown of Minneapolis. They were going so fast that everything seemed to be a blur. He knew it was for good reason. If Bill Thomas did get away, not only would they lose their suspect but also that all so important computer chip.

As they were making record time to the airport, Steve wondered why – or how – anyone could give up vital secrets and put so many people at risk. It was a selfish act of terrorism, conspiracy, and treason. Steve knew times were hard financially and that nothing else seemed to matter to a person after hitting rock bottom. The situation was even worse for Bill Thomas, compounded by his recent divorce and diagnosis of cancer. Steve obviously didn't know the details about Thomas's divorce, but if it involved something like infidelity, then Thomas was probably beyond feeling any remorse for his actions. He probably didn't have enough emotional feeling to perceive how his actions would affect others.

Steve wanted more answers but decided that this was not the time to inquire about the emotional status of Agent Thomas. They just needed to catch him before he got on a flight. Steve wanted to say so many things to Erica, but he feared that any disruption of her concentration might jeopardize their lives as she drove like a mad woman. He just stared at her instead from the passenger seat.

"Are you happy now, Dr. Carmichael?" she asked with a smile.

"Well, this is not what I hoped our second date would be like, but I will take what I can get." Steve chuckled. "But yes, I wanted to finish this business before we parted ways. Who knows? Maybe this could be the start of a partnership for future international espionage!"

Erica laughed. "Perhaps, but if I were you, I wouldn't quit your daytime job. You are a good doctor who loves his patients and work." She reached for his hand and gave it a gentle squeeze. Then she added with a warm smile, "I could see us being partners, just not work-related partners."

No sooner had she said this than Erica was pulling on to the airport road and racing by a line of cars that had pulled over for her siren. On the squad car radio, Steve heard voices from others who were already in the airport. "He must not have a gun. He just went through security, and nothing went off. I think he is headed down Terminal B. Don't know which flight he is headed for, though."

Erica picked up the intercom microphone and started rattling off orders. "This is Miller. Don't move in too close. We don't yet know what his plans are. He might be meeting some fellow enemies, and we don't want to startle them. This might be our only opportunity to nab more than just Thomas. Just keep a watchful eye on him. I'm just pulling up to curbside at the front entrance."

Another voice quickly followed Erica's. "I've got him in view. He hasn't glanced back once. Not sure if he is meeting anyone, but we will keep back until he is about to board the plane."

With the siren still blaring, Erica raced the car right up to the main entrance. She darted out of the vehicle and into the building without any hesitation.

Steve followed obediently.

She looked over her shoulder and said, "Please be careful, and promise if there are gunshots that you'll hit the deck and not be a hero!"

Steve laughed. "You are worried about me. That is so sweet!"

"Steve, promise me now! Otherwise, I will have you apprehended before you can get to the gates. I do care about you, and I will not lose you because of some stupid decision. Promise, Steve!"

"I promise!"

Chapter 53

Steve raced through the crowd, doing his best to keep up with Erica. She was dodging people left and right as she ran toward the security to Terminal B. As she approached, she waved her badge in the air and ran through the scanner without any resistance from the airport security agents. Then she quickly pointed back to identify Steve and told the airport security that he was with her, knowing he had neither a ticket nor a badge.

Steve saw the interaction between Erica and the security agent but slowed down to wait like every other person in line rather than cause a ruckus by butting in line. It actually gave him a minute to collect his thoughts about Erica. He was confident that she had the same feelings toward him, although she was a little conservative when it came to expressing her emotions. Perhaps because of her job or a bad relationship in the past, whatever the reason, Steve was just happy to know she acknowledged some attraction toward him.

He couldn't hear any particular commotion or gunshots. He knew they had to be cautious so as not to startle Thomas and scare him or his associates off into the wild, but still Steve expected a small gun battle. However, things seemed very quiet beyond the security checkpoint.

A few people in front of Steve complained about the lady who just got to pass through, but Steve just smiled to himself. Little did they know, she was out to protect them in the long run.

It took a surprisingly short time for him to get through the line and security checkpoint. Soon he was a free man inside the airport terminal, racing down the corridor to find Erica and the rest of her gang, though he would have no idea who they were.

There was a possibility that Thomas too might not recognize the other agents in the airport, but he certainly would recognize Steve.

Steve was somebody that Thomas wouldn't really care to see. More importantly, Steve was still on this man's hit list. Would Thomas just pull out a gun and blow Steve's head off if they crossed paths? Odds of this were less likely since the man had already made his way through security without any hitches, but Steve slowed his pace so as not to draw extra attention to himself.

Steve tried to find Erica or one of her colleagues who may have looked familiar, but no one came into view. He nonchalantly made his way to the first gate and scanned the waiting area without success. Then he walked to the next gate and so on. He slowed his motor even more as he searched, not wanting to give away his identity to Thomas.

Steve was at Gate 17 when he realized he had inadvertently scanned right past her. He turned his head back to refocus on her, and her eyes met his but not with a romantic gaze. Her eyes looked angry, tough, and concerning. The nonverbal communication was clear to Steve. She briefly looked to her left, and he followed her gesture.

Sitting as patiently as any other paying customer was Bill Thomas. He seemed completely unaware of the agents around him and oblivious to the fact that he was about to be pounced by almost a dozen CIA agents.

Steve didn't need another warning. He slowly backtracked his steps and nonchalantly made an about face. He tried to look as though he were searching for a lost family, scanning the crowd around the neighboring gate. He shuffled away from Thomas' line of view.

Steve found a collection of payphones and computer outlets at a table two gates away. He found a comfortable spot to sit and observe from afar. He couldn't see Erica anymore, but he could see the gate where she and Thomas were.

Steve heard the loudspeaker announcing the boarding of American Flight 322 to San Diego. All the people around that Gate 18 stood up to inch closer to the gate. Thomas got up, stretched his body, and tried to make his way closer to the gate with everyone. He clearly had no idea what was about to happen. There weren't any indications that he was meeting anyone there, but Erica's team was waiting until the last few minutes before boarding just in case he connected with someone.

Thomas was about twenty people back from the ticket agent. Soon it was ten people. Then Steve noticed Erica and a few robust men creeping closer to Thomas, who was still unaware of his surroundings.

It happened when he was first in line at the counter. He was handing his boarding pass to the gal and- boom! Just like that, Erica's team descended on him. Several men began apprehending him while another read him his rights. The handcuffs were on in less than fifteen seconds.

The element of surprise had worked in the favor of Erica and her team. Thomas had expected his pursuers to be looking for him in transit from up north. He offered little resistance.

Steve finally approached Erica as Thomas was whisked away. Never once did Thomas lay eyes on him.

"I guess he wasn't planning on meeting anyone here, huh?" asked Steve.

"I can't help but wonder if the deal went totally sour once he couldn't get rid of you," Erica replied. "You were the last straw to his completion of the deal. We know they didn't want to take any chances if there were still potential leaks in this arrangement. I suspect he had made plans with another group that he was going to meet somewhere in California. We are going to send an agent acting as Thomas on the plane to see if he is approached by anyone. He has Thomas's cell phone as well as identification showing him to be Thomas. We will just have to see how that pans out."

"What about the chip?"

"Good question! We still need to find that little old thing. We will take Thomas in for questioning and examine him. I am heading over to his house now to go through the place and see if he left it there to save for later. I don't think he would take the risk of going through security at the airport and getting caught, nor do I think he would take it with him to meet someone because then there would be no security for his safe return. They could just kill him once he handed over the chip."

Steve argued, "He could have gone through security at the airport just like you did, waving your badge around and then flying through."

"Yes, you may be right, but I still think he was too smart to take the jewels with him while making a deal. He would have no collateral, and he would have to trust more strangers – and you learn early on never to trust anyone! Right, Carmichael?"

Steve knew she was teasing him.

They left the airport without any more commotion.

Her car remained parked right next to the door to the terminal. They climbed in and sped off to Thomas' apartment without any more conversation.

Both passengers were in their own little worlds, not really paying attention to the talk on the radio. Erica was talked out for the time being, and Steve was trying to piece everything together.

Despite no shared verbal communication, their hands found each other halfway between the driver and passenger seats.

Chapter 54

As they pulled up to Bill Thomas's residence, the radio blared. Both passengers remained lost in thought, their hands still clasped together.

Several other cars parked outside the moderate size apartment building. A few men were walking around the yard between the garage and the apartment itself. Steve understood that these were other agents working with Erica.

Erica gave one extra squeeze before releasing his hand and pulling herself out of the car. "What have we found so far?"

One of the men replied, "Not much in the garage. We're just getting started in the apartment. I don't know if we are going to find much here, but he could have hidden it anywhere. It's like looking for a needle in haystack. Seriously, he could have put it anywhere in the building: the walls, mattresses, furniture, electronics, the list goes on."

Erica walked by him as if she didn't want to listen to anything he was saying, but she knew he was absolutely right. "Then let's start taking down the walls!"

Steve took his place behind Erica. This was her show, and he didn't want to get in the way. As she made her way inside to talk to the other agents, Steve went off on his own. He didn't want to be dead weight, so he made his way slowly through the kitchen and up the stairs. The apartment was relatively empty, but Steve figured it was a result of the recent divorce. The poor guy had probably lost a fair amount of his belongings in court.

Two bedrooms were upstairs. The master bedroom had one of the bathrooms directly off the left-hand side, and the other was along the hallway that connected the two bedrooms and a den area. Steve didn't think the rooms were not a big deal. Even the master bedroom was kind of boring. No paintings hung on the wall, no decorations cluttered the bedrooms, and nothing too exciting enhanced either of the bathrooms. Steve quickly explored the complete upstairs but still didn't want to bother Erica in her investigation.

He returned to the master bedroom for more careful examination. He noticed a small television at the end of the queen-sized bed. The guy probably didn't need anything bigger at this point. Steve observed that the bed was made perfectly, as if no one planned to use it for some time.

A walk-in closet had a number of black suits hanging next to several shirts and sweaters and two trench coats. Steve chuckled to himself about this stereotypical attire of CIA agents. *Thomas had never gone undercover with those garments.*

Steve knew better than to touch anything. Anything in the building could be part of circumstantial evidence, and Steve certainly didn't want his prints anywhere close. He tried to imagine where the chip was stowed. It could be in any of the pockets of the clothes, under drawers, in sink plumbing- the list was endless. Steve knew they were going to have to examine the house room-by-room and foot-by-foot. He walked into the bathroom again, bland and boring. None of the drawers were open, so he walked back into the bedroom.

The television was on a stand that had two doors on the bottom. He gently kicked the right door to see if it was spring-locked. The door popped open to reveal six or seven DVDs. Steve bent down and noticed that four of them were stacked nicely. Three were comedies, and one was drama. Scattered in front of them were a few X-rated flicks. Oddly, they were still in their wrappers, except for one. Even that torn wrapper was lying in the cabinet. Steve stared at the titles for a minute. How strange that appeared, one open nudy flick with the wrapper still in the cabinet lying next to three other unopened nudy DVDs.

It felt especially weird because the rest of the room appeared to have been untouched for a period of time.

Steve didn't want to judge a recently divorced man. He gently pushed the door to the TV stand shut with his foot. Then he looked for something else to explore, wondering if he could possibly come across the computer chip and then be the hero in this tale of international espionage.

The room otherwise appeared to be perfectly normal. Everything was where it should be, tidy with no clothes or socks dangling from the furniture. It looked great if it were Steve's parents' room, but for a single guy it just seemed weird to have everything in perfect position and not messed up in the slightest.

Steve made his way to the other bedroom. It was quite smaller but just as clean.

He paced idly around the room, pondering what would happen if the chip wound up in the wrong hands. It could change the world forever. It could alter foreign policy with many countries and affect the lives of countless people. Steve didn't know what was on that chip, but its value was reflected by the number of people who had lost their lives and the many more who were working nonstop to find it.

As Steve thought, he walked over to a window and gazed outside. A few men were taping off a perimeter so that no one would enter the area until it was carefully scrutinized by the authorities.

He realized that the window itself could be a hiding spot. As he studied its frame, his imagination wandered. What if Thomas drilled a hole behind one of the few pieces of artwork that was in the house? What about the garage or outside or the yard? The possibilities were endless.

Steve wondered *why* Thomas would hide it. Why would he not take the chip with him? The chip on the black market would probably be worth millions. If the group he was working with wanted to bail on him, there would be some other slimy group that would pay for the information on that chip.

What would be the advantage of leaving that chip behind? Thomas could hide it and come back in a few years when the heat on him was gone. He could pick up the pieces of his life and attempt to sell his precious chip. The only problem with that would be that in two or three years, the info on the chip would be history and not be worth nearly as much. In the meantime, the United States would have a chance to make the appropriate changes in their foreign policy to lessen the consequences of the info on that chip.

What if Thomas still had the chip? All those people were working through the apartment, but the hunt would prove futile if he had the chip with him.

Steve knew the CIA would interrogate Thomas harshly to discover the exact location of that chip. He may not have been the most intelligent guy in the world, but he had been hired to be a part of the agency. He must have had a little common sense to get that far. Just a few rounds of bad luck compounded by a rough marriage had led him to make stupid decisions. If that wasn't enough, he had to go through cancer surgery. Such serious life changing events would cause some serious stress.

As Steve continued his thought process, he almost felt sorry for the guy. His sympathy didn't last long as he thought about the four people who lost their lives because of this idiot. Jake, Sue, Karla, and A.J. each lost their life just because of a selfish, lonely man.

Steve heard a commotion in the master bedroom. He hurried down the hall to find a few of the agents mulling over something at the bedside. At first, Steve thought they found something of value and important. They were jumping around and laughing initially. Then the laughing changed to this horrific moaning of disgust. Steve was almost afraid to walk any closer. He knew he was probably not even supposed to be there. He had arrived with Erica, but she was no longer in sight. What would they say to him, a true civilian wandering alone in the middle of an international espionage dilemma?

Still Steve had a genuine interest in the commotion and activity at the bedside. His interest was too much, so he inched his way toward the group of men. As he got closer, he picked up pieces of the conversation.

"That is just wrong for a man!"

"I think I am going to hurl…Yuck!"

The agents were standing in front of the left side bed stand. The bottom drawer was open, and inside was a clear plastic wrapper. *This guy sure likes to keep his wrappers,* Steve thought. One of the men wore a pair of plastic gloves and was dangling an apparatus from his fingertips.

Steve was astonished when he made out what looked like a dildo. *Why in the world would this guy want to use a dildo?* Steve acknowledged that there could be several reasonable explanations. The man had recently had prostate surgery, so everything might not yet be in working order. Maybe he was dating an insatiably lusty woman. Perhaps it wasn't his. The list could go on.

As Steve made his way closer to the table, however, the long list of possibilities grew very short. The odor emanating from the dildo wasn't from some wild sexual experience but rather foul, such as after having a bowel movement.

Now Steve was disgusted. He had only one gay friend, but they never discussed sexual experiences. Steve was never really interested in learning, and his friend respected Steve's straightness. Nevertheless, the first thing Steve thought after the stench hit him was that Thomas was gay.

Whether he was gay or needed help after prostate surgery, it was weird to see a dildo in a man's bedside table. The agents dispersed after they'd had their chuckle. They put the device where they had found it in the bedside table and left making rude comments and jokes about Thomas. Steve didn't really care so much, but as a physician, he felt sorry for this guy who had suffered a new onset diagnosis of prostate cancer and then surgery to remove a vital male sex organ.

After a few hours of roaming around the house and yard, Steve decided his time on the case was done. His mind was on his residency and getting back to work, learning how to be a surgeon. He knew that Erica wouldn't be a part of that world anymore. They could chat about a potential relationship later, but then she would be assigned another task by the CIA that would lead her to some other place.

With a sigh, Steve set off to Erica, which proved much easier than finding the chip. He finally tracked her down in the commons, talking to other agents who were looking through some of Thomas's belongings. Steve gently tapped her on the shoulder. "Hi there, stranger."

"Oh, there you are!"

She seemed pleased to see him, but he knew it was time to go. "I think I will get on my way now. You and your colleagues have a lot to go through before you call it a day!

Maybe when things settle down for you we could get together?"

Erica responded with a smile. "That would be great! I promise to call when this settles down. Hopefully we find the chip so we can arrest Thomas." She put down what she was holding to give Steve a huge hug and a gentle kiss. She whispered into his ear, "I promise to give you a call the moment this is done. I can't wait to spend time getting to know you." She hesitated and then added, "The real you. The Steve Carmichael that I started talking to months ago, the one that I really like a lot. Not to say I don't like you now, but you know what I mean!"

They both giggled and made promises to each other about when they would next get together. Erica assured Steve that the case would be solved in a few days and that she anticipated a little time off once the paperwork was complete. Steve listened patiently and then told her how much he was missing his surgery residency.

Promises were made, their intentions revealed, and they had nothing to hide anymore. They hugged once again before Steve made his way to the front. He glanced back over his shoulder at Erica to find her gaze lingering in his direction. She smiled, and so did he as their eyes met, nonverbally saying one last goodbye mixed with so many other thoughts and feelings.

Chapter 55

Steve knew the neighborhood and decided to take the bus back to his apartment. It would only be a fifteen-minute ride, and he was ready to get home. It was a cool autumn day with trees well past their color changes. The breeze felt nice, and dry leaves on the ground crackled as he walked on the sidewalk.

The people at the bus stop apathetically acknowledged his arrival. They had no clue what he had experienced over the past few weeks. Then again, he knew nothing about their lives and secrets either.

When the bus pulled up, Steve waited his turn to climb the short set of stairs and find a secluded seat with no one near. He wanted to collect his thoughts and plan the next few months. He wanted to focus on getting back to real civilization without having to chat with strangers about the weather or the news. He dropped his weary body at the back of the bus and then stared out the window.

His gaze became fixated on some point in the distance. It didn't mean anything to him, but the center point of focus gave Steve's brain a chance to rest and not concentrate on staying alive. He felt so much more comfortable knowing that he could go home and that no one would be out to find and kill him.

He was in a relaxed state of mind as the bus made its stops. Although mesmerized by nothing in particular, he felt as though he were in a vegetative state. His mind was numb, but he could not wait to get back to the life he was supposed to be living. *Very amusing,* he thought to himself as he remembered how frustrated he had been with all the hours of all he was putting in at the hospital. Now he could not wait to be that busy intern running around with barely any sleep.

The excitement became overbearing. Steve reached for his

cell and called the hospital to page Sally Jenson. She seemed like a logical place to start. Sally was likely to be in charge of the team following Jake's death. Despite all the drama that took place over the last few weeks, Steve was more than ready to get back to his work, patients, demanding attendings, miserable hours, and mundane boring life of a surgery intern.

He was still in deep thought reflecting about his normal life when a familiar female voice answered on the other end. "Hello, this is Dr. Jenson. What can I do for you?"

"I have an emergency," replied Steve. "I need a really good surgeon to help me out. You see, I have this big ugly toe that is killing me, and I think it should be removed. I mean, it is really big and infected and draining pus and smells and I just want the toe gone. Could you help me out, Dr. Jenson? I heard you were the best!"

"Carmichael, you are such a geek!" Sally laughed. "I didn't miss your sick sense of humor, but I really missed *you*! I'm so glad to hear your pathetic voice!"

"Feeling's mutual, you little bitch! When can I get started? I miss you all and really just need to get back there and work."

Sally responded, "Steve, seriously don't you think you need some time to yourself? When did you get back? You must be physically and emotionally exhausted. You really ought to take a few weeks off before we get you back to the grind of this hell hole."

"I'm ready!" Steve insisted. "I want to get the show on the road. All I've been doing the last few weeks is thinking about things, contemplating life and the screwed up people who are out there. I know I am ready! But if you want to keep me off call for about a year or so, that would be great. No argument from me there."

"It sounds like you *have* been thinking about it for a while, Steve. How about if we make a compromise: you take two days off and see a shrink to make sure that you are stable enough to deal with this shit here, and I will gladly take you back."

Steve didn't like the suggestion. "How about we agree on the two days and skip the shrink for now? If I lose it, then you can lock me up in a straitjacket for some serious counseling. I am telling you, Sally, I am ready right now! The two days is just for you."

Silence filled the other end as Sally contemplated the decision. She was quick to act on a surgical trauma case; she could make split-second, lifesaving decisions in regard to surgical issues, but when it came to serious social issues, she could take forever to make a choice.

Steve realized her original argument was probably correct: any person who had been through this huge ordeal would need some downtime to mend. But he was ready. He had spent a great deal time reviewing and reliving the moments and the turmoil he had suffered. He had analyzed it all, and he was ready to be a regular human being again.

He understood the daily stress of an internship, but he knew he was ready to get back to work. He didn't feel there was any concern for any post stress disorder after his experience. He knew that Sally was worried about him but also worried about the patients and the mistakes that he might make as a result of his recent adventure and stresses.

Steve ran out of patience. "Okay, Jenson. What is it going to be? I can't take this anymore. The silence is killing me!"

"That's just it, Steve," responded Sally. "I don't want anything to happen to any of the patients because you all of a sudden lose it or freak out. I am going against my better judgment, but fine. Take a few days off, and I'll put you back to work. But if there are any signs that you are about to lose it, no matter how small, I will personally take you in for a seventy-two-hour hold. Do you understand, Carmichael? No ifs, ands, or buts! Off we will go *immediately* to the psych department if you are starting to lose it."

"Deal!" It took Steve but a split second to give Sally a reply. "I'll get a couple of good nights of sleep and see you in two days, bright and early. Thanks again, Sally!"

Steve was delighted. He could focus on the bus ride with a great sense of relief. He was ready to be a doctor instead of a wanted man. The rest of the bus ride seemed short, and soon he was at his doorstep and walking into his apartment.

Pudge, who had been cared for by the neighbors during Steve's absence, almost knocked Steve over as he entered. They played together for several minutes before Steve made his way to the couch and plopped himself down. Pudge jumped on the couch right beside his master, and Steve turned on the TV. He wasn't listening or watching the show, but he was comforted by the ordinary feeling of just sitting in front of the screen.

The next two days passed quickly, and Steve was very lazy. He slept late each morning and worked out each afternoon. He tried to establish a routine but knew that once he began working again, his spare time for mundane things like sleeping late, working out, and being lazy would come to an immediate end.

That was okay with Steve. He had never planned on this interim break to play as an espionage agent in the first place, and he was ready to be a doctor again.

One habit that did return quickly was Steve's constant thoughts about Erica. The prospect of dating a woman like her, someone who would constantly be running around the country or world to resolve this or that issue, was exciting to Steve in a very weird way. He recognized the fact that she would be gone a great deal of the time, not to mention the danger she would most likely encounter on a routine basis. However, his schedule too would be continuously occupied by his residency, horrendous call schedule, and studying. The more he thought about it, the more comfortable he felt that this would be a perfect dating situation because they would both be so busy. He wouldn't have to worry about her sitting around waiting for him, nor would he find himself waiting idly for her.

Even as quickly as those two days went, he desperately wanted to get back to the hospital and work. The refrigerator was filled again, and the place was cleaned up. The laundry was getting done, and his normal life was back in working order. He called several friends and family to reconnect and discuss the excitement of the last few weeks. Some people wanted to know the graphic details, but others were just happy to hear that he was okay and made it through the ordeal without any harm to himself.

He never once heard from Erica but knew that she was busy. He contemplated calling her while getting the last few things ready for his first day back at work.

He knew that she and her crew were on a significant deadline to locate the chip with all the vital information on it before Bill Thomas was set free. After seventy-two hours, if there wasn't enough evidence to keep him incarcerated, they would have to release him. Once released, Agent Thomas would have no trouble finding a way out of the country and probably out of sight forever.

Steve genuinely missed Erica and just wanted to say hi before he resumed his hellish schedule. He decided to give her a quick call before he went to bed. Books organized, groceries stored, laundry done, lab coats washed, and time to rest.

Just after 9:00PM, Steve was ready for sleep. He couldn't come up with any more things to get done, and he was excited to head to the hospital in the morning. He crawled into bed, pulled the sheets and blanket up, and made himself comfy. Then he reached for the phone.

His intentions were halted by the phone ringing.

"Hello?" answered Steve.

"Are you excited to get back and be a workingman, you lazy son-of-a-bitch?" asked Erica. "I mean seriously, how much time do they give you off for annual vacation at that place? And really, you only started working there a few months ago. You sure do have a cushy job. Don't think you could ever cut being a secret agent, Carmichael. Although that does have a nice sound to it, 'Agent Carmichael.'"

They both laughed at the thought.

"Yeah, I start tomorrow! I am so ready to be a doctor again. So – did you get the chip?" Steve asked.

A silence on the other end seemed to last longer than necessary.

"Hello? Are you still there?" questioned Steve.

"Yeah, Steve. I'm here," Erica responded sadly. "We searched Thomas' stuff for the last two days – his apartment, his cars, bank deposit boxes, his office, everywhere, but we still can't find it. He won't say if he sold it to another private buyer, but if that information gets leaked out, we would have to pull so many agents from the field. We'd have to relocate some of our major military installations around the world, and that's just the start. It has been very disappointing because we know he is guilty as hell, but if we can't find that chip, he walks free tomorrow at noon!"

"Hey, I'm sorry, Erica. I know you and your team have been working nonstop on this issue. Something will show up.

You still have fifteen hours. Something is bound to show up that will help you nail this guy!"

"Thanks, Steve. You are always so positive. I really appreciate that."

Steve tried to change the subject to something a little more relaxed, "It was kind of funny that you called when you did because I was just picking up the phone to call *you*."

"Great minds think alike, Agent Carmichael," laughed Erica. "You should probably get some rest for your big comeback tomorrow. Let's talk in twenty-four hours so you can tell me about your day as a hero and I can tell you if we let an international spy go free."

"That sounds like a great plan, Erica. Don't give up! It might be a long night ahead, but it'll show up. Talk to you tomorrow. 'Night."

Steve hung up the phone and lay in bed for a while with his eyes wide open, thinking about Bill Thomas, Sally Jensen, Erica Miller, and work. At last, he closed his eyes and fell asleep.

Chapter 56

The night was short for Steve Carmichael. He tossed and turned for hours, his mind spinning. So many ideas and thoughts were revolving inside his head. He thought of Erica and her pals trying so desperately to find this so important chip, and he thought about being an intern again and becoming a surgeon. Then he revisited Jake and life before all this started. The thoughts continued all through his precious sleep time and through his REM time as well.

The alarm clock went off at five o'clock, as it had before his espionage days. For a brief moment, he questioned why he was eager to start this hell of a lifestyle all over again, with the early mornings, late nights, and sleepless call days. But after a few quick seconds, he remembered how excited he was to get back to the hospital.

He pulled himself out of bed and into the shower. He wasted no time getting ready. He wanted to get his morning routine done quickly so he could get to the hospital before six. He needed time to get a cup of coffee and say his hellos before the grind would start.

As he walked through the halls of the hospital for the first time in what seemed to be years, he felt like a celebrity. He got high-fives from people he had never really talked to and hugs from old staff that he hadn't seen for weeks. Nurses and other residents stopped him in his tracks to catch up as if they were long lost friends from childhood. Steve was amazed by the number of people he talked to as he made his way to the ICU to start rounds. The staff surgeons, who rarely give an intern the time of day, went out of their way to shake his hand and treat him like a real human being.

Steve knew this prestige would fade within a few hours as the grind started. Patients' labs, x-rays and progress notes would soon bear more importance than a few weeks of espionage work. After all, this was a hospital and not a third world country with international spies and agents moving about.

"Carmichael!" screamed Sally, giving him another shot of reality, "How the hell are you doing? You don't look any different." She hugged him. "And you don't smell any different. Actually, you smell like you have not taken call in weeks!" They both laughed, and she continued. "We will have to change that. Maybe we should have you take call every other night for a few months to break you back in and get that nice locker room smell to you!"

As they both laughed again, the rest of the team was beginning to gather.

Steve replied, "I wouldn't have it any other way, Dr. Jensen! Hell, let's just do a few days in a row since I am so rested and ready to go. You know, you snooze, you lose."

"Don't you worry about a thing, Steve. We have lots of time for you to get back into the groove of things around here. I don't want to burn out a good intern. You know they are hard to find these days. I mean, they take unannounced vacations, leave for weeks, and then give bullshit excuses like that they are running from international criminals and spies! No, we better take our time with you. We really need your type to hang around, so we don't want to hurt your sorry ass feelings by taking too much call!"

Steve smiled and tried to ignore her silly comments as rounds were starting. Sally reintroduced Dr. Carmichael to the team. Then, as if nothing had transpired over the last few weeks, they took off. Taking on the role of Jake as she had done since his death, Sally asked for labs and CT reports on the first patient, who was a trauma from the previous night. The medical students were still shaking in their boots beneath Sally's tough and aggressive attitude, asking for this and that and why this wasn't done and yelling at the resident from the night on call about why a blood gas was still pending at the time of morning rounds. "Don't be bullshitting with me if you don't know the labs! I don't have time to mess around with your lies. Either you have what I need or you don't!" screamed Dr. Jensen.

Steve smiled to himself and felt a sense of comfort as he felt right at home. How he missed all the abuse and condescending remarks of a surgery resident's life. He chuckled as the staff surgeon hadn't even started harassing the poor resident. Yes, Erica could round up spies and fight bad guys, but surgery training was a whole different arena for battle.

"Carmichael, where the hell is your mind at this morning? You already said your hellos, but your stardom is over now, so let's get back to reality if you can handle it. Can you please give us your full, undivided attention, kind sir?" shouted Sally.

Steve acknowledged passively with a head tilt that she sure had filled the shoes of Jake as chief resident. Rounds continued with the same energy and disrespect for the junior residents as they started. From patient to patient, order to order, and demand to demand, Sally kept the rounds moving with great swiftness toward the OR, which was waiting with her first operative case.

At the end of rounds, the chief resident would delegate the work to be done for the day. After the last patient was seen, Dr. Jensen motioned the team to surround her so she could give everyone their tasks for the day while she was in surgery. Everyone was taking notes as she rattled off the chore list. "And Dr. Carmichael, would you please stay focused today and try not to let all the celebrity shit steer you away from your priorities? Please go and see a Mr. Torklewood in room 320. He came in to the ER about an hour ago, and I told them to admit him to the floor for us to evaluate him. He came in with lower abdominal pain, so Steve, please do a full consult on him. Thanks." She continued down the list, spreading duties amongst everyone staying out of the operating room that day. Steve knew he wouldn't be invited to go to the OR for a while until he had earned his way back in.

After rounds and duty delegation, Sally took off to surgery, and the rest of the team went to the cafeteria for a cup of coffee and a quick breakfast. Steve debated just going to the consult or sitting with everyone on the team to bullshit for a while. He knew if he went to the cafeteria that he would be there for at least an hour with people asking about the last few weeks, the drama and the adventure, and he would never get out of there. Then he would see someone else and have to repeat the entire story all over again. He decided to bag the idea of breakfast and told his team that he'd just catch up with them at lunch. They quickly reviewed what needed to get done and went over a few labs, and then Steve was off to room 320.

The walk to Mr. Torklewood's room was much like the entire morning: people saying hi, giving him high-fives and knuckles, wishing him well, and expressing joy that he was back at work and out of harms' way. He would have spent more time chatting with people and answering their questions with dramatic details of the last few weeks, but then Sally's comments rang in his ears about being a celebrity and not getting the work done. Plus, there was this uncomfortable man who needed to be evaluated for abdominal pain, lying in his hospital bed, waiting for Steve to determine if he needed pain control and surgery. With that in mind, Steve continued on his way to the patient's room without pausing for any further interviews along the way.

Mr. Torklewood was a pleasant, plump gentleman who appeared to be in his fifties. He had a distraught look on his face as Steve walked into the doorway of his room.

The doctor knocked on the doorframe. "Good morning, Mr. Torklewood. Dr. Carmichael here. I hear you have been having a little belly pain."

As the man grabbed his lower abdomen and rolled toward Steve, he said, "Yeah, I had a pretty rough night. Never had pain like this before, doc. Went to bed feeling fine and then a few hours afterwards woke up with this excruciating pain in my gut." He pointed to his lower abdomen to show Steve exactly where the pain was located.

Dr. Carmichael asked all the appropriate questions: length of time, duration, recurrent episodes, description of the pain, and so on. The pain was localized in the left lower quadrant after watching a football game a few days ago with some friends eating a lot of junk food and popcorn. While Steve was listening intently to the answers, he thought it sounded like a case of diverticulitis. Nonetheless, Steve let him finish his story and then asked more questions centered on his surgical history and medical issues. Then Steve took out his stethoscope from his lab coat to conduct his physical exam. He continued like he had never left the hospital. He started with the patient's neck and continued to his heart and lungs and then the belly. There was exquisite tenderness in the left lower quadrant, and Steve was sure to be gentler to this area. As with all abdominal pain, especially lower abdominal pain, a rectal was warranted. No student, resident, or physician looked forward to this part of the exam, but it was not only required, it could also help pinpoint the reason for the pain and help with the diagnosis to determine need for surgery versus medical management.

Steve looked around the room in search for gloves. He found the box in the corner and began to explain to Mr. Torklewood what would happen next as he crossed the room. "Sir, I am going to have do a quick rectal exam on you just to make sure everything is ok down there in your rectum. It will just take a few seconds. You will feel a little pressure for a short bit and then it will be done." Steve knew the pressure was quite an understatement because he and his fellow classmates in medical school had practiced that exam on each other. That was *not* the highlight of school.

Steve motioned for the gentleman to roll onto his side and then reached inside the bedside stand to grab a bottle of lube. The room became instantly quiet as Steve said, "Okay, Mr. Torklewood, there will be a slight pressure here in your bottom." While Steve was conducting the rectal exam, Mr. Torklewood was very patient and cooperative.

As Steve made the finger sweep across the man's prostate gland, he froze. Steve didn't move, Mr. Torklewood didn't move, and for the patient the pressure was becoming a bit uncomfortable.

"Hey, doc! Are we okay back there?" asked the patient.

But Steve was frozen, his eyes wide open and he could feel his heart race along as if it were busting out from his chest. Another fifteen seconds went by with absolutely no change on Steve's part.

"Hey doc, are you okay?"

Steve quickly but gently removed his finger. His eyes were fixed on the corner of the room. Nothing was there, but Steve was lost in extreme thought. He methodically took off his gloves, not even looking at his hands. His eyes were still focused on the corner of the room in a blank stare. He slowly walked backward from the patient's bed.

Again, the man asked Steve if everything was okay.

Steve responded, “Huh? Sure, uh, sure. Everything is okay, Mr. Torklewood. I need to leave for just a moment. But don’t worry, sir. There was nothing wrong with your bottom. I think you have diverticulitis, but I will be back in a minute.” Steve quickly turned around and ran out the door toward the nurse’s station.

Steve ignored two residents who tried to say hello to him in the hall. He ran to the nurses’ station with fear written across his face. He frantically grabbed one of the phones on the desk and began dialing Erica’s office phone number. Sweat droplets formed on his forehead as if he were working out. He felt impatient when the phone was not answered immediately. After four or five rings, Steve finally heard a voice, but it was not a woman’s voice and definitely not Erica’s.

“Hello?”

“Where is Erica? This is Carmichael,” Steve demanded.

“I am sorry, but Erica stepped away from her desk. I can send you to her voicemail if that would be okay for you?”

“NO!” exclaimed Steve. “I need to speak with her immediately! Have her paged! I need to speak to her urgently! This is Dr. Carmichael, Steve Carmichael.” Steve could sense that person on the other side felt uncomfortable with his tone in his voice, so he quickly regrouped and tried again. “I am sorry, but I really need to speak to Agent Erica Miller now. I have some vital information that may affect national security if I don’t speak with her. NOW!” Steve raised his voice because he heard what he was saying and it actually scared him.

After what seemed to be eternity, Erica got on the line. “Steve! What’s wrong?” Her voice sounded anxious. “What is the big deal? Why are you being so rude on the phone?”

“Erica, do you still have Thomas in custody?”

"Yes, Steve, but I am afraid they are just getting the paper work together for his release. We found nothing at his apartment, office, or car. There is nothing there. We looked everywhere, Steve, but we need to let him go."

"Don't let him go, Erica!" Steve yelled frantically. "He has it. Don't let him out yet. You all couldn't find it at his apartment, office, or car because he has it, Erica!"

"That's impossible, Steve! They strip search each person who enters the jail. Then they go through all his belongings, shoes, underwear, belt, everything!"

Steve asked, "How much time do you have before he is released?"

"About ten minutes, I think."

"Erica, he has that chip on him. Actually, it's *in* him! He doesn't have a prostate, Erica. He had prostate cancer. He told me they removed his prostate with surgery. He doesn't have a damn prostate!"

"So who really cares, Steve?" Erica responded with annoyance. "A lot of men have their prostates out, Steve.

What's the big deal?"

"Erica, the man had porn DVDs and a dildo at his bedside. The dildo was opened and freshly used. It was gross and disgusting, but the point is that he doesn't have a reason to use it for pleasure. What do they do when they strip search him? I mean, how do they examine his butt?"

"They do a finger exam."

"Right! He used the dildo to push the chip up his bottom way out of reach from any digital exam. No one would be able to feel that! And then he would just hold going the bathroom for a few days. And after he was released, he would be able to expel it! Erica, order an x-ray now! I will guarantee that you will see it on x-ray!"

"Steve, that is the most absurd, gross thought one could ever imagine! That is disgusting!"

"Erica, just do it!"

"Fine, Carmichael. I will do it, but this is totally against my principles. I have never heard of such-"

Steve interrupted, "I know it's farfetched, and that's why he did it. No one in their right mind would ever come up with such a disgusting idea, but that would explain why you couldn't find the chip! Let me know what you find."

Steve hung up the phone. His forehead was very sweaty, and his underarms were dripping wet. He looked up for the first time since he had gotten on the phone and didn't even think about where he was having this most unusual conversation. The nurses, residents, and a few visitors were standing with their eyes and mouths wide open at the nurse's station. Steve awkwardly smiled at them and pulled himself up from the chair to return to Mr. Torklewood's room. As he was walking, he took a slight glance over his left shoulder to look back at the nurse's station. The eyes were still wide, and the mouths had yet to shut.

Steve could only smile to himself. That conversation to an outsider must have been quite impressive, since even Erica couldn't believe it. They must have had a difficult time following his end of the conversation. He quickly picked up his pace and went back into room 320.

Poor Mr. Torklewood had a few questions.

Steve, as if a huge weight had been lifted from his chest, sat on the bedside and began explaining the concerns that the doctor had for his patient and his probable diverticulitis. He explained the need for a CT and probable antibiotics for the infection and that surgery would be less likely to be needed at this point.

As he was discussing the information with the patient, Steve was paged overhead. He didn't rush to get the page; Mr. Torklewood had a few more questions, and it was Steve's job to make him feel more comfortable about his condition and the plan. Besides, he knew it was Erica, and he knew he was right.

After a few more minutes with the patient, Steve stepped up and off the bed, "Any more questions or concerns, Mr. Torklewood? Otherwise I am going to answer this page, and I will be back in a few hours to see how you are doing."

The man nodded in agreement, and Steve was on his way back to the nurse's station.

Just as he approached with all the eyes on him, he heard the page for a second time. "Dr. Carmichael, Dr. Steve Carmichael, please call star seven seven for an outside call."

He sat down at the station, his pulse racing. He picked up the phone and dialed star seven seven. "Hello?"

"Steve?" asked Erica.

"Yes."

"My boss wants you to come in to the local office downtown whenever you have a few minutes. He wants you to work for us, maybe as a consultant. You are amazing! You were right-on with your absurd idea, and only you could have come up with that!" she exclaimed.

Steve smiled. "And you didn't believe me for a second!"

"I tried to, but it was a little out there for me. I am sorry I doubted you. When can we go out and celebrate? We need to plan our second date. I am ready when you are, Dr. Carmichael."